WHO TALKS FUNNY?
A Book About Languages for Kids

WHO TALKS FUNNY?
A Book About Languages for Kids

Brenda S. Cox

LINNET BOOKS   1995

© 1995 Brenda S. Cox.
All rights reserved.
First published 1995 as a Linnet Book,
an imprint of
The Shoe String Press, Inc.,
North Haven, Connecticut 06473.

Library of Congress Cataloging-in-Publication Data
Cox, Brenda S., 1958–
Who talks funny? : a book about languages
for kids / Brenda S. Cox.
   p. cm.
Includes bibliographical references
and index.
ISBN 0-208-02378-X
1. Language and languages—Juvenile literature.
[1. Language and languages.]   I. Title.
P124.C69   1994
400—dc20   94-5379
                                    CIP
                                     AC

The paper in this publication meets
the minimum requirements of the
American National Standard for Information
Science—Permanence of Paper for
Printed Library Materials, ANSI Z39.48-1984. ∞

Designed by Abigail Johnston.

Printed in the United States of America.

To my Arab friends, who have
taught me a lot about language,
and my friends and teachers
who speak many other languages

CONTENTS

List of Figures and Tables ix
Acknowledgments xi

1. Who in the World Talks Funny? 1
2. Scarecrow or Bogle: Varieties of Language 14
3. Politics, Faith, and Forbidden Tongues: Languages and Loyalties 30
4. Conquerors, Slaves, and Immigrants: Language Contacts and Collisions 45
5. Clicks, Trills, and Umlauts: The Sounds of Language 64
6. Rhythm and Tone: The Music of Language 74
7. Divisible and Indivisible: Pieces of Words 81
8. Camels and Kangaroos, Cousins and Kings: A Word for Everything 88
9. The Blueprint of Language: Grammar 107
10. From Hieroglyphics to Alphabets: Languages in Writing 120
11. Learning Languages: You Can Talk Funny, Too! 138

Appendix 1 How to Say It: Greetings and Words in Many Languages 153
Appendix 2 Language Learning and Language Acquisition 181
Glossary 183
Further Resources: Want to Talk Funny? 192
Bibliography 197
Index 203

LIST OF FIGURES AND TABLES

Figures
1. Indo-European and Some of Its Daughter Languages   8
2. The Tones of Mandarin Chinese   78
3. Puzzle: Deciphering a Language   117
4. The ABCs in Space and Time   127
5. Writing Systems of the World   131

Tables
1. Who Speaks What: Major World Languages   3
2. Major Language Families   12
3. Name That Language   32
4. Languages Used in American Homes   61
5. States with the Most Non-English-Speakers in 1990   62
6. Sounds of English in the 1600s   72
7. Putting Together the Pieces: Language Types   87
8. Numerals in Different Languages   99
9. Critical Languages   151

ACKNOWLEDGMENTS

Many thanks to Sharon Stockdale (M.A., Linguistics) who reviewed this manuscript and gave me helpful comments relating to linguistics and to Chinese. Speakers of many languages also gave me information: Nancy Alardo (Cantonese and Mandarin Chinese); Lorenz and Gabi Biegel and Sabine Spranger (German); Per and Monica Carlsén (Swedish); Nettie and Leonard Chernila (Yiddish); Aga Farhadi (Farsi); Debbie Fenley (Indonesian); Sue Golder (Albanian); Dr. Miles Jones (linguistics and language learning); Kim Young-Ja (Korean); Le Thi My Dung and Le Thi Dei (Vietnamese); Elena Nickolaevna Al-Masani (Russian); Kristiina and Hans Nilsen (Finnish and Norwegian); Sally and Ramachandran (Hindi and Malayalam); Tasneem Raza (Urdu); Cari Reixa (Basque); Rabbi Brant Rosen (Hebrew); John Shindeldecker (Turkish); Witold Smolen (Polish); Larry Snider (Farsi); Vivienne Stacey (Urdu); Pacita Tadena (Tagalog); Monica Tsung Thluai and Dr. Than Htun (Burmese and Khmer); Mike Titus and Dick Johns (New Guinea Pidgin); Marina, Michelle, and Angela Van Dijk (Dutch); and Marie Jane Weirich (French). Thanks also to my mother, Mrs. Pauline Sneed, for research in the U.S. while I was overseas, and to the multilingual boys and girls of Sanaa International Christian Fellowship Youth Group. While I acknowledge the gracious help of all these people, any errors found here are the author's own.

> **Language is a city to the building of which every human being brought a stone.**
> Ralph Waldo Emerson

1
WHO IN THE WORLD TALKS FUNNY?

Since you were about two years old, you've been talking. Even earlier, when your parents told you, "Time to eat!" or "Let's go bye-bye!" you understood. Language has surrounded you all your life.

Imagine visiting a foreign country where you don't know the language. You walk through a park. Suddenly a policeman yells at you. He tells you at great length what you've done wrong, but it sounds like gibberish. You shrug your shoulders, and finally he waves you on. You're hungry now, and want to find a restaurant. You stop someone and point to your mouth to show hunger; he acts as if you're weird. Eventually you find a restaurant. But what does the menu say? You point to something at random and the waiter brings you the local delicacy: fried sheep brain. Never mind, it will be worse when he brings the bill and you can't read it. Hold out some money to him; if he's honest he'll take the right amount!

If it's difficult not knowing someone else's language, think what it would be like if there were no languages at all. People couldn't build cities, trade with each other, sing songs, or record history and scientific discoveries. You need language to work with people, make friends, and express your feelings. Through language you learn new ideas and tell others what you've learned and imagined. You even use language in thinking and dreaming! Can you think of anything you do that doesn't involve language?

Every group of people has a system of speech to communicate to each other what they think, feel, see, and know. It's a kind of code, which combines sounds and gives them meanings. For instance, you put together a *d* sound, a short *o* and a *g* sound to say "dog."

English-speakers agree this means a certain kind of animal. Speakers of other languages use different sounds to mean that animal. To them "dog" would be nonsense. If an Arabic speaker hears *kalb*, though, he thinks of the animal you call "dog." *Kalb* is the sound-combination that Arabs have agreed stands for that animal.

Languages were spoken long before they were written down. Some languages use alphabets that are quite different from ours, as you'll see in chapter 10. The word that sounds like *kalb* in Arabic is actually written كلب. Arabic, Russian, Khmer (Cambodian), Hindi, Greek, and many other languages have their own alphabets. In this book, words from those languages are written with the letters of our alphabet that come closest to the sounds of the letters in their alphabets. This is called "transliteration."

WHICH PEOPLE TALK FUNNY?

Each child learns a language as he or she grows up. A Vietnamese child raised by French parents would grow up speaking French, not Vietnamese. No one is born understanding any language.

More than 6,000 languages are spoken in the world today. Every group of people on earth has a language that meets its needs. In some countries many languages are spoken. The people of India speak more than 400 languages! These languages come from at least five different language families. (Table 2 shows some language families.) Hindi and English are India's official languages. Fourteen other languages are used by state governments of India, and sixty-seven languages are used in its schools!

Some tongues are the official languages of several countries. Spanish ranges from Mexico down to Chile, and across the ocean to Spain. Arabic is spoken in at least thirty-five countries. English is spoken by more than 300 million people as a first language, and by millions more as a second language.

The language used by the most people is Mandarin Chinese. It has about 930 million speakers. On the other hand, some languages are spoken by only a few hundred people: perhaps less than the number of kids in a medium-sized school! The Tatuyo language, for example, is spoken by only 350 South American Indians in Colombia. Some other American Indian languages are only spoken by one or two elderly speakers; when those people die, their languages will disappear.

What languages have you heard spoken? Do you have friends who speak Spanish, Vietnamese, Polish, or French? Most Americans originally came from other countries, and some still speak the languages of those countries. The language you learn from your parents when you first begin to speak is called your "mother tongue," "first language," or "native language."

Languages besides English are spoken in every state of the United States. In most of them a wide variety of languages are spoken. In California, for instance, there are large groups of people who speak Spanish, Italian, German, French, Japanese, Yiddish, Chinese, Portuguese, Korean, Vietnamese, Tagalog (a language of the Philippines), and other languages!

In Montana, farther inland, Native Americans still use the lan-

TABLE 1
WHO SPEAKS WHAT: MAJOR WORLD LANGUAGES

	Native Speakers	Total Speakers	
Mandarin Chinese	827 million	930 million	☺☺☺☺☺☺☺☺☺☾
English	319 million	463* million	☺☺☺☺☾
Hindi	327 million	400 million	☺☺☺☺
Spanish	326 million	371 million	☺☺☺☾
Russian	172 million	291 million	☺☺☾
Arabic	182 million	214 million	☺☺☾
Bengali	184 million	192 million	☺☾
Portuguese	167 million	179 million	☺☾
Malay-Indonesian	49 million	152 million	☺☾
Japanese	125 million	126 million	☺☾
French	72 million	124 million	☺☾
German	98 million	120 million	☺☾

Reprinted with permission from *The World Almanac and Book of Facts 1994*. Copyright © 1993 Funk & Wagnalls Corporation. All rights reserved.
*According to other estimates, there may be as many as 800 million English-speakers in the world today.

guages Chippewa, Cree, Blackfoot, Crow, Teton-Sioux, Assiniboine, Flathead (Salish), and Kutenai. During Montana's history, it has taken in groups speaking Arabic, Basque, Bulgarian, Chinese, Czech, Danish, Dutch, English, Finnish, French, Frisian, German, Greek, Hmong (a language of Vietnam and Laos), Hungarian, Italian, Japanese, Korean, Lao, Norwegian, Polish, Russian, Serbo-Croatian, Slovak, Slovenian, Spanish, Swedish, Vietnamese, and Yiddish! Some of those groups still speak their own languages. Others now speak only English.

ARE ALL LANGUAGES ALIKE?

All languages are alike in some ways. All use sounds to communicate (except for sign languages, which use hand motions instead). People put sounds together into words with meanings. Every language uses words to describe *things*, like "horses," and *actions*, like "run." Speakers of any language can talk about the past and future, ask questions, and give commands.

Languages are also different in many ways. Each language has its own patterns, called its grammar. (Chapter 9 explains more about grammar.) Spanish-speakers say *la casa roja*, which translates literally (word for word) as "the house red." In English you would say "the red house." The pattern in English is to put descriptive words (adjectives) before nouns; in Spanish, adjectives come after nouns.

Languages all use sounds, but not always in the same way. An African bushman uses clicks as parts of words. The Chinese use musical tones to change the meanings of words. All languages also build words, but each in its own way.

HOW DID PEOPLE START TALKING FUNNY?

Linguists, people who study language, have come up with many ideas. A nineteenth-century linguist, Max Müller, gave these theories funny names which linguists still use. Some of these ideas seem pretty silly today. The "bow-wow" theory says the first words were copies of what people heard in nature. When a man heard a dog bark, he called the dog a "bow-wow." The "pooh-pooh" theory is that language started with people's exclamations when they felt surprised ("oh!"), afraid, hurt ("ooh!"), or happy. According to the "sing-song" theory, language came from primitive chants—songs made up around the campfire. Followers of the "yo-he-ho" theory believe that language began with grunts made by people working hard—lifting heavy stones and saying "Heave! Ho!" for example.

These theories don't really explain much. If dogs were first called something like "bow-wow," how did we end up with words as different as the English word *dog* and the Arabic word *kalb*? Or if we started with "ooh" and "ow," how did nouns, verbs, and sentences develop?

People have wondered about language origins for a long time. Did all languages come from the same origin? The eleventh chapter of Genesis, in the Bible, tells a story about languages. It says that in ancient times people all spoke one language. Therefore they could cooperate on huge projects. They chose to build an enormous tower to defy God. So it is recorded that God "confused their languages" to keep them from working together. Society fell apart without a common tongue. People scattered around the world, each group taking a unique language with it. These languages were the roots of today's big language families. From the name of this tower, Babel, comes our word *babble*, which means "to talk on and on meaninglessly."

None of these ideas can be proven. Most modern linguists accept that there is really no way of knowing how language began. Because people began talking long before they started writing, there is no record of the first languages. The oldest written records we have are markings on clay tablets from the area that is now Iraq. They are from about 3500 B.C. By comparing ancient languages that were recorded, historical linguists can get a good idea of what the languages before them were like. But the very oldest languages they can reconstruct were not simpler or more primitive than today's languages. In fact, many of them were far more complex!

Some languages are related to each other. All the languages we speak now may have developed from fewer than twenty early languages. No one knows for sure whether those languages all came from one original language, although some linguists believe they must have. When one language develops into several others, it is called a "parent language." The languages that came from it are called "daughter languages." Groups of related languages are "families."

How do linguists know that a group of languages are related? After all, they don't usually sound the same. English is distantly related to Russian, but an English-speaker and a Russian-speaker can't understand each other! You can understand some words from very closely related languages, though.

Speaking to your dad early in the day you could say *God morgon, fader* in Swedish, or *Goedemorgen, vader* in Dutch. Can you guess what the German words *Mann, Hand, braun,* and *Haus* mean in English? (That's right: "man," "hand," "brown," "house.") Be careful, though. The German *überall* does not mean "overall"; it means "everywhere." And German *bald* has nothing to do with your head; it means "soon."

To find out which languages are related, linguists compare the oldest written records of various languages. This is called historical or comparative linguistics. Linguists look for similar words for basic things like numbers, family relationships, and body parts. They compare the way words are put together. Two languages with similar basic words and grammar are usually from the same family.

For instance, the English word *two* came from the Old English word *twa*. This sounds like Russian *dvah*, French *deux* (pronounced something like *d* plus the *u* sound in *put*), and Dutch *twee*, all of which mean "two." The Japanese "two," *ni*, and the Chinese "two," *èr*, are clearly not related to the English word *two*.

INDO-EUROPEAN LANGUAGES

English and its relatives came from the ancient Indo-European language. It is called Indo-European because the languages which developed from it stretch geographically from India to Europe. This language was never written down. Linguists have figured out what it was like by studying the languages that developed from it. They have even learned about the people who spoke it. The Indo-Europeans probably lived in a cold climate, since all Indo-European languages have similar words for winter, snow, and rain. English "snow" is German *Schnee*, Russian *sneg*, Sanskrit *snih-*, and Gothic *snaiws*. They also had words for mountains and mountain streams, which makes some linguists think the Indo-Europeans lived in the Caucasus Mountains east of present-day Turkey. Others think they may have lived in northern Europe. The Indo-Europeans did not live on the coast, since there is no common word for "sea" in the Indo-European languages. They had cattle, sheep, horses, dogs, grain, arrows, farming tools, weapons, and other things for which English-speakers still use words like theirs.

The language closest to Indo-European that is still spoken today is Lithuanian. Its grammar is very complicated, like Indo-European grammar was, and it is very similar to the ancient Indian language called Sanskrit.

At some time in pre-history the Indo-Europeans split into bands of people who settled in different places. Their language began to change. Some groups encountered the ocean and made up words to describe it. Others came across new animals, or invented new ways of doing things, and added words to their language. As groups lost contact with each other, they began pronouncing words a little differently. Some substituted one sound for another. For instance, the sounds we write as *t* and *d* are similar, made in the same part of the mouth. Many linguists think that the Indo-Europeans used a *d* sound in their word for the number ten. The *d* changed to a *t* in some languages, as in English *ten*. It became a *z* in German *zehn*, but stayed a *d* in Spanish *diez*, French *dix*, and Sanskrit *dasa*.

People began using words in different orders and in different ways. Some said words more quickly, leaving out some syllables. Some groups borrowed words from the languages of people they met in their wanderings.

At first these bands of people could still understand each other, although they spoke differently. They were speaking "dialects" of

FIGURE 1
INDO-EUROPEAN AND SOME OF ITS DAUGHTER LANGUAGES
(dead languages in parentheses)

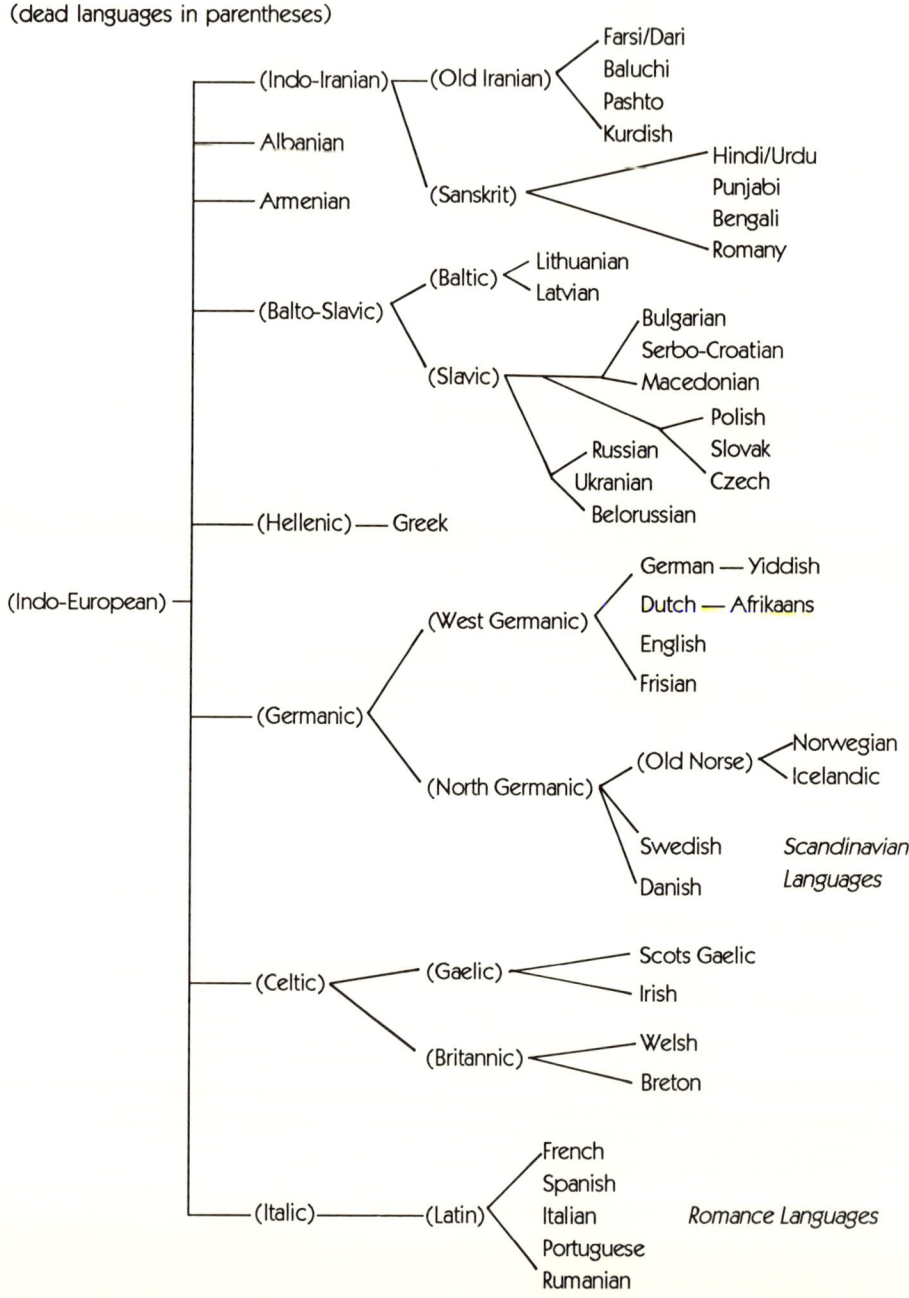

the Indo-European language. Over time, their speech changed so much that they could no longer communicate. Then they were speaking new languages.

ENGLISH, OLD AND NEW

One of these languages was Germanic. Modern German, Dutch, Swedish, English, and other languages are its daughters. Like all living languages, these languages are still changing. Only about forty percent of English words come from Anglo-Saxon, or Old English, the Germanic language which was the earliest form of English. The rest have been borrowed from French, Latin, Greek, and other languages at various times. In the Old English of about 1200 A.D., the Lord's Prayer begins: *Fader ure þu þe eart on heofonum.* In the English of the 1600s this was written, "Our Father who art in heaven." In modern English it is "Our Father in heaven." The word order is different: now we say "Our Father" instead of *fader ure*. The letter "thorn" (þ) was used for the sound *th,* and that letter is no longer in our alphabet. The pronunciation of all the words has changed. What do you think English will sound like after another 400 years?

The history of English is the history of England. The legendary King Arthur probably did not speak English at all. The stories about him may be based on a Celtic king or chieftain of the sixth century who fought against Saxon invaders. He and his countrymen could not keep the invaders out. The Anglo-Saxons pushed the Celts back to Scotland, Wales, and Ireland, where their languages (Scots Gaelic, Welsh, and Irish Gaelic) are still spoken today. When the Anglo-Saxons settled in England, beginning in 450 A.D., they borrowed only a few words from the Celtic Britons like *glen, druid,* and *down.*

Scandinavian Viking invaders took over parts of England between 750 and 1050 A.D. England was ruled by the Danes from 1013–1042 A.D. after King Sweyn of Denmark defeated the English King AEthelred "the Unready." AEthelred's nickname comes, not from the modern meaning of *unready,* but from an Old English word

ENGLISH'S CLOSEST RELATIVE Living near the Angles and Saxons, and perhaps even invading England with them, were a group of people called Frisians. They still live in what is now northern Holland and western Germany. The Frisian language is the closest living language to English. It sounds very much like what linguists believe Anglo-Saxon, or Old English, sounded like before the Norman invasion. Can you understand these Frisian words: *kat, need, goed, jo, boat, rein, ko*? They mean "cat," "need," "good," "you," "boat," "rain," and "cow."

unrede, meaning "lacking advice." The first two letters of his name were the old English letter *Æ*, which looks like a combination of *a* and *e*, and sounded like the *a* sound of *cat*. The Viking conquerors brought most of the *sk-* words into English, like *skin, sky*, and *skill*, as well as words as common as *are, they, them*, and *die*. But the Vikings, perhaps since they tended to settle in an area and take local women for their wives, absorbed the local culture and language more than they changed it. Within a hundred years or so the Vikings were speaking English.

The Vikings also took over an area of northern France called Normandy, and began speaking their own dialect, or variety, of Old French. Their French-speaking descendants, the Normans, invaded England in 1066 A.D., led by William the Conqueror. For the next 333 years all the kings of England spoke French as a first language. The noblemen, officials, and church leaders used French and Latin, while the common people continued to speak English. A huge range of words, from *jolly* and *joy* to *curfew* and *royal* were adopted from French into English. These words were changed to sound more English, and sometimes they changed meanings. For example, the French word *poupée*, which means "doll," became the English word *puppy*. The English of 1066 to about 1476 is called Middle English. The year 1476, when William Caxton brought the printing press to England, can be considered the beginning of modern English. English has continued to grow through contact with other languages. In the fifteenth and sixteenth centuries, for instance, Renaissance scholars borrowed many scientific words like *telegraph* and *atmosphere* from Greek and Latin, and they became part of English.

French, which gave English so many words, is a "Romance language." This doesn't mean it's romantic, but that it comes from the language of Rome: Latin. The Roman Empire ruled much of Europe for about 500 years (from about 30 B.C. to 476 A.D.), taking their language everywhere. The Latin spoken in different areas gradually changed into separate dialects, which developed into separate languages. Because the Catholic Church preserved Latin, linguists can easily see how it changed into its daughter languages. The Latin *candēla* (candle) became the French *chandelle*, the Portuguese *candeia*, and the Italian and Spanish word *candela*.

OTHER LANGUAGE FAMILIES

Indo-European is the largest language family. Sino-Tibetan, the second largest family, includes the many dialects of Chinese and the languages of Thailand, Burma (Myanmar), and Tibet. Arabic, Hebrew, and others are in the Semitic family. Malayo-Polynesian languages are spoken in the Pacific Islands, including Hawaii, Indonesia, and New Zealand.

Finnish is spoken in Europe but is not Indo-European. Norway and Sweden, right next to Finland, speak Germanic languages so much alike that Norwegians and Swedes can understand each other. Finnish, though, is an entirely different language distantly related to the language of Hungary, far to the south.

The thousand or so languages of Africa have been grouped into four or five families. Australian aborigines use about 230 languages, all related to each other. About 900 languages are spoken today by the Indians of North, Central, and South America and the Caribbean, while hundreds of others have died out. Linguists have classified these American Indian languages into anywhere from three to 152 families! Many languages of the world need to be studied more before we'll know their family relationships.

Some languages, called "isolates," have no known relatives.

TABLE 2
MAJOR LANGUAGE FAMILIES (with a few members of each family)

INDO-EUROPEAN
Indo-Iranian: Sanskrit, Hindi, Gujarati, Marathi, Punjabi (India); Urdu (Pakistan); Bengali (Bangladesh); Sinhala (Sri Lanka); Romany (Gypsies); Farsi/Dari (Iran/Afghanistan); Pashto (Afghanistan, Pakistan); Kurdish (Turkey, Iraq, Iran, Syria); Baluchi (Pakistan)

Armenian

Albanian

Greek

Slavic: Bulgarian; Serbo-Croatian; Slovenian; Macedonian; Czech; Slovak; Polish; Russian

Baltic: Lithuanian; Latvian

Romance: Latin; Italian; French; Spanish; Portuguese; Rumanian

Celtic: Welsh; Breton (France); Irish Gaelic; Scots Gaelic

Germanic: Norwegian; Swedish; Danish; Icelandic; German; Frisian (Netherlands); English; Dutch; Flemish (Belgium)

AFRICA/MIDDLE EAST
Afro-Asiatic: Coptic (Egypt); Berber (North Africa); Somali; Hausa. *Semitic:* Arabic; Hebrew; Aramaic; Amharic; Tigrinya (Ethiopia)

Nilotic (Africa): Dinka; Maasai; Luo

Niger-Congo (Africa): Kikuyu; Mossi; Senoufo; Wolof. *Bantu (Africa):* Swahili; Zulu; Xhosa; Shona; Tswana

Khoisan (southern Africa): Bushman; Hottentot; /xam

ASIA
Austro-Asiatic (Southeast Asia): Khmer (Cambodia or Kampuchea); Vietnamese; Mon (Thailand, Myanmar)

Dravidian (South India): Kannada; Malayalam; Tamil; Telugu

Caucasian: Georgian (former Soviet Union); Circassian (Russia, Middle East)

Ural-Altaic: *Finno-Ugric:* Finnish; Saami (Lapland, northern Scandinavia); Hungarian; Estonian. *Turkic:* Turkish; Uzbek; Kazakh; Uighur (China)

Sino-Tibetan: Tibetan; Burmese (Myanmar); Chinese languages or dialects including Mandarin, Cantonese, Wu, Min, Hakka, Xiang, Gan

Tai: Thai; Lao (Laos)

OCEANIA
Malayo-Polynesian: Bahasa Indonesian/Malay; Tagalog (Philippines); Malagasy (Madagascar); Maori (New Zealand); Hawaiian; Javanese; Fijian; Tahitian

Australian aboriginal: about 230 languages, all related

Papuan: about 740 languages of Papua New Guinea, several families

THE AMERICAS
About 900 languages which can be grouped in various ways. These are some of the groups used (there are many others):

Macro-Algonkian: Natchez; Muskogean or Creek; Seminole; Choctaw; Blackfoot; Cheyenne; Shawnee; Delaware; Ojibwa or Chippewa

Eskimo-Aleut: Inuit; Yupik; Aleut

Macro-Siouan: Iroquois; Mohawk; Cherokee; Crow; Dakota or Sioux

Na-Dené: Athabascan; Navajo; Apache; Tlingit

Hokan: Mohave

Azteco-Tanoan: Nahuatl; Shoshoni; Comanche; Hopi; Paiute; Papago-Pima

Mayan: Yucatec; Quiché; Cakchiquel

Oto-Manguean: Mixtec; Zapotec

Tupian: Tupi-Guaraní (Paraguay)

Quechumaran: Quechua

Cariban: Carib

Macro-Chibchan: Colorado

ISOLATES
Unrelated to other languages; there are about fifteen others in addition to these:

Korean

Japanese

Basque (Spain, France)

Their structure and vocabulary are not like other known languages, and we have no record of the languages they developed from. Korean, Japanese, and the Basque language spoken in Spain and France are all quite different from any other language. They may have been part of larger families long ago, but all their relatives have died out. Basque may be the last survivor of the languages spoken in Europe before the Indo-Europeans arrived. Some linguists think that Korean might be distantly related to the Turkic languages, or that Korean and Japanese might be distantly related to each other. But so far these connections have not been proven. Other languages, each spoken by only a few thousand people, also seem to be isolates: Burushaski and Nahali of India, Gilyak of Russia, Ainu of Japan, and the Zuni, Kutenai, Keres, and Tarasco languages of Native American tribes. A number of dead languages, like Iberian, Sumerian, Etruscan, and some American Indian languages are also considered isolates. However, if linguists had more information they might be able to connect them with other languages.

How do languages die? Sometimes they gradually change into other languages and the original is no longer spoken. Latin, for example, has been replaced by the Romance languages derived from it. You can still learn it, but no one speaks it as a "mother tongue" anymore; it's a "dead language." Other languages die when the people who speak them are conquered and begin speaking the conqueror's language. Children learn the new language in school, or are forced to learn and use it, and forget their first language. Sometimes the people who speak a language die out. In 1962, for example, the Trumai Indian language of Venezuela was nearly wiped out by a flu epidemic: only ten speakers were left alive. Hundreds of American Indian languages have been lost in these ways.

Languages that are alive are always changing, just as people are. And the beginning of language change is the growth of dialects.

> **We ain't what we want to be, and we ain't what we're goin' to be, but we ain't what we wuz.**
>
> South Carolina mountain proverb

2

SCARECROW OR BOGLE: VARIETIES OF LANGUAGE

Do you have friends who don't talk the way you do? A boy from the South might say *y'all*. A girl from another part of the United States might say *you guys, youse guys* or *you all*. When you eat chicken, do you wish on the *wishbone, pulley bone,* or *lucky bone?* Do your friends greet you with *Hey!* or *Hi!* or *What's goin' down?* Do you say *cah* or *car, wash* or *warsh, greecey* or *greezy?*

These words could tell a linguist what dialect of American English you speak. For instance, people from the North usually say *greasy* as *greecey,* while southerners say *greazy.* A dialect is the way a group of people uses a language. All people speak some dialect of their language. Each dialect uses some of its own special words and pronounces and puts them together in certain ways.

If someone speaks differently than you do, you might say that she or he "has an accent." That means that they pronounce words in a certain way. But if the person also uses some different words and puts together sentences in different ways than you do, a linguist would say that the person speaks a different dialect, or variety, of your language.

No two people speak exactly alike. That's why you recognize friends' voices on the phone. You also have favorite words and expressions which you use a little differently from other people. Your own particular variety of your dialect is called an "idiolect." It's probably not very different, though, from the way your family and other people in your area speak.

In the book *The Grapes of Wrath* by John Steinbeck, a girl says to her new friends, "I knowed you wasn't Oklahomy folks. You talk queer kinda—that ain't no blame, you understan'." Her friend replies, "Ever'body says words different. Arkansas folks says 'em different, and Oklahomy folks says 'em different. And we seen a lady from Massachusetts, an' she said 'em differentest of all. Couldn' hardly make out what she was sayin'."

How many dialects have you heard? Are they from regions of the country, or states, or even just areas in your city?

DIALECTS OF ENGLISH

Three main groups of dialects—eastern (or New England), midwestern, and southern—are spoken in the United States. (Some linguists also include a midland dialect between New England and the South.) There are also many smaller dialect areas within these big groups. Nowadays, though, television, radio, telephone, and travel are decreasing many differences between American dialects.

In other countries, English is spoken with much more variety than we have in the United States. In different parts of the English countryside a scarecrow is called a *bogle, flay-crow, mawpin, bogeyman, rook-scarer,* or *guy*. A Scotsman might say *Ah've kenned yon man geyly echt years*, meaning "I've known that man almost eight years." The Scottish *braw bairn* is the American *good kid, fine young'un,* or *chile*. A few old plurals, long dropped from the rest of English, are still used in Scotland: *kye* for "cows," and *een* for "eyes."

Many sounds and words in American dialects came from England. English was changing as the first British people came to America. The New England settlers, as they traded with London, copied changes in the speech of upper-class Londoners. They began to say the letter *a* with an *ah* sound, like the *a* in *father*. They dropped *r*'s after *a*, and added *r*'s to other words. These Englishmen might say, "Fahthuh had an idear: staht nee-uh the pahth to the gah-den." ("Father had an idea: start near the path to the garden.") Many New Englanders still speak this way.

Southerners developed their own dialects. They leave endings off some words (*good mawnin'* instead of *good mahning,* and *nex' bes'* for *next best*) and stretch vowels in a drawl: "Aahm doin' faahn, dee-ah." ("I'm doing fine, dear.")

People from northern England settled in the midwestern and western parts of America. They did not have much contact with England, like the people who lived on the eastern and southern coasts did, and so they did not copy changes going on there. They pronounced all their *r*'s and used a short *a* (as in *cat*) in words where people from southern England used an *ah* sound. This dialect is the standard pronunciation of English that you hear on network television. It is used in the midwestern and western United States and many other areas.

Each of these areas can be divided into many dialects. For instance, Rhode Islanders speak their own version of a New England accent, with pronunciations like *sar* for "saw," *Vitchud* for "Richard," and *di'int* for "didn't."

In the Appalachian Mountains, people still use some expressions that were common in Shakespeare's day or earlier. Today's Appalachian *hisn, hern, ourn* for *his, hers,* and *ours* were used in fifteenth-century England. *Ax* for "ask," *dar* for "dare," and *et* for "ate" were common pronunciations in earlier times, and mountain people still use them. Their language has changed over time in other ways, though, just as all dialects do.

Some odd English spellings came from British dialects. *Bury,* for instance, is spelled as if it were *burr-y,* because it was pronounced that way in Southwest England. But today's pronunciation, *bear-y,* was used in Southeast England.

Dialects use words differently. In some parts of England and America, the *-s* is left off verbs. People say "she like him," or "it go very fast." In other areas, *-s* is added to all verbs. You might hear "I likes it," or "we goes home."

An Irishman might say, "I come to your house yesterday and done the work." Irish English sometimes puts words together as the old Irish Gaelic language does, saying "I do be going to school," or "I wonder what is gone with them" ("I wonder what happened to them"). The Scottish say "it needs washed," rather than "it needs washing." This expression is still used in parts of Pennsylvania. "I be gwine now," used in some British dialects for "I'm going now," has also traveled to parts of America.

Sometimes people who speak different dialects can't understand each other, even though they are speaking the same language. Would you like to be called a *dag* or a *hard case*? In New Zealand a *dag* is a good man. A *hard case* is a person with a sense of humor! New Zealanders have also picked up a few words from the Maori tribespeople who are native to their islands. *Kit* is from the Maori word for "basket," and *hoot* means "money."

Australians have also borrowed words from Australian aboriginal languages. (Aboriginal languages are the languages of the aborigines, the people who have been living in Australia since before European colonists came.) If your Australian friend said she saw a *dingo* and a *jumbuck* by the *billabong* on the *big scrub,* would you know she saw a wild dog and a sheep by the creek on the prairie? *Billabong* and *jumbuck* are aboriginal words. Would you understand her if she said *give it a burl,* "try it," or *she'll be right,* "it'll be okay"?

As you can see, dialects can lead to some problems in communication! If you met a British boy named Edward, your conversation might go something like this:

Edward: "Do you go to a *public school?*"
You: "Yeah."
Edward: "Is it *dear*? Does it cost a lot to go there?"
You: "Of course not!"
Edward: "Well, the public school I go to is very dear. I'm in the first *form.*"
You: "Is that like the sixth grade?"
Edward: "I don't know. Why don't you come visit me at my *flat?*"
You: "Your what?"
Edward: "My flat, where I live. It's on the *first floor;* you take the *lift* to get to it. We can play *draughts* or *noughts and crosses* before dinner."
You: "What are you having for dinner?"
Edward: "*Tinned* beef, *courgettes,* and *chips,* with *trifle* and *biscuits* for *pudding.*"

You: "What kind of beef? With tin in it?"
Edward: "No, it comes out of a *tin*. You *chuck* the tin in the *rubbish bin* when you *wash up*."
You: "Rubbish?"
Edward: "Yes. A *lorry* takes away the rubbish to the *tip*."
You: "Lorry? Who's she?"

Did you understand the British words, in italics? In Britain a *public school* is private, and usually expensive (*dear*). Government-supported schools (which Americans call "public schools") are called *state schools* in Britain. A *form* is an American "grade," though British forms are numbered differently than American grades. A *flat* is an "apartment," and the *first floor* is the first one above the ground floor: Americans call it the "second floor." You take a *lift*, an "elevator," to go up. *Draughts* are "checkers," and *naughts and crosses* is a game of "tic-tac-toe."

For dinner Edward was having what you would call "canned beef" (*tinned beef*), "zucchini" (*courgettes*), "French fries" (*chips*), "cake and custard" (*trifle*) and "cookies" (*biscuits*) for "dessert" (*pudding*). The British call our "potato chips" *crisps*.

Finally, if Edward were speaking American English he would have said you throw a "can" in the "trash can" when you "wash the dishes," and a "truck" (*lorry*) takes the "trash" to the "dump."

Canadians, who were ruled by the British until the early 1900s and are still part of the British Commonwealth, use some British and some American words. They wear British *braces* and eat *porridge*, rather than wearing "suspenders" and eating "oatmeal." But they put American "gas" in their "trucks" and fix them with "wrenches," rather than the British style of putting *petrol* in *lorries* and working on them with *spanners*.

Most words are the same in various dialects. But they are often pronounced differently. A Scotsman may say *ah* for "all," *wuzni* for "wasn't" and *wilni* for "won't." Some dialects add extra syllables. If an Irishman wants to sell a sure cure for a girl, he says it is a *shuwirr kiyuwirr* for the *girril*.

Cockneys are working-class people from the East End of London

SHIBBOLETHS   Dialects have been used to catch spies! The Bible, in the twelfth chapter of Judges, tells of a time when two tribes, the Ephraimites and Gileadites, were at war. The tribes spoke Hebrew with different dialects. The Gileadites used a *sh* sound, but the Ephraimites didn't. To find out if someone was an enemy, the Gileadites made him say *shibboleth*, which means "river." If he said *sibboleth*, because he couldn't pronounce the *sh*, they would know he was an enemy and kill him. But if he could say *shibboleth*, with the *sh*, they let him go. Now the term *shibboleth* is used to describe words or customs that distinguish one group of people from others. For instance, the words *soda, tonic, cola,* and *pop* are shibboleths. People from the East of the United States usually ask for a *soda*, while those from the West usually get *pop*. Bostonians drink *tonic*, and many southerners enjoy *cola*. Which do you say?

who speak their own distinct dialect. (The name Cockney comes from the Middle English word *cokeney,* which meant "cock's egg," slang for a townsman.) Cockneys drop most *h*'s, saying *'e 'ad an 'orrible 'eadache* and *geddoud of 'ee',* "get out of here." A Cockney calls a "lady" a *lie-dy,* and says *Oi moit* for "I might."

London Cockney dialects also use special words called "rhyming slang." They call a "hat" a *tit-for-tat,* a "table" *Cain and Abel,* and "money" *bees and honey.* Can you make up your own rhyming slang to use as a code with your friends? Some London dialects use a backward slang which is another kind of code: *eno* is "one," *yob* is "boy," and *xis* means "six"!

Dialects have their own pronunciations: *good mawnin'* or *good mawerning.* They can differ in grammar: "Who dat man?" or "Who is that man?" Or they can use special words: "I drove him home," or the southern "I carried him home." But people speaking different dialects of the same language can usually understand each other.

DIALECTS IN SPACE AND TIME

Sometimes dialects are separated by geography—mountains or rivers. These keep people from being in close contact with each other and influencing each other's dialects. But often there is no clear boundary where one dialect stops and the next begins. If you traveled from Germany to Holland, listening to the dialects spoken in villages along the way, you would find they change only slightly from one town to the next. The people in each town can easily understand the people in neighboring towns. Close to the border, you would hear people speaking dialects halfway between Dutch and German. The people speaking German on one side of the border would easily understand the people speaking Dutch on the other side of the border. These border Germans might find it hard, though, to understand a dialect of German spoken in Austria, on the other side of their country. Still, the Austrian and the German read and write the same language, while the Dutchman and the German do not.

An old Hindi proverb says, "Language changes every eighteen or twenty miles." This is quite true in India, where many different languages are spoken and each has its own panorama of dialects. It is not true, though, in the United States. The United States is a much younger country than India, and people here have not been very isolated from each other. So we have fewer differences in languages and dialects over much larger distances than many other countries.

Dialects develop over time. The more isolated people are from each other, and the longer they have been isolated, the more their speech differs from other speakers of their language. For instance, in very mountainous countries, like Switzerland and Yemen (Middle East), people tend to live in small communities which do not communicate with each other. They develop many dialects which differ a lot from each other. In countries where communication is easier, people mix with each other more, hear each other's speech, and read each other's writing, so they tend to speak like each other.

The British have been speaking some form of English since the Angles, Saxons, and Jutes invaded England more than 1,500 years ago. For the next thousand years, Britain was divided into various parts, which did not have good communication with each other. Only since 1476 has the English language been printed, so that the written word was widely spread and helped standardize the language. England and Wales have only been united since 1536. Scotland was added to the United Kingdom in 1603, when James I, son of Mary, Queen of Scots, became king of England, Scotland, and Wales. So for most of their history, the British were developing different varieties of English which had little chance to influence each other.

Beginning in the 1600s, many of these varieties were transported to America. But since people speaking different dialects of English were living in communities together (for instance, there were about thirty different dialects of English spoken on the *Mayflower*), people began to speak more alike. Since the 1800s we have had inventions like radio, telephones, and television which enable us to hear the speech of people from faraway places. In the past 200 years, trains, then cars, then planes have made it easy for people to travel all around the country. Some places that were once difficult to reach, like the Appalachian Mountains, developed distinctive dialects which are hard for outsiders to understand. They kept forms of words that were being dropped elsewhere, because they weren't in contact with other English-speakers. Areas that have been settled the longest, like New England and the South, have the most noticeable dialects. In some areas, dialects were influenced by other languages spoken in the area. But in general, there is much less variety among American dialects than there is among British dialects.

SOCIAL DIALECTS: HIGH AND LOW

Any group of people that doesn't mix much with other groups develops its own way of talking. Your dialect may show your ethnic group or social class. A Cockney girl in the movie *My Fair Lady* sold flowers on the streets of London. Her Cockney dialect showed that she was poor and uneducated. But when a linguist taught her standard English, the dialect of the upper class, she was accepted into high society and thought to be royalty!

Dialect is not something a person is born with. Everyone learns to talk the way those around him speak. A white boy raised in an area that is mostly black will speak with the dialect of the black people around him. A Spanish girl raised by an Irish family will speak English as the Irish do, with no trace of a Spanish accent.

All dialects are equally useful for explaining what you want to say. A person's dialect doesn't show how smart he is. But for people of many different backgrounds to communicate with each other, both in speech and in writing, it is useful for them to all agree on one dialect. That dialect is the "standard" form of a language. In English the standard form is not defined and enforced by an organization like the "academies" that regulate standard French and Czech. Instead it is a form of English that most educated English-speakers agree on. Standard English is constantly changing, like all living languages. It is not a clearly-defined set of words and structures. You can hear standard English from newscasters on television or the radio, college professors and schoolteachers, and many other educated people. Most books, including this one, are written in standard English. Children are taught standard English in school. For instance, you learn not to say "ain't" and to say "he came" or "he comes" instead of "he come." This variety of English will help you communicate with other English-speakers from different backgrounds. It can also help you to get better jobs, since most people think that a speaker of standard English is better educated and more intelligent (though this is not necessarily true) than people who speak other dialects.

How does one dialect come to be standard? In some countries, like Norway and Greece, the standard form of a language is decided by the government. That form is then taught in the schools and used in print. Standard German and Polish are combinations of various regional dialects. Often the standard dialect is the dialect of the people thought to be the "best" in a society—those who have the most money, power, and education. Other people, wanting a better position in society, copy the speech of those above them. Standard

French developed from the dialect of Paris, which is the cultural, economic, and political center of France. The same thing happened in England. The speech of the upper-class people in London, especially those who were part of the royal court, was copied by scholars, writers, and schools. Printed materials, which were mostly produced by educated Londoners, spread this dialect across the country. Eventually upper-class London English became a standard for the country, taught in the schools and copied by everyone who wanted to speak and write "well." Standard British English is often called "the Queen's English" or "B.B.C. English," after the British Broadcasting Corporation. B.B.C. television and radio announcers use standard British English and spread it around the world.

Standard English is a little different in different countries. Standard American English, standard Scottish English, and standard Australian English all developed from the standard English of England, but they occasionally use different structures and different vocabulary. For instance in standard American English we use the word *elevator*, while in England the word *lift* is standard.

Standard English does not have to be pronounced in a certain way, and it is often pronounced like the speaker's own dialect. However, some pronunciations are preferred because they sound more "high-class" than others. In England the preferred pronunciation is called R.P., or "Received Pronunciation," which is the accent "received" by students in English private schools (which the English, of course, call *public schools*). In R.P., the *a* in *path* would be pronounced like the *a* in *father*, and *part* would be pronounced *paht*. The preferred pronunciation in America, on the other hand, is a midwestern accent, with all the *r*'s pronounced and a flat *a* sound (as in *cat*) rather than an *ah* sound in words like *path*.

Even standard dialects change. The preferred pronunciation of English in England seems to be changing now. More upper-class people are using words and sounds from what used to be lower-class dialects. For instance, some of them are using Cockney pronunciations, like replacing *t*'s, *p*'s, and *k*'s with the sound in the middle of *uh-oh*, and saying *bu'er* for "butter" and *te'nical* for "technical." This is probably because British society has changed, and "class" is not so important any more. People who don't want to look like upper-class snobs are changing their speech so that they sound more like everyone else.

Standard English developed mostly without official intervention. But sometimes standard languages are specifically chosen and controlled. Basque is spoken in four provinces of southern France and three provinces of northern Spain. Its speakers are trying hard to keep it alive. But each province has a different dialect. In the 1970s a standard Basque dialect, Euskera Batua (*Euskera* is the Basques' own name for their language and *Batua* means "unified"), was created. The Basques hope that this standard language will make it easier for them to keep their language alive, since it makes it easier for Basques from different provinces to communicate with each other.

Standard English, like other languages, includes a range of speech appropriate to different occasions. The written language is more formal and structured than spoken language usually is. The language used in a history text or in a mystery story, the language of a college lecture or a Sunday School class, the language of a woman speaking to her boss or a child speaking to his friends—all these can be standard English, but with different words and sometimes different grammar. Which of these would be a more formal style of English: "I'm really worn out" or "I am extremely fatigued"? The second, of course, is more formal and more likely to be used in writing than in speech. The differences are not so extreme, though, that we would call them different dialects. English does not have a set of words that only belong to one level of speech or another.

Some languages do use two different dialects, with different sets of words, which could almost be considered different languages. This is called "diglossia," which means "two languages." There is "High German" and German "dialects," "classical Arabic" and "colloquial Arabic," and "high" and "low" forms of Greek and Tamil (a language of India). For a sermon, political speech, lecture, or news broadcast, the "high" form of a language is used. In everyday conversations, the "low" language is used.

Some words are pronounced differently in "high" and "low" languages. The word *ist* ("is") in high standard German is pronounced *isch* in Swiss German dialects. Both speakers, though, would use the high form, *ist*, in writing.

Compare the sentence "I can't go to the house" in high classical Arabic: *La 'astatee'u an 'athhab ilal manzili*, with the Jordanian low colloquial Arabic: *Ma ba'dar 'aruuH il bayt*. The words and grammar are quite different. (Arabic is not written with our alphabet; these sentences are transliterated to show you approximately how they sound.) Most Arabs write in the classical language, using their colloquial dialects just for speaking.

Why do some languages have high and low forms? Sometimes, as in German and Basque, high and low forms of a language develop because, over time, very different dialects of the language have developed. One dialect is chosen or created (by choosing forms from several dialects) to be the high language. Everyone then learns that dialect in school. The high language may be a form of nationalism, keeping people united and thinking in terms of "our country" and "our language." It may also be a matter of practicality. It would be very inconvenient to only be able to talk to people in nearby villages, and to have to read books written in unfamiliar dialects.

A high language may also develop, as it did in Greece, when people use an older form of the language for church, government, writing, and other formal uses. The high language of Greece is called Katharevousa, which means "purifying" Greek. It was put together in an attempt to revive ancient Greek, with its complex grammar, and get rid of the "impurities" which had crept into the language—borrowed words from Italian, Turkish, and Slavic languages. This language was the official language of Greece which all schoolchildren had to use from 1834 to 1976. Now Dimotiki (the everyday low language) is the official language, but Katharevousa is still used for official documents and scientific books.

People often think that an older form of a language must be "better" than newer, changing forms. Their use of the older form shows their respect for tradition and the past. In Greece, in 1903, there was rioting when the New Testament was translated into the "low" language. Many people thought that it did not show respect to the Bible to read it in everyday language. They believed that only the "high" Katharevousa language was appropriate for religious use.

MEN AND WOMEN, BOYS AND GIRLS

Occasionally women and men speak different dialects of the same language! Even in English men and women talk a little differently. For instance, women more often use expressions like "oh, dear," "we had such a nice party," or "it was so lovely." In a few languages, men and women use different dialects.

Women in Japan can choose to use the "feminine" style of Japanese. This style has been taught to Japanese women since the early eleventh century as a way of being gentle and submissive and showing their special position in society. In feminine style women say *atashi* for "I" rather than *watakushi* (used by men and women) or *boku* (traditionally used only by men). Women use nouns in the "polite form," which start with *o-*. For instance, they say *osakana* for "fish" rather than *sakana*. Special words and different intonations are used in "feminine" sentences. Women in Japan are much more likely than men to use "honorific" speech, which shows that the person they are talking to is more important than they are.

Nowadays, Japanese women can choose their style of speech. Some use the feminine style when talking about their children or their home. They discuss business in a neutral style, used by both men and women. Japanese women who want to emphasize that they are equal to men may use the more assertive men's style. Some schoolgirls use *boku*, the men's word for "I," to show that they are as important as men. Japanese men, on the other hand, sometimes use feminine language to show gentleness and consideration.

In the Cheyenne Indian language, a man says "yes" as *haáhe*, while a woman says *héehe'e*. Nowadays men sometimes use the women's "yes." This probably means that the roles of men and women in Cheyenne culture are changing. Language change often follows changes in culture and customs.

If you want to say "thank you" to a Hopi Indian, you say *kwakwha* if you're a boy, *askwali* if you're a girl. The Hopis think it's quite funny if you use the wrong word, as if you'd forgotten whether you were a boy or a girl!

Yukaghir is a Siberian language whose speakers traditionally lived in nomadic bands, living by hunting and fishing. In Yukaghir a word with a *tj* sound in the men's dialect is said with a *ts* by women and children and a *chj* by old people. So during a man's lifetime he uses three different dialects: the women's version when he is a child, the men's version as an adult, and finally the old people's version! From this we can guess that a man in Yukaghir society probably has three distinct roles in life (as a boy, a man, and an old person), while Yukaghir women have one role as girls and women, and then when they are old have about the same place in their society as old men do.

The people who first studied the language of the Carib Indians, who live in the Lesser Antilles islands near South America, said that the women and the men spoke different languages! Actually, the men use many words and expressions that women understand but don't use. The women have their own words and phrases which a man would be ridiculed for using. The Indians claim that when the Caribs first conquered their islands, they killed all the men living there. They kept the women, who spoke an Arawak language, for their wives. Words from the Arawak language are still spoken by women but not men.

Some linguists doubt this story. They think that Carib, like some other languages, developed male and female dialects because of "taboo" (forbidden) words. Their religious beliefs allowed only men to say certain words. The women then had to develop other words to use instead of those taboo words.

SLANG, SWEARING, AND JARGON

Other varieties of language are not dialects but are words or phrases used only by specific groups of speakers. "Slang" is informal language used by a group of people, usually young people. Some of the words are new, made-up words, and others are shortened words or familiar words used in new and exaggerated ways. You probably use slang with your friends. If you say you "aced" a test, think someone is a "hunk," want to "split," or call something "groovy," you're using slang. Most slang disappears after a few years (like "groovy"!). What are some slang words you use? Can you think of any that you used to use that are out of style now? Every language has its own slang, which changes all the time.

Although most slang words disappear before they ever become widely used, sometimes slang words become part of the language. Shakespeare brought 1,700 new words into standard English. Many of them were slang in his time. *Assassinate, bump, fireworks, lonely,* and *hurry* were all slang words in Shakespeare's day, and were brought into everyday language through his plays. Some more recent words that started out as slang and now are listed in the dictionary as standard words are *cab* from *cabriolet, cop* for *policeman,* and the worldwide favorite *okay,* a slang word which was probably invented in the 1830s, though no one knows for sure where it came from.

Some slang words are also swear words, or profanity. These are words that most people in a society think are bad, rude, immoral, or irreverent. They are related to things that are taboo, things that people prefer to avoid talking about. In English and many other languages, swear words usually refer to filth, actions that are forbidden, or things that are sacred. Some languages, including many American Indian languages, do not have swear words (except perhaps borrowed ones). The Basques joke about all their swear words coming from Spanish. Either Basque had no swear words to start with, or else the words they had have been lost and replaced by words used by the Spaniards who surround them. Other languages have taboo words for the left hand, for certain relatives, or for some animals. In Norway any reference to the devil is very profane, while in Germany a word meaning "pig-dog" is a nasty insult. In most languages "euphemisms," or milder, more socially acceptable words, develop in order to avoid taboo words. *Heck* and *darn* are English euphemisms. In the 1800s in the United States, *leg* was a dirty word; *limb* was used instead. During the same time period, *pants* were known as *unmentionables,* or even *unwhisperables*!

Every occupation has its own variety of language, a kind of shorthand called its "jargon." Can you "translate" this oil business telex? "WOW. MORE DOWNTIME ON THE LAY BARGE—ROUGHNECKS IN THE DOGHOUSE." It means, "Waiting On Weather. Work on the barge laying submarine pipelines has been held up again, and the drilling crews are taking shelter."

Sports also have their own jargon. If you're a basketball player or fan, you may be able to understand this account: "The home team forces a turnover and runs a three-on-one fast break down the court. The guard lobs the ball into the paint where the forward slam-dunks it through the hoop." That means, "The team that's playing on its own court steals the ball from the other team and quickly dribbles (bounces) and passes the ball down the court before the other team can get into position, so that three offensive players and only one defensive player are at the other end. The guard (a player in a certain position) throws an arcing pass over the defense player which comes down in the painted rectangle under the basket, where the forward (another player) jumps above the basket and throws the ball down through the basket." See how jargon made the first description much shorter and simpler?

There are many varieties of language. Your speech may show where you grew up and what social group you belong to. Dialects give language variety and color, and they change quickly. A year from now, if you move to a different part of the country, you may find yourself speaking a different dialect!

A language is a dialect with an army and a navy.
popular saying

3

POLITICS, FAITH, AND FORBIDDEN TONGUES: LANGUAGES AND LOYALTIES

DIALECT OR LANGUAGE?

What makes a language a language and not a dialect? When did the dialect of Latin spoken in Spain become the Spanish language, and when did the Old Norse (Viking) dialect spoken in Norway become the Norwegian language? The answer is both linguistic and political. Latin was spoken in the area we now call Spain from about 206 B.C., when it was conquered by the Romans. As the Latin spoken in Spain became more and more different from the Latin spoken in France, the Spanish and French dialects of Latin were developing into separate languages. The Catholic Church recognized in about 813 A.D. that Latin was no longer all one language, and Emperor Charlemagne decreed that sermons should be given in the Roman dialects rather than in Latin. Finally, when the Spanish began to think of themselves as a people and a nation, separate from other nations, their Latin dialect became "a dialect with an army and a navy," and they called it the Spanish language.

Political boundaries often define languages. Norwegian is very similar to Swedish and Danish, its neighboring languages in Scandinavia. The people of Sweden, Norway, and Denmark, speaking their own languages, can usually understand each other. You might say they're speaking dialects of a Scandinavian language. But each country has its own customs, culture, and political system. A Norwegian would never say that he was speaking a dialect of Swedish, or vice versa. So these nations are said to speak different languages, not different dialects. (Look in appendix 1 to see how much alike Swedish and Norwegian are.)

Culture can define languages, too. Slovaks and Czechs speak languages which are ninety percent alike, although their alphabets are a little different. They were united for many years in one country, Czechoslovakia. But since they are culturally different and consider themselves separate ethnic groups, they continued to call Czech and Slovak languages, not dialects. They now have separated into their own countries, the Czech Republic and Slovakia.

Dutch of the Netherlands and the Flemish language of Belgium are also alike enough to be called dialects of one language. They are written alike but pronounced differently. But each group of people sees its language as part of its own unique culture and identity. Language has been a sensitive issue in Belgium, since it is about thirty-three percent French-speaking Walloons in the South, toward France, and fifty-five percent Flemish-speaking Flemings in the North, toward Holland, plus about one percent Germans in a small area bordering Germany. (The rest of the Belgians are from a variety of backgrounds.) Since 1966 Belgium has had four official language regions—one where French is the official language, one where Flemish is the official language, one German area, and a bilingual French/Flemish area around Brussels, the capital city. In school, children study most subjects in the official language of their area (usually their first language) and are also required to study another major language of their country as a second language. The Belgian government knows that their country will only stay together if each nationality feels that its language, and therefore its identity, is being protected.

Serbs and Croats speak languages which are so similar that both languages are usually called Serbo-Croatian. But they use different alphabets, because they traditionally belong to different branches of Christianity. The Catholic Croats use a Roman alphabet like ours, while the Orthodox Serbs use a Cyrillic alphabet, like Russian's. The word "young," for instance, would be written *mlad* by Croatians and млад by Serbians, but pronounced the same. They use different alphabets because the central authority of the Catholic faith is in

TABLE 3
NAME THAT LANGUAGE

Many groups of people call their languages something quite different from what others call them. Try to guess where these languages are spoken: Zhong Wen, Putunghwa, Khmer, Español, Cymraeg, Farsi, Dari, Deutsch, Nederlands, Magyar, Dakota, Euskera, Nihongo, Inuit, Nama, Ying wen.

Zhong Wen	Chinese, literally "Middle Language," the language of the "Middle Country" (China).
Putonghua	Mandarin Chinese, "common standard language"
Khmer	Cambodian
Español	Spanish
Cymraeg	Welsh
Farsi	Persian, spoken in Iran
Dari	Persian, spoken in Afghanistan
Deutsch	German
Nederlands	Dutch
Magyar	Hungarian
Dakota	Sioux
Euskera	Basque
Nihongo	Japanese
Inuit, Inupik, Yupik	Eskimo
Nama	Hottentot, spoken in southern Africa
Ying wen, Yong-o, Eigo, Tieng Anh, Angrezi, Engraji, Angolul, Engelsk, Ingilizçe, Ingleezi, Inglés	English: what it is called in Chinese, Korean, Japanese, Vietnamese, Hindi, Bengali, Hungarian, Norwegian, Turkish, Arabic, Spanish

Rome, where our Roman alphabet developed, while Orthodox Christians of eastern Europe use the Cyrillic alphabet developed by Orthodox missionaries to Russia (see chapter 10). Muslims of the area, in Bosnia, also speak Serbo-Croatian, writing it with the Roman alphabet. The Serbs, Croats, and Muslims used to be united in one country, Yugoslavia, but have now separated into several republics.

Forms of language that linguists would call dialects may be called languages because of politics, culture, or religion. On the other hand, forms that are linguistically different enough to be languages may be considered dialects because of politics and history. People refer to the "Chinese language." You hear about the "Mandarin dialect" of Chinese, or the "Cantonese dialect." In reality, people speaking these dialects cannot understand each other at all! In Mandarin Chinese, "five" is *wŭ*; in Cantonese, *ngh*. The many Chinese languages are related, but quite different.

All these languages are called Chinese for two reasons. First, politically, they're all spoken in the country of China. Second, they're all written alike! Chinese writing uses symbols for *words* rather than *sounds*. A Chinese person sees a symbol and thinks of a word in his own dialect. If you draw a picture of a red dog, and a Spanish boy sees it, he says *perro roja*. You communicated without speaking the same words. In this way a speaker of Mandarin Chinese sees the symbol 男人, which he knows means "man," and he reads it as *nán rén*. A Cantonese speaker sees the same symbol, thinks of "man," and reads it as *nam yun*.

FAITHS OF OUR FATHERS AND MOTHERS: HOW RELIGIONS AFFECT LANGUAGES

Many people's first loyalties are to a religion, rather than to a nation. Serbian and Croatian get their alphabets from two faiths, Roman Catholic and Eastern Orthodox Christianity. In South Asia, two languages are separated by religions which differ much more radically from each other: Islam and Hinduism. About 325 million people, mostly in India and Pakistan, speak Hindi or Urdu. Speakers of these two languages can understand each other so well that some linguists call Hindi and Urdu two dialects of one language called Hindustani. (See appendix 1 for examples of Hindi and Urdu words.) People of the Muslim religion in India and Pakistan call their language Urdu. Since Arabic is important in Islam, Urdu-speakers have borrowed many words from Arabic, as well as Persian. Urdu uses a modified Arabic alphabet, written from right to left.

Most speakers of Hindi, the national language of India, follow the Hindu religion. The ancient holy language of Hinduism, Sanskrit, uses a script called Devanagari, which is written from left to right like English. (See example of Hindi and Urdu scripts in chapter 10.) Hindi is also written with the Devanagari script. It uses many words originally from Sanskrit, especially when written in a formal style. The literatures of Hindi and Urdu are quite different. But everyday spoken Hindi and Urdu are very similar.

Sanskrit, an Indo-European language very distantly related to English, is preserved in holy writings of the Hindu, Buddhist, and Jainist religions. Hindu priests believed that their rituals might not work if they did not pronounce their hymns exactly as the originals were pronounced. So Sanskrit was spoken, unchanged, by Hindu priests until the end of the Middle Ages. It is still used as a literary language.

Religions that place a high value on tradition and history often preserve the languages of their holy books and worship services. The Catholic Church has kept Latin in use for centuries. Latin was the language of the Roman Empire. When the empire fell apart, speakers of Latin across Europe became isolated from each other and their dialects developed into Romance languages like French, Spanish, and Italian. The Catholic Church in those countries continued to use Latin for religious ceremonies. By the Middle Ages, Latin was the language of educated people, who used it to communicate with scholars of other countries. (It is still used by scientists today in naming their discoveries. The scientific names of animals and plants are usually from Latin.) Since the 1960s, Roman Catholic services have been held in local languages rather than in Latin, but Latin continues to be an official language of the Catholic Church. In the same way, the Ge'ez language of Ethiopia died out in the ninth century but has been preserved, and is still used today, in ceremonies of the Ethiopian Orthodox Church.

Christians have also helped preserve living languages in many remote areas. Because they believe it is important for people to be able to read the Bible in their native languages, Christian missionaries have gone to many parts of the world and developed alphabets for previously unwritten tongues. Then they print basic readers, Bibles, and other literature in those languages. Missionaries have developed alphabets for languages of Hawaii and other Pacific Islands, Australian aborigines, and remote areas of Papua New Guinea, Africa, South America, and many other parts of the world. Having their languages in writing helps people value their own languages and cultures, and makes it less likely that they will lose them.

Muslims place a very high value on the Arabic language. They believe that their holy book, the Qur'an (or Koran), was written in heaven before the beginning of time and that its words descended from heaven to their prophet Muhammad between 610 and 632 A.D. The flowery literary Arabic of the Qur'an is considered the best language, the language of heaven. Any translation of the Qur'an is called an "interpretation," since the true Qur'an can only be written in Arabic. This is unlike the Christian view of the Bible, which Christians believe to be God's Word in whatever language it is translated into. Muslim ritual prayers, called *salaat*, must be recited in Arabic, no matter what the first language of the speaker is. After saying the ritual prayers, though, Muslims may pray personal prayers in their own languages.

Because Arabic is so important to Muslims, the Arabic language spread with the spread of Islam. At first Arabic was spoken in the Arabian peninsula (what is now Saudi Arabia and the surrounding countries). From 632 to 750 A.D. the Muslim caliphate (leaders of Islam after Muhammad's death) spread their empire, by both conquest and peaceful means, until it included the whole Arabian peninsula, Palestine, Syria, Egypt, Libya, Iraq, North Africa, Spain and Portugal, parts of Armenia and Persia (Iran), and lands east to the borders of China and India. Most of the people in these countries converted to the Muslim religion. The Arabs settled among them, marrying local women and starting colonies. The countries of the Arabian peninsula and North Africa began using the Arabic language when they converted to Islam, and they still speak Arabic today. (Some minorities in North Africa still speak their original

Berber languages, but most of them also speak Arabic.) These Arabic-speaking countries feel a sense of unity today, although they are independent countries, because they share a common language.

Areas a little farther from the Arabian peninsula, like Persia (modern-day Iran), Pakistan, and Turkey, kept their own languages when they became Muslim. Through contacts with Arabs and Arabic religious writings, however, they borrowed huge numbers of Arabic words. They also adapted the Arabic script, a flowing alphabet written from right to left, for their languages. (See chapter 10 for examples of Arabic, Farsi, and Urdu scripts.) Over half the words of the Persian language Farsi came from Arabic. Languages from Indonesian to Spanish include Arabic words because of the influence of Islam. The Muslim Moors who ruled Spain and Portugal from the eighth to the fifteenth centuries did not require the conquered people to accept Arabic, but Spanish and Portuguese borrowed hundreds of words from Arabic at that time. The Spanish words range from *mezquino* (from Arabic *maskeen*, "poor") to *álgebra* and *alcohol* (from Arabic *aljabr* and *alkuhul*). *Al-* on the beginning of many words, in English as well as Spanish, is from Arabic *al-*, meaning "the." Many scientific and mathematical ideas developed among the Arabs before Europeans became interested in science. In the eleventh to fourteenth centuries, Europeans learned many scientific ideas from the Arabs and borrowed words to describe them. So words like *algebra* and *alcohol* entered Latin, the language of learning at that time, and from Latin they came into English.

Arab traders also spread Islam to parts of Africa. Swahili is a Bantu language used as a "lingua franca," a common language used between people of different languages. Tribes speaking many languages in East Africa use Swahili to communicate with each other. Arab Muslim traders spread Swahili and added Arabic words to it, like *kitabu* from Arabic *kitab* (book), and *jirani* from Arabic *jiran* (neighbors). Even the name *Swahili* comes from an Arabic word, *sawaaHil*, which means "coasts, seashores."

Even though the Muslim religion has spread the Arabic language and Arabic words, not all Arabic-speakers are Muslims. (And many Muslims do not speak Arabic, though they use Arabic for religious practices.) Sometimes people who refused to take the conqueror's religion still ended up speaking the language, in order to communicate with those around them. For hundreds of years after Muslims conquered Egypt, the Egyptian Coptic Church clung to their Christian religion and their Coptic language, descended from the ancient Egyptian of the Pharoahs. Coptic was widely spoken until at least the sixteenth century. Today, however, it has died out as a spoken language and is used only in rituals of the Coptic Church. Egyptian Christians now speak Arabic like their Muslim neighbors. Christians and even Jews in Arabic-speaking countries usually speak Arabic.

Aramaic, the language Jesus spoke, has managed to survive for two thousand years in a few small villages in Syria. Surrounded by a sea of Arabic, these people cling to their native tongue. Their favorite phrase is *lo bo Alo*, "if God wills it." The same phrase is popular in Arabic as *in sha' Allah*.

The Mourner's Kaddish, an important prayer of the Jewish religion, is still said today in Aramaic. Much of the Talmud, a book which interprets Jewish law, is also in Aramaic. Most Jewish prayers, though, are said in Hebrew, the ancient language of Judaism. The Jewish Scriptures (which Christians call the Old Testament) and other religious writings are read and studied in Hebrew. Jewish people did not spread Hebrew around the world, though, as Muslims did with Arabic. Instead, Jewish people in different countries developed their own languages and dialects, based on local languages but influenced by Hebrew. The Jewish language based on French, called Zarphatic, and the Jewish language based on Italian, Italkian, died out about a thousand years ago. Jews of Spain and Portugal and their descendants spoke Dzhudezmo (or Ladino), which is similar to Spanish, and Portuguesic, which is related to Portuguese. Many early Jewish immigrants to the United States spoke Dzhudezmo. Few American Jews use it now, but there are still about 100,000 Dzhudezmo-speakers in Israel. The Jews of Yemen speak their own Jewish dialect of Arabic, with Hebrew words and expressions mixed in. They write their version of Arabic with a Hebrew script rather than the Arabic alphabet.

The Yiddish language, sometimes considered a dialect of German, developed among Jews in central and eastern Europe around 1100 A.D. Mixed in with a base of about seventy percent German words are many words from Hebrew, Slavic languages, and a bit of Latin, French, Italian, and English. (Compare the Yiddish, German, and Hebrew words in appendix 1.) Yiddish is written with the Hebrew alphabet. Most Jewish immigrants to the United States, from the 1800s until about the 1960s, were Yiddish-speakers.

Yiddish has contributed a number of words to English, including *bagel, chutzpa* (nerve, gall), *klutz* (clumsy person), and *kosher* (proper). The *-nik* ending on words like *beatnik* and *no-goodnik* came from Yiddish, which borrowed it from Russian. We also use some expressions which started out as direct translations from Yiddish expressions: "I need that like a hole in the head," "get lost," "excuse the expression," "how come?" and "smart he isn't." Most Jews in the United States no longer speak Yiddish, but many use their own Jewish dialect of English. This dialect includes words, phrases, and pronunciations from Yiddish.

The Jews developed their own languages in Europe for two reasons. First, they lived in communities where they had much more contact with fellow Jews than with other Europeans. Second, their Scriptures and religious teachings are mostly in Hebrew. Hebrew is a Semitic language which developed about 3,000 years ago. It was used by Jews in Palestine until it died out in about 200 A.D., when it was replaced by Aramaic and Greek. After that it was not spoken as anyone's first language, but Jews kept using it as a religious and literary language. It was revived in the early 1900s, and was made the official language of the state of Israel in the 1940s. The Hebrew language was chosen to unite Jews immigrating to Israel from many different lands with many different native tongues. It gives them an identity related to their religion and their new country rather than to the lands they came from. Religion and politics have changed Hebrew from a dead language to the native tongue of many Israelis.

PROVERBS

An entire book of the Jewish Scriptures is called "Proverbs." It includes wise sayings such as "A gentle answer turns away wrath, but a harsh word stirs up anger" and "Pride goes before destruction." Many cultures store their wisdom in the proverbs and sayings of their language. The Poles say *nie od razu Kraków zbudowano*, "Cracow was not built all at once." (Cracow is an important city in Poland.) That's like the English proverb "Rome wasn't built in a day." To the Mossi of Africa, "the underwear of today is worth more than the trousers of tomorrow." That means, "a bird in the hand is worth two in the bush." The Swahili proverb *Ulimi hauna mfupa* means "the tongue has no bone," or, "it's easier said than done."

Proverbs can show family relationships. An English proverb says "a daughter is a daughter all her life, but a son is a son 'til he takes a wife," implying that a girl's first loyalty is to her parents. But in Arab culture, a son usually continues living with his parents after he is married, and his children are raised in their home, while a daughter moves to her husband's family's home. So the Arabs say, *ibn il'ibn ibni, wa bint ilbint bint innaas*. "The son of my son is my son, and the daughter of my daughter is someone else's daughter."

Some proverbs show what a culture values. In Korea they say, "even for a sheet of very thin paper, it's better for one person to lift each side." That means that cooperation is always important. The Russians say, "the ones who don't risk, don't drink champagne." You can hear the Hispanic emphasis on hospitality in the proverb *donde comen seis, comen siete*, "where six can eat, seven can eat." In English that's like "there's always room for one more." Arabs value patience and peace, saying "patience is beautiful," "hurry is the sister to destruction," and *fulaan kathiir ilharaka qaliil ilbaraka*, "the person of much motion has little blessing." Sometimes proverbs contradict each other, showing two points of view within a culture, or perhaps a desire for balance. The Arabs also say *kul haraka fiiha baraka*, "all motion is blessed." Russians say "the slower you go, the farther you'll get," but "latecomers only get bones."

Many proverbs are the same in different cultures. The Swedes say *sådan fader såden son*, "like father like son," as well as "all is not gold that glitters" and "it is no use crying over spilt milk."

Some proverbs are used to laugh at people who are foolish. In Arabic, you can say "he wants meat from his sheep and he wants his sheep walking." In other words, "he wants to have his cake and eat it too." Swahili-speakers are cautioned, "don't curse the crocodile before you have crossed the river," while the Chinese say, "don't set out unarmed to fight a tiger."

Many proverbs show what is special about a culture, how it is different from others. As the Russian proverb says, "what is healthy to a Russian is death to a German."

CANADIAN LANGUAGE LOYALTIES

In Canada, language identifies and divides two cultures with different histories and different religions. Canada was first explored and colonized by the French, starting with the colony of Port Royal in 1605. It was called New France until 1763, when the British won it in the French and Indian Wars. During those wars, the eastern coastal area of Canada, which the French called Acadia and the British called Nova Scotia, was taken by the British. In 1755, the British governor expelled 10,000 French Acadians who would not swear allegiance to Britain. A few thousand of those made their way down to Louisiana, which was also controlled by the French at that time. Their descendants, living in isolated communities in the marshes and *bayous* (waterways) of South Louisiana, still speak French today. They are called Cajuns, short for "Acadians." Their dialect of French is an old form mixed with some English, German, Spanish, and Indian words.

When the British took over New France, they renamed it Canada (probably from the Huron-Iroquois Indian word *kanata*, meaning "village" or "community"). Most of the French lived in the eastern area, which is now the province of Quebec. After the Revolutionary War, many people who were still loyal to the British king left the United States and moved up to British Canada. From the beginning there were conflicts between the British and French Canadians, who had different religious (British Protestant, French Catholic), social, and legal systems, and of course different languages. Today Canada still has two official languages: French and English. The Canadian French dialect is at least as different from the French of France as American English is different from British English.

LANGUAGES AND LOYALTIES

In Canada, as in many countries, speakers of different languages have struggled over how much power each group should have. The government of Quebec in the 1960s had the slogan *Maîtres chez nous*, "Masters of our own house." In 1976 Quebec banned languages other than French on signs and required that French be used in most schools and businesses. The "language police" even took down "Merry Christmas" signs and destroyed "Dunkin' Donuts" bags because they were marked in English. These laws were ruled illegal in 1988. The Supreme Court of Canada said Quebec could make French the main language of the province, but not its only language. Quebec is still eighty percent French-speaking, and some of its people would like Quebec to be independent from the rest of Canada. The question of how independent they will be has not yet been answered.

WORTH FIGHTING FOR: PERSECUTED LANGUAGES

Language gives groups of people identity and keeps their cultures alive. When one group of people is trying to control another, they often try to wipe out the subject people's language.

When the Angles, Saxons, and Jutes conquered England in the fifth century, they pushed back the native Celts, with their Celtic languages, to the far north and west of the country. But the Celts hung onto their languages: Scots Gaelic, Irish Gaelic, Cornish, Welsh, and Manx. Breton was spoken on the coast of what is now France. These languages are all very similar. French onion sellers used to come to Wales in the summer. Speaking Breton, they could talk with their Welsh-speaking customers.

Over the centuries, under persecution, the languages declined. Cornish, which was spoken in Southwest England, died out in the 1700s. Now people are working to revive it, and about a hundred people speak it as a second language. Manx was spoken on the little Isle of Man, which lies between England and Ireland. Manx became extinct during this century, but a few people are trying to revive it, too.

In 1800 things looked good for Irish Gaelic, or Erse. More than half the people of Ireland spoke Irish Gaelic. Then Ireland came completely under the rule of England. The schools, with parents' cooperation, began to push children to speak only English. Gaelic-speaking children were ridiculed. Brothers and sisters were encouraged to spy on each other and keep each other from speaking Gaelic. Each child had to wear a stick on a string around his neck. Every time he used an Irish Gaelic word, his parents would cut a notch in the wood. At the end of the week, the schoolmaster punished the child according to how many notches there were on his stick.

Today few Irish people, about 120,000 out of a total population of 3,600,000, speak Irish Gaelic. Now that Ireland is an independent country, the tide has turned, and Irish is being taught in all the schools. People who speak Gaelic at home even get a special grant of fourteen dollars a year. It's not much, but it shows that the Irish are trying to save their traditional language. Only time will tell whether Irish Gaelic, and neighboring Scots Gaelic, will survive.

Similar efforts were made to wipe out Welsh and Breton, but they have survived in spite of persecution. Today about a million people speak Breton. Around a quarter of the people living in Wales still speak Welsh. The schools teach Welsh, and a popular television station broadcasts only in Welsh.

Even in the United States some children have been forced to stop using their own languages in school. In the early 1900s, Cajun children who used French words on school grounds were punished by being whipped or made to write lines. Some Native American children were required to go to boarding schools where they were not allowed to speak their own languages. Their teachers did not see themselves as cruel. They were trying to give children the English skills they needed to get along in American life. Today, though, educators believe that children can learn standard English fluently without giving up their native language or dialect. Some children are being taught in their own languages along with English. This is called "bilingual" (two-language) education.

Most people love their native tongues. The Basques of northern Spain and southwestern France are united by their common language in their struggle for independence. The area where Basque is spoken has shrunk over the centuries, but Basques are determined to keep their language alive. While Francisco Franco ruled Spain from 1939 to 1975, the Basque language was forbidden. Basque was not allowed in the schools. Books in Basque were burned and Basques were not even allowed to have names in their own language. In 1979, after Franco's death, Basques won the right to use and study their own language along with Spanish. They now have their own regional government, called an *autonomía historica* (Spanish for "historical autonomous area"), which is responsible for education, health, transport, and other regional concerns.

Schoolchildren in the Basque area are now required to study the Basque language until they are fourteen years old, or they can study in Basque their whole time in school. The government gives Basque-speakers an advantage in getting government jobs. One television channel broadcasts in Basque, but only a small percentage of the population are fluent enough to watch it. Unfortunately, during Franco's rule many Basque children grew up speaking Spanish rather than Basque, and it is a very difficult language to learn as an adult. A few Basque people still want their own independent country.

The Basques are quite proud of the complexity of their language. They say that the devil once tried to learn their language so he could tempt them. He worked at it for seven years, and finally gave up in disgust. In another story, Basques say the devil uses their language to fight with his mother-in-law!

Another self-governing province of Spain is Catalonia. Catalonians speak the Catalan language. Catalan is closely related to Spanish and so is much easier for Spanish-speakers to learn than Basque is. About ninety percent of the Catalan people still speak Catalan, although their language was also suppressed under Franco.

Most Gypsies speak their own language, called Romany. They have some very distinct dialects because they have lived in different parts of the world for a long time. The name Gypsy comes from the word Egypt, since people once thought Gypsies came from there. *Romany* sounds like it has to do with Rome, but it actually comes from the Gypsy word *rom*, meaning "male Gypsy." *Rom* came from a Sanskrit word, *domba*, "a low-caste male musician." By studying the Romany language, linguists have discovered that Gypsies actually came originally from Northwest India. Although Gypsies had forgotten their own origins, their language kept the clues!

Politics has often drawn national boundaries between people with a common language. The Kurds spread across Iraq, Iran, Turkey, Syria, Russia, and Lebanon. Armenians live in Armenia, Iran, Syria, and Lebanon. Baluchi-speakers live in Pakistan, Afghanistan, Iran, and the Arabian peninsula. Each group holds onto its language, dreaming of—and sometimes fighting for—a nation of its own. Language unites people and helps preserve their unique cultures and identities.

> Language is the archives of history.
> Ralph Waldo Emerson

4
CONQUERORS, SLAVES, AND IMMIGRANTS: LANGUAGE CONTACTS AND COLLISIONS

LANGUAGES AND EMPIRES

Languages travel around the world with their speakers, affecting and changing each other. Sometimes one language enriches another. Sometimes one language destroys another.

Conquest of nations almost always affects language. The conquerors, if they don't have much contact with their original country, may learn the language of the conquered country and forget their own. That's what happened to the Normans in England. Or, the conquered people may forget their own language, as many North African Berbers did when the Arabs conquered them. Sometimes the local language absorbs the conquering language by borrowing from it until the original language is radically different, as English was after absorbing words from Norman French, and as Persian and Urdu were after contact with Arabic.

China, the great political and cultural power of the Far East, influenced the religions, arts, governments, and languages of the countries surrounding it. China ruled Vietnam for a thousand years, from 111 B.C. to 939 A.D. During these years of domination, many Chinese words were added to Vietnamese. Korean and Japanese were also strongly influenced by Chinese. More than half of Japanese words, and part of Japan's writing system, came from China.

From the 1400s to the 1800s, the European countries took it upon themselves to conquer, colonize, and "civilize" the world. They carved Africa into pieces. The British, Italians, French, Belgians, Germans, Portuguese, and Spanish each controlled sections.

By 1980 all the countries of Africa had gained independence from European powers. However, the Europeans, through various treaties and agreements, drew the boundaries of most modern African countries. They did not divide them according to language, culture, and history, as most of the countries of Europe are divided. Most African countries are made up of many tribes, speaking many languages, who do not always live peacefully together. The groups speaking a common language are often too small to establish countries of their own. African languages spoken by larger groups are usually spoken in a number of countries, crossing foreign-made borders. These countries often use European colonial languages as their official languages, since there are many local languages. Languages used between people with different native tongues are called "trade languages" or "lingua francas." (*Lingua franca* is Italian for "French language," since French was often used this way.)

English is the official language of Zimbabwe, which used to be part of British Rhodesia. Two African trade languages, Shona and Ndebele, are also used by speakers of the nineteen languages of Zimbabwe. Angola, which was ruled by the Portuguese until 1975, uses Portuguese for its official language, while its people speak forty-two different languages. It would probably not be practical to split up this country into forty-two tiny countries, so it is helpful to have some common language. The countries of North Africa do not need an internal lingua franca as other African countries do, since most of their citizens speak some dialect of Arabic. But Tunisia, Algeria, and Morocco still use French, and sometimes English, for business and government work. In some African countries, including Kenya and Tanzania, the African language Swahili is used as a trade language along with English. The Germans lost their colonies during the two World Wars, and the countries they once ruled now use French or English.

Why are European languages usually used to unite these countries, rather than African languages? One reason is that the colonial powers ran schools in many countries, teaching in their own European languages. So the educated, upper-class leaders of many African countries speak European languages with each other. Also, even after the African countries became independent, they wanted to develop systems of education, communication, and transportation like those of European countries. They became dependent on the U.S., Russia, and European countries for financial and technical aid. To communicate with western countries, these "developing nations" usually use French or English. French and English developed into international languages because France and England were colonial powers, and because of the United States' wide influence in giving aid to other countries.

The situation in South Africa is different than in other African countries, since about a quarter of South Africa's citizens are descended from Europeans. Dutch settlers called Boers (from the Dutch word for "farmer") began to settle there in 1652. Since they were isolated from their home country, and ruled by the English for a while, their Dutch dialect developed into a new language called Afrikaans. Its grammar is simpler than Dutch grammar, and it includes many words borrowed from English, German, and African languages. It was not a written language until the mid-nineteenth century. In 1925 it became an official language of South Africa, along with English. From 1948 until 1994, South Africa had a system called *apartheid,* which is Afrikaans for "apartness." This system kept different racial groups separate and allowed only whites to have real power. Blacks were required to use Afrikaans, but they preferred to learn English to help them communicate with educated people outside their country. Now that the system has changed in South Africa, and blacks are beginning to be treated equally with whites, the country has chosen eleven official languages, adding nine black African languages to Afrikaans and English. English may end up as the main language of the country, since it is already used as a lingua franca between blacks who speak different languages.

Europeans did not send large numbers of immigrants and settlers to their colonies in Southeast Asia, as they did to South Africa and other areas, so they did not influence those countries or their languages as much. The French ruled Indochina (now Cambodia, Laos, and Vietnam) from 1862 to 1954. Those countries now use their own languages. The Dutch, who ruled Indonesia from 1602 to 1945, imposed their language temporarily on Indonesia. Indonesia is a country of more than 3,000 islands in Southeast Asia, whose people speak more than 700 languages—certainly a difficult country to unify! When the Indonesians became independent, they rejected Dutch and chose Bahasa Indonesian as a national language. Bahasa Indonesian was developed from a Malay dialect that was already used as a trade language. The Indonesian government launched a concentrated campaign to educate all the island tribes in Bahasa Indonesian. It looks like they will be successful; the Indonesian language is helping to unify the country.

English is probably the most widely used lingua franca, and it continues to spread. The more countries that use it, the more people want to learn it. One reason the English language is so widespread is that the British Empire at one time spread around the world, including the United States, Canada, Australia, India, Pakistan, and parts of the Middle East. In 1914, at its largest, the British Empire included about one out of every four people in the world! Most of those people were exposed to or affected by the English language. English still helps unify multilingual India, which uses Hindi and English as its national languages.

India has tried, since its independence from Britain in 1947, to make Hindi its one national tongue. But the Dravidian languages spoken in southern India are not Indo-European like Hindi and English. Speakers of Dravidian languages like Telugu fought for years to have separate states in India according to their languages. By 1956, all of South India was organized on the basis of language. Still there is conflict between native speakers of Hindi, who want the whole country speaking Hindi, and speakers of other languages, who want to use English as a common tongue.

English-speakers from India have their own dialect. An Indian would say "the three of them were healthy" as *de tree of dem were helty.* "It was a pleasure" comes out *eet was a pleshur.* They say *I am doing it,* meaning "I do it all the time," and *when I will come* for "when I come." They sometimes use words from Indian languages, like "he went to the *gudwarra* to have a *darshan,*" meaning "he went to the temple to worship."

Australia had a much smaller original population than India, and Great Britain sent many more colonists there. After the American Revolution in the 1770s, when the new United States would no longer receive people the British didn't want, British colonists began arriving in Australia. The languages of the original Australians, the aborigines, were mostly replaced by English. About 200 Australian aboriginal languages are still spoken by small groups of people. At least fifty Australian languages have died out. Most of the rest are close to extinction. Only about fifty aboriginal languages have more than 100 speakers, and only four have more than 1000 speakers today.

LANGUAGE COLLISIONS IN THE NEW WORLD

The original languages of the Americas were also pushed aside by European languages. The French, English, and Spanish in North America, and the Spanish and Portuguese in Central and South America, arrived as conquerors and immigrants after Columbus happened upon the "New World" in 1492.

The original inhabitants of the Americas were misnamed by Columbus, who called them "Indians," thinking he had reached the East Indies. That name caught on and is now commonly used, like the name of America itself (which was mistakenly named after Amerigo Vespucci rather than after Columbus, who arrived earlier). The Native Americans, or "American Indians," spoke at least a thousand different complex languages. Many of these were wiped out after Europeans arrived. Diseases carried by explorers and conquerors killed off some tribes and their languages vanished. Some tribes died out through wars or being overworked as slaves. Other groups were absorbed into larger groups of Indians, like the Quechua-speaking Incas, and lost their languages.

However, languages spoken in a country before it is conquered do not disappear easily. The original inhabitants of a country often stay together, either by choice or involuntarily (like the Native Americans on reservations) and resist being absorbed into another society and language. In 1900, more than four hundred years after

Columbus arrived in the Americas, almost half of the Indians in the United States still did not speak English. Many others were bilingual, speaking their Indian language and English. In recent times, though, many North American Indians have been educated in English and have lost their native tongues. Navajo is the only North American Indian language whose number of speakers is increasing. Many people are trying to keep Native American languages alive by setting up programs to teach Indian children in their own languages. It would be sad if more of these languages were lost forever.

Mexico, Central America, South America, and some of the Caribbean Islands are called "Latin America" because they use the Spanish and Portuguese languages which are descended from Latin. After Columbus' discovery of the West Indies in 1492 for King Ferdinand and Queen Isabella of Spain, the Spanish and Portuguese divided the New World with a treaty in 1494 that gave the eastern part of South America (now Brazil) to Portugal and the rest to Spain. The Portuguese explorer Pedro Cabral landed in Brazil in 1500, and the first Portuguese colony in the Americas was started in Brazil in 1532. The Indians of Brazil were very spread out, and huge numbers of Portuguese immigrants came to Brazil over the years. Today sixty percent of Brazilians are descended from the Portuguese and most of the rest are mixed races. Less than one percent are Indians. Almost all Brazilians, except for some isolated Indian tribes, speak the Brazilian dialect of Portuguese.

To take what Spain considered her part of the New World, the Spanish government sent Cortes, who conquered the Aztecs of Mexico in 1519, and Pizarro, who conquered the Incas of South America in 1532. Spanish government and the Spanish language were imposed on the conquered Indians. However, when the conquerors arrived, there were many more Indians in Spanish areas of Central and South America than there were in North America or Brazil. That made it easier for the Indians to keep their own languages. Most of them today speak Spanish along with their original languages.

All the Spanish-speaking countries of Latin America are now independent, and some recognize Indian languages as national languages along with Spanish. (Latin Americans, of course, speak their own dialects of Spanish.) In Mexico and Central America large groups speak Maya, Zapotec, Mixtec, and the Aztecs' Nahuatl. In Paraguay, the Indian language Guaraní is the first language of most of the population, while only a few percent speak Spanish as a first language. Most people know and use both languages, though, and they are both official languages. Guaraní is usually used in the countryside. Spanish is taught in the schools. In the cities, Paraguayans use Spanish for formal occasions and for distant relationships, while Guaraní is used informally between friends.

American Indian languages are used in the same way in other countries. Over six million South American Indians speak Quechua, the language of the Incas. In Peru, Quechua is an official language along with Spanish. In Bolivia about thirty-seven percent of the people are Quechua Indians and about twenty-four percent are Aymara Indians; Quechua and Aymara are official languages along with Spanish. Quechua and Aymara, like Guaraní in Paraguay, are spoken mostly in the countryside, while Spanish is used in the cities in official and formal situations. The Caribbean Islands that were colonized by Spain, like Cuba and Puerto Rico, use their own dialects of Spanish.

Many languages collided in what is now the United States. American place names show the history of these collisions. The hundreds of American Indian languages that were first spoken here left names ranging from *Connecticut,* which comes from the Algonkian word *quinnehtukqut,* "beside the long tidal river," to *Oklahoma,* from a Choctaw word meaning "red man," to *Alaska,* from an Aleut word thought to mean "land that is not an island." (The Aleuts live in the Aleutian Islands, which trail from the tip of Alaska.) The French first explored and settled the Louisiana Territory, which is now the central United States. They left the name *Louisiana,* named for King Louis XIV, and such city names as *Baton Rouge* (French for "red stick"). The Spanish settled Florida and the Southwest, including much of Texas. *Florida* is Spanish for "flowered," and two thousand American cities and towns still have Spanish names, like *San Diego* (*San* means "saint"). Other nationalities have left names like the

Catskill Mountains (in New York) from Dutch *kaaterskill*, "wildcat creek," and Anaheim (California) from German "home on the Ana (River)." The British, who started the thirteen English-speaking colonies, gave us names like *New York* (after the duke of York) and *Georgia* (after King George II). As the United States spread across the continent, English became the dominant language, and most (though not all) French- and Spanish-speakers, as well as many Native Americans, began speaking English.

South America also has French- and English-speaking areas. France, Great Britain, and the Netherlands each claimed colonies on the northern coast of Brazil: French Guiana, British Guiana, and Dutch Guiana. Today British Guiana is the independent country of Guyana, but English is still its official language. Its people are mostly descendants of slaves brought in to work on the sugar plantations, and of Indian, Portuguese, and Chinese immigrants. French Guiana is called an overseas department of France, which means it is a part of France with representation in the French government. Its official language is French. Dutch Guiana is now independent Suriname. Its official language is Dutch. Most people of all three Guianas, though, speak creole languages: Guyanese Creole English, French Guianese, or the Suriname creole, Sranang Tongo or Taki-Taki.

PIDGINS AND CREOLES: NEW LANGUAGES FROM OLD

"Creole" languages like Taki-Taki began as "pidgin" languages. Pidgins are simplified languages which develop when people of different languages are thrown together and have to live and work together. Pidgins are based on some unifying language which gives them their basic structure and words, but they use words and forms from other languages as well. When children of pidgin-speakers grow up speaking the pidgin as their first language, it develops into a creole language.

In the Caribbean Islands, the European conquerors first put local Indians to work on their plantations. The Indians soon died of disease and overwork, and the Europeans brought in African slaves.

These Africans spoke many languages in their home countries and had to work out new ways to communicate with each other and with their overseers. Islands colonized by France, like Haiti and Martinique, developed pidgin languages based on French, with African, English, and Spanish words added. Former British colonies like Jamaica and the Bahamas use English-based creoles. People of the Netherlands Antilles, which belonged to Spain and then Holland, speak a Portuguese-based creole called Papiamento, with words from Spanish, Dutch, and African languages.

Pidgin and creole languages have developed in many parts of the world. Chinese and British traders spoke a pidgin using English and Chinese words in a Chinese word order. Africans, Eskimos, and groups of Native Americans have used pidgins between tribes speaking different languages. Slaves may have brought a West African pidgin language to the New World, where it influenced the development of other pidgins. Pidgin languages have their own rules and words. They are not "broken" English or French. They are simpler than other languages, which makes them easy to learn.

"Tok Pisin" (also called New Guinea Pidgin or Neo-Melanesian) is a creole language which has been spoken for about a hundred years in Papua New Guinea, a Pacific island nation where 700 different languages are spoken. (See examples of New Guinea Pidgin in appendix 1.) Tok Pisin is based on English, but uses many words from other languages. For instance, Tok Pisin uses the Polynesian word *kaikai* to mean "food" or "meal," the Malay *susu* for "milk," and the German word *rausim* for "throw out."

Tok Pisin only has five vowel sounds, and words like *tok* (talk) and *wok* (work) rhyme. There are no *sh, ch,* or *f* sounds. This makes the language easy to pronounce for people from different backgrounds. But it can be confusing. The word *hat* can mean "hot," "hard," "hat," or "heart"!

Pikinini, a word borrowed from Portuguese, means "child" in many pidgin languages. Rather than creating separate words for "son," "daughter," "puppy," and "piglet," pidgin combines words. In Tok Pisin, *pikinini man* means "son," and *pikinini meri* means "daughter." (The word *meri* for "woman" comes from the name

"Mary.") *Pikinini dok* means "puppy," and *pikinini pik* is "piglet." Pidgins often use long, cumbersome expressions. Tok Pisin for "hymn" is *singsing bilong haus lotu*, "song of a house of worship." A public library is *haus buk bilong ol man/meri*, "house of books belonging to all men and women."

Tok Pisin is not just simplified English; some parts of it are quite different. English has only one word "we," for instance, but Tok Pisin, like other languages of the Pacific, has several. *Mi* means "I" or "me"; *mipela*, the plural, means "me and someone else who's not here." *Yumi* means "me and you, the person or people I'm talking to." *Mitupela* means "the two of us; me and the person I'm talking to." *Yumitripela* is "the three of us; me and the two people I'm talking to." So Tok Pisin "we" is much more exact than English "we."

Pidgin languages can only express basic ideas. But creoles are complete languages, able to communicate anything their speakers want to say. They are as "good" as any other language. Children who grow up speaking creoles speak them much faster than their parents spoke pidgin. They develop new words so they can talk about whatever they want to. The phrase for "fighter," *man bilong pait*, becomes *paitman*. While pidgins often can't put a verb in the past or future, creoles find a way to do it. *Baimbai*, from the English "by and by," becomes *bai*, which means future tense. So a creole speaker of Tok Pisin would say *tumora bai mi go long taun*, "tomorrow I will go to town."

Some people in Jamaica are struggling to make their creole language an official language. They want street signs in Jamaican Creole, which would say, for instance, *No Ton Rait* for "No Right Turn," and *No Paak Betwiin Dem Sain Ya* instead of "No Parking Between These Signs." Scrabble, Monopoly, and other games have been translated into Jamaican Creole, to encourage people to use their own language more. The Bible has even been translated into creole languages. In New Guinea Pidgin, "Jesus is the Son of God" is written *Yesus i pikinini bilong God*.

Because all pidgin and creole languages have some things in common, some linguists believe that they all came from one early

THE LORD'S PRAYER IN NEW GUINEA PIDGIN (TOK PISIN)

Note: Pronounce *i* either as short *i*, as in *givim* [give him] or as long *e*, so that the word *i* sounds and means something like "he" and *inap* sounds like *eenup*, meaning "enough." *E* can be short *e* as in *mipela* [we], which sounds almost like "me-fellow," or pronounced like long *a*, so *olsem* sounds like "all same," and *tekewe* sounds like "take away."

English	Pidgin
Our Father who art in heaven	Papa bilong mipela, yu stap long heven
Hallowed be thy name	nem bilong yu i mas i stap holi.
Thy kingdom come	Kingdom bilong yu i mas i kam.
Thy will be done on earth	Mipela i mas bihainim laik bilong yu long graun
as it is in heaven.	olsem ol i bihainim long heven.
Give us this day our daily bread	Nau yu ken givim mipela kaikai inap long dispela de.
And forgive us our debts	Na yu lusim ol rong bilong mipela
As we forgive our debtors.	olsem mipela i lusim ol rong ol man i mekim long mipela.
Lead us not into temptation	Na yu no bringim mipela long traim,
But deliver us from evil.	tasol tekewe mipela long samting nogut.
For thine is the kingdom and the power and the glory forever. Amen.	Kingdom na strong na biknem i bilong yu tasol oltaim. Tru.

Matthew 6:9–13 from *Nupela Testamen na Ol Sam*, Port Moresby, New Guinea: The Bible Society of Papua New Guinea, 1980.

pidgin language, probably a Portuguese-based pidgin called Sabir which was spoken by seamen in the Middle Ages. However, not all pidgins seem to have had enough contact with other pidgins for this to be true. Another theory is that all languages tend to simplify in the same ways, dropping the use of *to be*, for example, when they need to be simplified (as when they are spoken to small children or foreigners).

Several creole languages are spoken in the United States by small groups of people. In Hawaii, an English-based pidgin developed in the nineteenth or early twentieth century among Asian plantation laborers. This language, now a creole, includes words from the Hawaiian language as well as Japanese, Chinese, Portuguese, and languages of the Philippines. More than half a million Hawaiians speak this creole, though most of them can switch to standard English when necessary.

Pidgins developed much earlier on the mainland. When Louisiana was a French colony in the eighteenth century, Louisiana Créole French developed. The basic vocabulary is French, with many African words added. This language is used today by about 70,000 people, including African-Americans and Houma Indians in Southwest Louisiana, as well as a few speakers in Texas and California. Cajun French-speakers, who speak a dialect of French rather than a creole language, live in the same area. Since they have a lot of contact with each other, the Creole language and Cajun dialect seem to be coming closer together, and may eventually become one language.

On the coasts of South Carolina and Georgia, about a quarter of a million African-Americans speak a creole called Sea Islands Creole English or Gullah. This language developed among slaves working in the rice plantations, mostly on isolated islands, in the 1700s. About fifty years ago, a study showed that Sea Islands Creole had about 6,000 words and phrases from African languages. Some are translations. For instance, the phrase *sweet mouth* means "to flatter." This phrase probably came from the African Twi language which uses *no ano yede*, "his mouth is sweet," to mean "he is a flatterer." Other African words were directly borrowed into Sea Islands Creole. *Goober,* for "peanut," and *cooter,* for "turtle," are from West African languages. Over the past fifty years, though, Sea Islands Creole-speakers have had a lot more contact with English-speakers, and have stopped using many African words.

AFRICAN-AMERICAN DIALECTS

African-Americans today speak dialects ranging from Sea Islands Creole to standard English. Somewhere in between is a dialect linguists call Black English Vernacular, or BEV. ("Vernacular" means dialect.) This dialect of English is used mostly by black Americans in the inner cities. It's not used very consistently. Sometimes speakers use BEV patterns in one sentence and standard English patterns in the next. As with any language or dialect, speakers use different speech styles for different situations.

BEV uses some patterns from African languages and the pidgin languages developed by slaves. For instance, BEV-speakers tend to leave off the standard English *-s* on verbs, as in "he learn" or "she walk." They sometimes leave out the words *is, am,* or *are* in sentences where they would be contracted in standard English. Instead of "she's married," they might say "she married." On the other hand, they add the word *be* to show that something happens habitually. "He sick" means "he's sick right now," while "he be sick" means "he's not healthy, he's sick all the time." The opposites of those sentences would be "he ain't sick" (right now) and "he don't be sick" (usually). *Been* before a verb can be used to show something that has been going on for some time, like "I been know your name." Sea Islands Creole uses one word, *ee,* to mean both "there's" and "it's," while BEV occasionally uses the word *it's* for both meanings. For instance, speakers might say "it's a new boy in my class."

BEV-speakers sometimes use double negatives, like "ain't nobody comin'." That's not considered standard English nowadays, but double negatives were commonly accepted in Old English, up through Shakespeare's time, and are still used in many other languages. The use of *ain't* instead of "isn't" is also not standard, but it is used in many American dialects.

BEV-speakers sometimes use different pronunciations of words than standard English. *D* may be substituted for *th* in words like *the, they,* and *those* so they are pronounced like *duh, day, doze.* This is also true in a common New York dialect. New Yorkers, though, would pronounce *th* in the middle of a word as *d,* saying "other" as *udder,* while BEV-speakers might say *uvvah.* Final letters are often dropped in BEV, like the *-r* of *other.* A BEV-speaker might also say *las'* for "last," *han'* for "hand," and *learn* for "learned."

Most BEV pronunciations and expressions are also used in other dialects of English. Many are also used in creole languages. Some linguists believe that BEV developed from American and British dialects of English and became a distinct dialect because its speakers were generally separated from whites. Most linguists, though, believe that the special features of BEV came from African languages and slave creoles. Some characteristics of BEV then spread to white dialects, especially in the South, where whites and blacks were in contact with each other.

It was many years before linguists recognized BEV as an orderly, well-developed dialect, just as good for communication as standard English. The law recognized BEV as a separate dialect, not just "broken English," in 1977. In that year, some African-American parents challenged the school board of Ann Arbor, Michigan, claiming that their children were doing badly in school because a "linguistic barrier," BEV, was keeping them from having equal educational opportunity. The court ruled that the school board had to help teachers identify children speaking BEV and use knowledge of the children's dialect to help them learn to read standard English. For instance, the teacher might explain to the child that "desk" has a final "k," which is silent in BEV, just as she explains to the class that "lamb" has a silent "b" in standard English. Since then, other school districts have started similar programs.

IMMIGRANT LANGUAGES: THE AMERICAN MELTING POT

Most African-Americans are descended from Africans who were brought involuntarily (against their will) to the Americas. "Immigrants," on the other hand, are people who leave their native country and move to a new country, usually voluntarily (by their own choice), to stay. Immigrants have brought many languages to the United States. The English, Spanish, French, and Dutch were the first European immigrants to settle in North America. In the 1700s and 1800s, most other immigrants to the thirteen colonies were from Northwest Europe, including Germans, Irish, and Scots-Irish. Scandinavians from northern Europe came in the 1880s, and mostly settled on farms in the countryside. In the late 1800s many Chinese came to work in the oilfields and help build the railroads. Between 1882 and 1965, their immigration was forbidden or tightly restricted. There were also brief immigrations of Japanese and Koreans to the U.S., mostly to Hawaii and California in the 1880s. After 1900 the majority of immigrants were from eastern and southern Europe, including Italy, Greece, Poland, Hungary, and Russia. Mexican immigrants have come all along, both legally and illegally, to find jobs and better lives in the U.S.

In 1965 a new law opened the doors for all ethnic groups to immigrate to the U.S. more easily. Since then hundreds of thousands of immigrants have arrived. After the Vietnam War ended in 1975, a wave of Vietnamese, Laotian, and Cambodian refugees entered the country. By the end of the 1980s, about half of all immigrants to the U.S. were Asian, mostly from Hong Kong, Japan, Korea, the Philippines, and Southeast Asia. The Chinese immigrants mostly speak Cantonese Chinese, rather than the standardized national language, Mandarin Chinese. About a quarter of current immigrants are Spanish-speaking people from Latin America, especially from Mexico and Cuba. Many Spanish-speaking Puerto Ricans have also moved to the mainland, especially to New York City, but they are not considered immigrants since they are U.S. citizens. In smaller numbers, immigrants have probably come to the United States from every country of the world.

Most immigrants coming to the United States are ready to learn a new language and culture and blend in. At the same time, being strangers in a strange land, immigrants tend to cluster together. People coming to join relatives and friends in the U.S. naturally want to live near them. They form communities like the "Chinatowns" and "Little Italies" of New York City and Boston. Mexicans have communities in cities of Texas, California, and other parts of the country. Many Cubans and Haitians make their homes in sections of Miami, and Puerto Ricans are concentrated in New York City. In Orange County, California there is a "Little Saigon" where Vietnamese immigrants congregate, and Los Angeles has a "Koreatown" and "Little Tokyo." In these areas and many others like them, a visitor may hear no English at all. Outside of the cities, there are whole villages and towns in the midwestern and western U.S. started by immigrants who all came from the same country. What immigrant communities are there in your city or area?

Even in these communities, children of immigrants to the United States usually become bilingual by learning English in school. They may translate for their parents and help them learn English. Their parents often encourage them to speak English at home. If the children stay in a community of people from their parents' home country, they may keep speaking their parents' home language as well as English. But if they leave that community, or if the community is not committed to speaking the old language, their children (the immigrants' grandchildren) usually do not learn their ancestors' language. Except for a few words they hear from their grandparents, they often speak only English.

Descendants of immigrants who live in their own communities sometimes speak English with a strong accent, using sounds and rhythms of their original language, and mixing in words from the language of the "old country." Some communities, like Greek Americans and some Hispanic Americans, have strong ties to their original countries. New immigrants come in, people travel back for visits, and newspapers, magazines, and radio programs are available in their original languages. Those communities tend to keep some form of their original language.

Religion can also help people to keep their original languages. Germans of the Mennonite religion came to America in the late 1600s to escape persecution in their home country. They first settled in Pennsylvania, where they were called "Pennsylvania Dutch." They did not speak Dutch, but German, which is called *Deutsch* in

TABLE 4
LANGUAGES USED IN AMERICAN HOMES

Top 25 languages, other than English, spoken at home by Americans over age five, in 1990

Language	Total Speakers	Language	Total Speakers
1. Spanish	17,339,000	14. Hindi, Urdu, and related	331,000
2. French	1,703,000	15. Russian	242,000
3. German	1,547,000	16. Yiddish	213,000
4. Italian	1,309,000	17. Thai	206,000
5. Chinese	1,249,000	18. Persian	202,000
6. Tagalog	843,000	19. French Creole	188,000
7. Polish	723,000	20. Armenian	150,000
8. Korean	626,000	21. Navajo	149,000
9. Vietnamese	507,000	22. Hungarian	148,000
10. Portuguese	430,000	23. Hebrew	144,000
11. Japanese	428,000	24. Dutch	143,000
12. Greek	388,000	25. Mon-Khmer	127,000
13. Arabic	355,000		

Reprinted with permission from *The World Almanac and Book of Facts 1994.* Copyright© 1993 Funk & Wagnalls Corporation. All rights reserved.

German (or *Dietsch* in the Pennsylvania Dutch dialect). Their non-German-speaking neighbors thought *Deutsch* meant "Dutch," so they gave them that name. The Old Order Amish are the most conservative branch of the Mennonite Church. Most Old Order Amish still speak their German dialect, which developed from dialects of southwestern Germany, at home. In church they use High German, and in contact with outsiders they use English. There are large Amish communities in Pennsylvania, Ohio, Indiana, and Kansas, as well as Amish towns in other states of the U.S. and in Canada. Because of their religious beliefs they live and dress in old-fashioned ways, wearing plain clothes and avoiding inventions like electricity and automobiles. They preserve their way of life by living in communities without much contact with outsiders. Their isolation and respect for tradition also help keep their language alive.

However, the less conservative branches of the Mennonite Church have gradually switched over to English. They speak a distinctive dialect of English, influenced by German expressions. They are known for phrases like "outen the light" and "make the light out." "Make the light out" is a direct translation of the Pennsylvania Dutch *mach de Licht aus,* which in High German would be *mache das Licht aus.*

English can also influence the way immigrants use their original language. For instance, Puerto Ricans living in America sometimes use English words mixed into Spanish sentences. These words usually are words that describe things they didn't have in Puerto Rico, or that are related to customs that are different in New York than in Puerto Rico. For instance, one study shows that Puerto Ricans on the mainland usually say *la factoría* for "the factory," rather than

• •

TABLE 5
STATES WITH THE MOST NON-ENGLISH-SPEAKERS IN 1990

In 1990, as reported in the Census of that year, the United States had 31,844,979 people (about 13% of the total population), who spoke a language other than English at home. These twelve states had the most people, age 5 and over, who speak a language other than English at home.

State	Non-English Speakers	% of State Population
California	8,619,334	31.5
Texas	3,970,304	25.4
New York	3,908,720	23.3
Florida	2,098,315	17.3
Illinois	1,499,112	14.2
New Jersey	1,406,148	19.5
Massachusetts	852,228	15.2
Pennsylvania	806,876	7.3
Arizona	700,287	20.8
Michigan	569,807	6.6
Ohio	546,148	5.4
New Mexico	493,999	35.5

Other states with more than 10% non-English-speakers: Alaska (12.1%), Colorado (10.5%), Connecticut (15.2%), District of Columbia (12.5%), Hawaii (24.8%), Louisiana (10.1%), Nevada (13.2%), Rhode Island (17.0%). Every state is at least 2% non-English-speaking.

Reprinted with permission from *The World Almanac and Book of Facts 1994.* Copyright © 1993 Funk & Wagnalls Corporation. All rights reserved.

• •

the Spanish *la fábrica*, and *la boila* for "the boiler," which they wouldn't have in Puerto Rico but which is called *la caldera* in Spanish. Puerto Ricans say *lonchar*, "to lunch," for the quick and simple American lunch, instead of Spanish *almorzar*, which they would use for a larger and more leisurely midday meal. Sometimes Spanish words are also used in sentences as they would be in English. For instance, a Puerto Rican in the U.S. is more likely to say *me lavo <u>mis</u> manos*, "I wash <u>my</u> hands," rather than the standard Spanish *me lavo <u>las</u> manos*, "I wash <u>the</u> hands."

American English has had close contact with many languages. Most have brought words and phrases into English. A tremendous variety of American Indian languages were here first. They left a legacy of words ranging from *raccoon* to *wigwam*. Immigrant languages have also influenced American English with many borrowed words and expressions. These expressions enter American dialects where large groups of immigrants live. Yiddish words and expressions are most common in New York, where the largest Jewish community in the world lives. Louisianians often use words and expressions from the Cajun and Creole French communities who live among them, like *lagniappe* for "a little something extra," and *sauce picante* for a dish cooked in a spicy sauce. American English has been enriched by many languages, as American society has been enriched by many cultures.

> **The ear tends to be lazy, craves the familiar, and is shocked by the unexpected.**
> W. H. Auden

5
CLICKS, TRILLS, AND UMLAUTS: THE SOUNDS OF LANGUAGE

When you listen to a person speaking another language, you will hear sounds you don't recognize. No two languages use exactly the same sounds. Even the ones that seem familiar, like *b* or *k*, are pronounced a little differently in each language. The study of the sounds used in languages is called "phonology."

You can produce thousands of different sounds with your mouth. Babies try out all kinds of noises. When babies make sounds that aren't used in their parents' language, no one is interested. But when they say *da-da*, everyone is excited, so they say it again. *Ma-ma*, *da-da*, and *ba-ba* are among the first sounds all babies make, and most languages have given those words meanings like "mother" and "father."

English uses about fifty different sounds. Many letters can be pronounced in different ways, like the sounds of the letter *a* in *ball* and in *bat*. Letters combine to make sounds like *sh, ch, th,* and *ow.* Some languages use fewer sounds than English does. Australian aborigines speak Mowring with only three vowels and nine consonants. Hawaiian has eight consonants and ten vowel sounds. On the other hand, there are about seventy distinct sounds in Vietnamese. The Khmer language of Cambodia uses fewer consonants than English, but more than twice as many vowel sounds (thirty). Even so, four English vowel sounds (*i* as in *bit*, *e* as in *bet*, *a* as in *bat*, and *oo* as in *book*) are not close to any in Khmer!

You use your mouth, tongue, throat, lips, teeth, and nose to make language sounds. Feel the Adam's apple in your throat as you say *zzzzzz* and then *sssssss*. The vocal chords in your throat vibrate when you say *z*, but they don't for *s*. That's why linguists call *z* a "voiced" consonant and *s* a "voiceless" consonant. Try to feel the difference between *t* and *d* and between *g* and *k*. Can you tell which sounds are voiced? The *d* and the *g* are voiced consonants; *t* and *k* are voiceless.

You put your tongue against your teeth to say *th*, or farther back in your mouth for *t*. The back of your tongue moves up when you say *k*. A Northwest American Indian language, Tlingit, makes twenty-one consonants in the part of the mouth where you produce only *k*, *g*, and *ng*. To make consonant sounds, you stop or slow the breath coming through your mouth. Sounds where the breath is stopped, like *p*, are called "stops." When you put your tongue almost to the roof of your mouth, not quite touching it, you pronounce sounds like *sh* and *s*. These sounds, made by slowing your breath, are called "fricatives." Combinations of a stop and a fricative are called "affricates." *Ch*, for instance, is a combination of the sounds written *t* and *sh*. For vowel sounds, like *a* in *cat*, you don't slow your breath at all.

When you change the sound *j* in *joke* to a *ch* sound, you get a word with a different meaning: *choke*. So you can see that *j* and *ch* sounds are both used for meaning in English. Linguists call such sounds "phonemes." Phonemes are sounds that distinguish one word from another in a language. If you gurgled and then said *oke*, you wouldn't be making a different word. The gurgling sound has no meaning in English—it is not a phoneme of English. In some languages, though, like Arabic and some dialects of German, this sound *is* a phoneme; it's used to make words.

The letter *p* is pronounced two different ways in English. Hold your hand a little way in front of your mouth. Now say "I pat." Did you feel a puff of air? That's called "aspiration," and linguists write it with a little *h*: p^h. Now try saying "I spat." There is no puff of air, since *p* following an *s* is not aspirated. *P* and p^h are different sounds used in English, but they are not phonemes. If you say *pat* with or without the puff of air, you do not make two different words.

In Korean, though, *p* and p^h are phonemes. *Pita* means "cut," and

$p^h ita$ means "bloom." It is hard for an English speaker to hear the difference between those two words, but to a Korean the difference made by the puff of air is quite clear. In Korean, though, the change from *th* to *d* does not create a new word as it does in English. So it is hard for a Korean to hear the difference between English words like *thing* and *ding*.

CONSONANTS: CLICKS TO TRILLS

In Southwest Africa, the Khoisan languages, including Xhosa, Zulu, Hottentot, Bushman, and others, use grunts and clicks as consonants. Dutch settlers who met members of the Khoi-Khoin tribe in South Africa called them Hottentots, because their clicks sounded like *hateran en tateran*, "stuttering and stammering."

The *X* in Xhosa stands for a click with the sides of the tongue, like you might make to get a horse to move. The / in "/xam," the name of another language, represents the tip of your tongue clicking against your teeth. You might do that when you feel sorry for someone ("tsk, tsk"). Try saying *oXo* (an *o* sound like in *off*, then a click with the sides of your tongue, then another *o*) or *a/a* (an *a* sound, like in *father*, then a click made with the tip of your tongue against your teeth, then another *a* sound). When you throw a kiss you are making another "click" sound. These sounds use the air in your mouth. All English sounds, on the other hand, are made with air you breathe out from your lungs. You'd have to learn forty-eight different click sounds to speak the !Xū language of Africa!

Sounds can be borrowed from one language to another. The Khoisan languages of Africa are totally unrelated to the Bantu languages. But the Bantu languages spoken in areas near the Khoisan languages have borrowed the idea of using clicks as language sounds. Some languages of India, which aren't related to each other, have unusual sounds called "retroflexes," where the tongue is curled backwards to the roof of the mouth. One language developed the sound, and the others started using it, too. Should we borrow the sound of throwing a kiss as a new letter in English?

Many language sounds come from the back of the throat. Cockneys and Scots substitute another sound for the *t* in the middle of *bottle*. We could write it *bo'el*. The same sound is in the middle of *uh-oh*. It's a quick closing of the throat called a "glottal stop." This consonant is used in Arabic, Hawaiian, Mandarin Chinese, Thai, Tagalog (Philippines), and most American Indian languages. The Navajo word for father, *shizhé'é*, has a glottal stop between the last two *e*'s.

Here is another way to speak with air trapped in your mouth. Hold your breath with your mouth open. The "glottis" (space at the back of your throat) is closed. Say *p*, holding your breath; do you feel a little explosion of air? This is a "glottalized consonant." Many American Indian and African languages, as well as languages of Russia's Caucasus Mountains, make words with glottalized consonants.

All languages use sounds made with air coming out of the lungs. In many languages people also talk while breathing in. Try making a *b* sound while pulling air into your mouth. You can hear sounds like this in some American Indian, African, and Australian languages, the Sindhi language of India and Pakistan, Khmer of Cambodia, and others.

German, Dutch, Russian, Vietnamese, and Arabic use rasping sounds in the back of the throat as consonants. Make a *k* sound with your tongue not quite touching the roof of your mouth. Now say it farther and farther back until it is coming from the back of your throat. It sounds something like an angry cat, or the sound of clearing your throat. The Scottish pronounce the *ch* in *Loch Ness* this way. Anglo-Saxons (whose language developed into English) wrote this sound: *gh*. Try saying *night* and *through* with a rasping sound where the *gh* is. That sound has disappeared from English, so now the *gh* is silent.

The Dutch pronounce *sch* at the beginning of a word as an *s* combined with this raspy sound. This is a difficult combination for non-Dutch people to say. In 1940, when Holland was overrun by German spies, suspected spies were asked to say the place-name Scheveningen. Only the Dutch could say the *sch* correctly! Do you remember the term used for a word like this? It's a shibboleth.

Watch out for the letter *r* in other languages. Americans make an *r* by cupping the tongue. Spaniards flap or trill the tongue against the roofs of their mouths. The French and Germans vibrate the uvula, a flap of skin at the back of the throat, as if they were gargling. Some Australian aborigine and Indian languages curl the tongue back. The sound that linguists call an *r* in Japanese sounds like the *t* in *city*. The Chinese equivalent of *r* can be pronounced almost like the *s* in *measure*, or sometimes like the *ir* in *shirt*.

Even in dialects of English, *r* is pronounced different ways. In England and Australia, an *r* between two vowels is just a tap of the tongue, so that *very* sounds almost like *vedy*. In Ireland, *r*'s are rolled, like the *rrrrrr* sound you make playing with cars. In Scotland, *r*'s are trilled more strongly. Try saying "very regular roaring" with a rolled *r*, then with a trilled *r*.

English consonants combine in certain ways, like *tr, st,* and *cr*. Words begin with *kp* and *gb* in many West African languages. Can you say *kpa* without making an *uh* sound between the *k* and the *p*? Or try the Swahili for "coconut," *mnazi*. It's two syllables: *mna-zi*. *Mbwa* (dog) or *ndiyo* (yes) are also tricky; don't say *umbwa* or *indiyo*! How about the Russian combinations *shch* and *vstv*? "Hello" in Russian is a tough one: *zdravstvuytye*. (Remember that Russian is not written with our alphabet; this is a transliteration into the closest letters from our alphabet.) The Aztec language, Nahuatl, gave English the words *tomatl* and *xocoatl*, but lazy tongues made them "tomato" and "chocolate"!

Some words seem to be without vowels. Say the Kota (South India) word *anjrchgchgvdk*. (It means "because of the fact that [someone] will cause [someone] to terrify [someone]"!) Here are some others to try (the Kota word above and the Shilh below are transliterations):

nmnmk'	animal (American Indian Bella Coola language)
prncrc	dust (American Indian Yurok language)
ttss	to fall asleep (Moroccan Berber language Shilh)
trzy	three (Polish)
wczesny	early (Polish)
vrt	garden (Serbo-Croatian; *r* is a vowel.)
ngngenda	I go (African Luganda)

Fortunately, some combinations are easier than they look. For instance, the Scots Gaelic word spelled *dealbh* is actually pronounced *deal-uv.*

In English, you might pronounce the name of the town of Llano, Texas as *Lawn-oh*. But in Spanish *ll* is pronounced *y,* so the Spanish pronunciation of the town's name would be *Yahn-oh*. A town in southern Wales called Llanelli is pronounced with the Welsh *ll,* something like *thlanethli.*

You say the *rr* in "Merry Christmas" like any other *r* in English. But in Spanish *rr* is a longer trilling sound than *r.* So *pero* means "but," while *perro* is a "dog"! (That means that *r* and *rr* are phonemes in Spanish.) In some languages double consonants are held longer than single consonants, like the *d d* in *mad dog*. In Italian, for instance, *fatto*, pronounced *faht-toe,* means "fact"; *fato,* pronounced *fah-toe,* means "fortune" or "destiny." Double consonants are also lengthened in Japanese, Farsi (Iran), Arabic, Finnish, and Hungarian.

Language sounds change over time. Several hundred years ago, *nation* was pronounced with a *ty* sound: *natyon*. *Sh* has replaced the *ty* sound. People used to say *sugar* and *sure* as *syugar* and *syure*. The British still pronounce *tissue* as *tisyue*, while Americans say *tishoo*. British people and Australians keep this *y* sound in words like *picture* (*piktye*) and *future* (*fyutye*).

VOWELS

How many vowel sounds are used in English? Did you say five: *a, e, i, o, u?* Wrong! We have five letters for the vowels, but at least fourteen vowel sounds (more if you include all the dialects of English). For instance, the letter *a* stands for the sounds in *fat, fate, far, fall,* and *fang*. Fortunately, most other languages represent each vowel sound with only one spelling.

You can recognize dialects by the way a person pronounces vowels. Most American vowels are a combination of sounds. If you say the *a* in *plate* slowly you can hear an *eh* and an *ee* sound. A combination of two vowel sounds like that, starting with one vowel sound and sliding into another, is called a "diphthong." The Irish

THE PERFECT CODE

The Navajo language is so utterly different from European and Asian languages that it was used during World War II as a military code. Navajo Marines sent radio messages around the Pacific in their own language, a secret code that was never cracked.

pronounce this vowel as a pure sound, not a combination. They use *eh*, like the *e* in *let*, but drawn out longer. So an Irishman says "baby breaks plates" as *bebi breks plets*. Spanish vowels are also pure sounds. There are only five of them: *a, e, i, o, u*. They sound somewhat like *ah, ay, ee, oh,* and *oo* (as in *too*).

French, Portuguese, Navajo, Bengali, and other languages say some vowels through the nose, the way you say the consonants *n* and *m*. These are called "nasalized" vowels. In the French word *son* (sound), the *n* is silent; the *o* is pronounced through the nose instead. It sounds something like *sohng*, without the *ng*. Try saying the Navajo word for horse, *tłį́į́*. Say it like *tinin*, but without quite pronouncing the *n*'s. Both *i*'s are said through the nose.

In English some vowels, like *oo*, are said with rounded lips, others not. If you say *oo* with a big smile, or *ee* (as in *feet*) with rounded lips, you are making "umlauted" vowels. These are vowels whose sound has been changed by the sound that comes after them. Many umlauted vowels were originally followed by an *i, j,* or long *e* sound (like the sound of the *y* in *happy*). Over time the following sound was dropped, but the vowels are still pronounced as they were when the *i, j,* or *e* sound was there. Some of these vowels are marked with a special sign called an *umlaut*. It looks like two little dots over the letter: *ü* or *ö*, for example. Vietnamese *ư*, Turkish *ö*, German *ü*, and French *u* are all pronounced by rounding the lips for *oo*, while saying *ee* with your tongue instead!

Japanese, Finnish, Dutch, Hungarian, Navajo, and other languages use double vowels. Some are pronounced twice as long as single vowels. Others are pronounced twice, as two separate syllables. The Japanese *obasan* means "aunt," while *obaasan*, with the *a* drawn out longer, means "grandmother." In Finnish, *tapaan* is "I meet"; be careful to hold the *aa* a long time, or you'll be saying *tapan*, "I kill"!

English vowels have not always been pronounced as they are today. The word *life* was pronounced in Shakespeare's time (the 1500s) as *layf,* and in the Middle English of the 1300s was said *leef.* The word *name* was pronounced *nomay* (with the *o* of *hot,* and the *e* pronounced like *ay* instead of being silent) in the 1300s, and *nem* 200 years later. Around 500 years ago, about the time that Europeans were settling the Americas, most English vowels changed in the "Great Vowel Shift." Over a period of about 200 years, most of the vowels in English moved forward in the mouth. For instance, the *oo* sound of *moose* became the *ou* sound of *mouse,* and the *o* sound of *boat* changed to the *oo* sound of *moose.* That means that *mouse* used to be pronounced like we say *moose* today, and *spoon* used to be pronounced as if it were *spone.* No one knows why this happened, and it happened so gradually that people didn't notice while it was going on. We can tell that the sounds of vowels changed by looking at misspelled words, which usually reflect how words really sound, and by comparing words that rhymed in the writings of authors like Shakespeare in the 1500s and Chaucer in the 1200s.

The Great Vowel Shift produced some odd spellings. Words we spell today with an *ea,* like *clean* and *meat,* used to be pronounced with the *a* sound of *clan* and *mat.* Words spelled with an *ee,* like *green* and *meet,* were pronounced with the *a* sound we now use in *grain* and *mate.* Now both *ee* and *ea* are usually pronounced the same, but they're still spelled differently!

At the same time as the Great Vowel Shift, other radical changes were taking place in the pronunciation of English. Unstressed *e*'s on the ends of words like *name* were lost, as well as sounds like the *k* and *gh* of *knight.* This process changed what we call Middle English into modern English.

FOREIGN ACCENTS

Since every language has its own sounds, people often don't pronounce a second language perfectly. It's easiest to say the sounds of

72 WHO TALKS FUNNY?

• •

TABLE 6
SOUNDS OF ENGLISH IN THE 1600S

There are many ways that linguists can tell that the sounds of a language have changed. Some of the evidence for sound change in English comes from homophone lists and rhyming dictionaries. Homophone lists are lists of words which are pronounced the same. These lists were used to teach spelling. Rhyming dictionaries give words that rhyme, so that poets can use them in writing poetry. From these clues, linguists know which words sounded alike in the 1600s. From other sources they figure out exactly what the words sounded like.

Homophone lists of the 1600s showed these words being pronounced the same, at least in some dialects:

| east / yeast | form / farm | knots / gnats | coffin / coughing | hole / howl |
| though / thou | bath / bathe | past / paste | own / one | sheep / ship | ask / ax |

Rhyming dictionaries of the 1600s showed that in the standard, accepted English of the time these words usually rhymed with each other:

eight / height / slight / straight / bait
plant / want
aunt / chant / slant / haunt / taunt
good / hood / food
ear / bear / tear / smear / wear
here / there / where
bread / bead / plead / dread / read
beak / break / steak / weak
dough / through / trough / cough*

*These words did NOT rhyme with owe, doe, and fro, so linguists know they still had some form of a raspy X or breathy H sound on the end.

• •

your first language. So someone may speak English with a German "accent" (using some German sounds in the place of English ones), or speak Spanish with an American English accent.

Spanish has only five vowel sounds, while English has about fourteen. So Spanish-speakers may say *keet-ayn* for "kitten," since their language does not have the *i* and *e* sounds used in *kitten*. On the other hand, it's hard for English-speakers learning Spanish to make their vowels short and clear. If you use English vowel sounds in Spanish, you'll sound like a Spaniard with a southern drawl!

The Hawaiian language has few consonants. So Hawaiians can't pronounce English using only sounds from their language. For

"Merry Christmas" they would have to say *Mele Kalikimaka*. (Of course most Hawaiians today speak English as a first language and have no trouble with its sounds.)

Many languages do not have the English *j* sound. Spanish *j* is pronounced as an *h*. But Spanish has a *ch* sound, which is close to *j*. So a Mexican talking about "George's giant giraffe" might say *Chorcha's chian chirahf*. Germans, Poles, and Russians do the same. French, Portuguese, and Filipinos usually use the sound of *s* in *measure* instead. They would talk about *Zhorzh's zhiant zhiraf*. The Finnish use the most convenient sound from their language, making it *Dzordz's dziant dzirav!*

Germans pronounce *w* like an English *v*. So someone with a strong German accent would say, "Do you *valk* on *vater* or *svim kvickly?*" ("Do you walk on water or swim quickly?") People from Hungary, Greece, and other countries also have trouble with the English *w*. An American speaking German, on the other hand, might mispronounce the German *es macht nichts aus*, "it doesn't matter." The *ch*'s are all said in the back of the throat, rather than in the front of the mouth like *ch* in *church*.

Fortunately, no one has to speak a foreign language with an accent. People of every race have the same kind of lungs, vocal chords, and mouths. You don't have to sound funny in a foreign language; you can pronounce any language correctly if you work hard enough. When you learn another language, listen carefully to its sounds, watch the mouth of your teacher, and practice until you sound like he or she does. Remember, no other language sounds the same as your first language!

> **Talking is like playing on the harp; there is as much in laying the hand on the strings to stop their vibrations as in twanging them to bring out their music.**
> Oliver Wendell Holmes, Sr.

6
RHYTHM AND TONE: THE MUSIC OF LANGUAGE

Every language has its own music. If you listen to people who speak another language, you will hear that not only do they pronounce some letters differently than you do, but the whole rhythm and tone of their speech is different from yours. In each language, sounds are combined in a unique way into syllables, words, and sentences.

SYLLABLES

Words in English can have one syllable, like *what* and *it*, or many syllables, like *discombobulated* or *polysyllabic*. A syllable is a piece of a word which has only one vowel sound. The vowel sound may be written as one vowel, like the *a* in *bat*. Or it may be written as several vowels, like the *a* in *bait* or the *oy* diphthong in *boy*. *Bat, bait,* and *boy* are all one-syllable words. But *batboy,* which has two vowel sounds, is a two-syllable word.

Most words in Chinese and Vietnamese are only one syllable long, while words in Japanese are often many syllables long. *Watakushitachi,* the common Japanese word for "we," is quite a mouthful: six syllables!

Every syllable in Japanese must end with a vowel or *n*. You can split the word above: *wa-ta-ku-shi-ta-chi*. When the Japanese borrow words from English, they make the syllables fit their own pattern. So "football," which has two syllables ending in consonants, becomes *fo-to-bo-ru* in Japanese (there's no *l* in Japanese, so they substitute their nearest sound, *r*). "Ink" becomes the Japanese *in-ki*. The Swahili language of Africa also does this, making "police" into *po-li-si* and "train" into *tre-ni*.

In Spanish, French, Swahili, and Italian most syllables end with vowels, which gives these languages a gentle, flowing sound. Languages like English and German sound harsher, since they often end syllables with consonants or groups of consonants (like *much* and *asked*).

RHYTHM

The rhythm of a language depends on which syllables and words are said most forcefully, or "stressed."

British English and American English don't always use stress the same way. The British say *reSEARCH, adVERtissment,* and *laBORatry,* while most Americans say *REsearch, ADverTISEment,* and *LABratory.* (The syllables in capital letters are stressed.) *SECretry* and *NECessry* also lose a syllable in British, while Americans pronounce all the syllables of *secretary* and *necessary* with about the same stress.

English sometimes uses stress to distinguish between words. You *preSENT* a *PREsent* to your friend. A star *reCORDS* new *REcords*. The factory *exTRACTS* vanilla *EXtract*. In Navajo, *ta-DI-gis* means "you wash yourself," while *TA-di-gis,* the same word with different stress, means "he washes himself." In Cheyenne, *o-O-na-ha'-e* is a "frog," while *o-o-na-HA'-e* are "frogs." The Hindi *gi-LA* means "throat," while *GI-la* is "wet."

In many languages, like Polish, Swahili, Welsh, and Nahuatl (the language of the Aztecs), the second-to-last syllable of the word is usually stressed. So the Polish word for "Excuse me," *Przepraszam,* is pronounced *pshehPRAHshahm*.

Czech and Slovak have what is called a "staccato" rhythm (quick, short bursts, like a machine gun), because they accent the first syllable of every word. In English and Russian the stress is unpredictable; you have to hear the word to know which syllable is said most strongly.

Spanish and Portuguese usually stress the last vowel to come before a consonant (unless there's an accent mark somewhere else). Spanish *CA-sa* (house) and *fe-li-ci-DAD* (happiness) follow this rule. Latin Americans speaking English will sometimes use the same kind of stress, saying *base-BALL, se-VEN,* and *li-BER-ty.*

Japanese accents each syllable of a word equally. In sentences, some words which you might consider unimportant, like *in* or *of*, are stressed. This creates A rhythm WHICH sounds quite strange TO English-speakers. (Try reading that last sentence stressing the words A, WHICH, and TO.)

Words in a sentence can be stressed by saying them more loudly and forcefully than other words. This can even change the meaning of a sentence. "Tell me the TRUTH" (not a lie) is different than "Tell ME the truth" (whatever you may have told HIM). German and Czech also emphasize words this way.

PITCH

Italian, Russian, Yiddish, and Polish use pitch to emphasize words or syllables. This means that they say the stressed word on a higher or lower note than the rest of the sentence.

Pitch, the musical tone of the voice, is also used in English sentences. The pitch of your voice usually drops at the end of a statement like "I have nothing more to say." It usually rises at the end of a question: "What did you say?" The tone rises and falls in other sentences: "How should *I* know?" "Don't say I didn't *warn* you!" In Vietnamese, this kind of stress can change a question to an exclamation. The same Vietnamese words are used to say, "How many people?" and "So many people!" The pitch and stress of the words show the difference.

English occasionally uses tones to express emotion. You could answer a simple question with a flat "No." The tone drops a little as you say it. Or if something shocks you, you might say "No!" with your voice at a higher tone. Or if you don't believe something, you say "No!" with the tone dropping much lower.

Try that again with the word *what.* Say this conversation aloud: "I just saw it."

"What?" (rising tone, meaning "I didn't hear what you said")
"I just saw it."
"What?" (falling tone, meaning "What did you see?")
"A flying saucer."
"What?!" (very high tone, meaning "Are you crazy?")
See how the tones changed the meaning of the word?

Each language has a characteristic tone at which it is usually spoken. The "music" of Greek, Spanish, and other Romance languages is higher than the music of American English. British, Irish, and Indian dialects of English are also spoken a bit higher than Americans speak, on the average. But German, Russian, and other Slavic languages rumble along two or three tones lower than our speech.

TONAL LANGUAGES

More than half the world's languages use tones in a more important way. These are called "tonal" languages. In tonal languages musical pitch is as important as consonants and vowels in telling you what a word means.

The people of Southeast Asia could be said to sing, rather than talk, since Thai, Lao, Vietnamese, and Burmese are all tonal languages. The Chinese languages or dialects and all their relatives are tonal, too.

In Mandarin Chinese, you might think the word *ma* meant "mother." It does if it's said at a high tone (tone^1, also written *mā*). If you say *ma* at a medium tone going higher (tone^2, *má*), though, it means "hemp," a plant used to make rope. If you start low and go down and then up (tone^3, *mǎ*), still saying the word *ma*, it means "horse." And if you start on a high note and go low (tone^4, *mà*), *ma* means "to scold." So a Chinese person could say, "Mama^1 qi ma^3. Ma^3 man. Mama^1 ma^4 ma^3." (The numbers show the different tones.) It means, "Mother rides horse. Horse slow. Mother scolds horse."

Different Chinese languages, or dialects, have their own tone systems. In fact, two villages in China, only a few miles apart, may have different tone systems.

FIGURE 2
THE TONES OF MANDARIN CHINESE

Try playing these notes on the piano and saying *ma* on each set of notes. This will show you how the tones compare with each other.

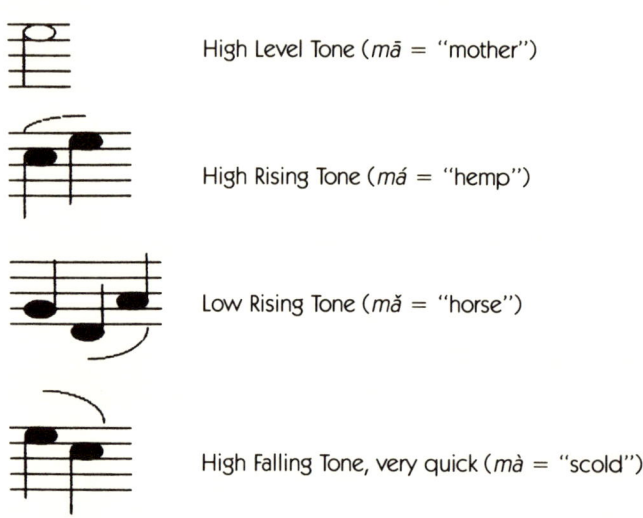

Vietnamese words can have six different tones. Said with a level, medium tone, *la* means "shout"; with a high tone going up, *lá* means "leaf"; starting low, going a bit lower and then higher, *lã* means "not interesting"; starting low and going lower, *là* means "like, resembling"; starting high and going down *lả* means "exhausted," and on a low, even tone *lạ* means "strange." So if you say you're "not paying attention" with the wrong tone, people may think you're "strange"!

In Thai, if you got thick mud on your face in your uncle's rice paddy, you'd use the word *naa* four times. *Naa* on a high pitch is "uncle"; with a medium pitch it means "rice paddy." Start high and go low and you've said "face." Do the opposite and *naa* means "thick."

Thai, Mandarin Chinese, and Vietnamese are examples of languages with gliding tones; they change pitch during a syllable.

Other languages, like Zulu and Hausa in Africa, use flat tones which differ in being higher or lower than the tones of other words or syllables in a sentence. In the Shilluk language, spoken near the Nile, *yit* said on a high tone means "ear"; *yit* on a low tone means "ears."

Languages also have different numbers of tones. Zulu has only two, high and low. The Punjabi language of India uses low, medium, and high tones. Mandarin Chinese uses four tones. The language of the Hmong tribes of Southeast Asia uses seven tones. Cantonese Chinese has three tones for syllables ending in *p, t,* or *k,* and six tones for other syllables!

Sometimes pitch can make small changes in the meaning of a word, rather than making it a totally different word. In Cantonese, *nöy* on a high tone means "woman," while a rising *nöy* means "daughter." In Mandarin Chinese, *mai* with a rising tone (tone^3) is "to buy." *Mai* with a falling tone (tone^4) is the opposite: it means "to sell."

Many of the Indian languages of both North and South America use tones. Navajo and Cherokee are both tonal languages. In Navajo, a vowel with an accent mark means that syllable is said on a high tone; a vowel without an accent mark indicates a low tone. If you want to say that your brother put a belt around his waist, you use *biní*, with a low then high pitch, to mean "his waist." If you say *bíní* all on a high pitch, you've put the belt around "his nostril"!

Hundreds of African languages are tonal. Nearly all the words in the 300 or so Bantu languages are distinguished by high and low tones. In the Tongan language of Zambia, *bapá,* with the second syllable high, means "they give." *Bápa,* with the first syllable high, means "they gave." Even the English-based creole language Krio, used in Sierra Leone, has some words that are different depending on their tone. This is because Krio uses some African words and has been influenced by the African languages used along with it.

TEMPO

Tones are the musical notes of language, and syllables and stress give it rhythm and volume. What about tempo? Are languages spoken at different speeds?

Of course different speakers speak at different rates, just as some people's voices are higher or lower than others'. But compare the average rates of some spoken languages. The French fly along at 350 syllables a minute. The Japanese at 310 and the Germans at 250 are a little slower. English has a medium rate, getting out about 220 syllables a minute. Most of the languages of the South Seas, like Hawaiian, are drawled along at a sleepy pace: only 50 syllables a minute. One estimate says American women average 175 words per minute, while the men only go through 150. (Notice that's words, which on the average are longer than syllables.)

Every language has a music all its own, and every speaker plays it a little differently. When your friends are speaking, listen for the melody!

> **When spider webs unite, they can tie up a lion.**
> Ethiopian proverb

7

DIVISIBLE AND INDIVISIBLE: PIECES OF WORDS

Words can break into pieces. If you accepted that *unquestioningly* (without doubt or questions), you used a word with four pieces. *Un-* means "not," *question* is something you ask, *-ing* makes it something you are doing, and *-ly* makes the word an adverb, so it can tell *how* you accepted the idea. When an Eskimo says, "I will hunt a big caribou," he uses a word with even more pieces: *Tugto-ssuak-siok-niak-punga*.

Linguists call the study of the pieces of words "morphology." Each piece that has a meaning is a "morpheme." A morpheme may have only one syllable, like *-ing*, or it may have more than one syllable, like *question*. Some words, like *Elizabeth*, are made of only one morpheme, since they have no parts with separate meanings. *Elizabeth's* still has the same number of syllables as *Elizabeth*, but it is made of two morphemes: the name *Elizabeth*, and *'s*, which means "belonging to."

ROOTS AND AFFIXES

Words, like trees, grow from "roots." The root of a word is the basic word you start with. The root of *unquestioningly* is *question*. The other pieces, called "affixes," are fixed onto the root. *Un-* is a "prefix," since it comes *before* the root. (The prefix *pre-* means "before," so a "prefix" is "fixed before" the word.) And since they come *after* the root, *-ing* and *-ly* are "suffixes" (from the Latin word *suffigere*, "to fasten underneath").

Some languages work on words from the inside. In English you change m<u>a</u>n to m<u>e</u>n to make it plural. The Khmer language of Cambodia sticks an "infix" inside *kdaw* (hot) to make *ka<u>m</u>daw* (heat). *Criep,* "to learn," plus the infix *-um-* makes *c<u>um</u>riep,* "to inform." In Sioux, *cheti* means "to build a fire." Add *-wa-*, meaning "I," and you get *che<u>wa</u>ti,* "I build a fire."

Affixes are used in many ways. In English, *un-* or *dis-* at the beginning of a word makes its opposite: *<u>un</u>satisfied, <u>dis</u>agreeable.* Albanian uses *s'* to make opposites. *Kuptoj,* which means "I understand," becomes *<u>s</u>'kuptoj* (say *skoop-toy*), "I don't understand."

English and Spanish use the suffixes *-s* and *-es* to make one thing into more than one. *Dog* becomes *dog<u>s</u>, libro* (book) becomes *libro<u>s</u>* (book<u>s</u>). Arabic sometimes uses the suffix *-at* to make plurals. *Hafla* (a party) is fun, but *hafla<u>at</u>* (parties) are even better! For other plurals Arabic changes the inside of the word, like the English *goose/geese.* Don't just read a *kitaab* (book), read *kutub* (books).

African Bantu languages use prefixes to tell what kind of thing they're talking about. In Swahili, words about humans start with *m-* if they're singular, *wa-* if they're plural. *<u>M</u>tu* means "person," *<u>wa</u>tu* means "people." *<u>M</u>zungu* is a white person, *<u>wa</u>zungu* are white people. *<u>M</u>wamerica* is an American, while *<u>M</u>kenya* is a Kenyan.

Ki- is a prefix used for certain objects and creatures, and *vi-* gives the plural. *<u>Ki</u>tana* means "comb" and *<u>ki</u>dani* means "necklace." How would you say "combs" and "necklaces"? (*<u>Vi</u>tana, <u>vi</u>dani.*) This prefix is usually used for small things, like *<u>ki</u>toto* (infant) and *<u>ki</u>mo* (monkey). But it's also the prefix on *<u>ki</u>boko,* which means "hippopotamus"!

Prefixes like *ki-* and *vi-* are added to other words besides the noun. The ending *-dogo* means "small." *<u>M</u>toto <u>m</u>dogo* is a "small child" and *<u>ki</u>su <u>ki</u>dogo* a "small knife." *-Zuri* means "good." Can you figure out how to say a "good knife" or a "good child"? (*<u>Ki</u>su <u>ki</u>zuri, <u>m</u>toto <u>m</u>zuri.*)

These prefixes are even added to verbs, so that in Swahili they say *<u>ki</u>boko <u>ki</u>lila <u>ki</u>jidudu,* "the-hippo it-ate a-bug." Pretend that English used noun prefixes like these. Say, as in Swahili, that *wa-* means humans and *mi-* means plants. Then "big, strong men planted three tall trees" would come out, "<u>wa</u>big <u>wa</u>strong <u>wa</u>men <u>wa</u>planted <u>mi</u>three <u>mi</u>tall <u>mi</u>trees."

Some languages double words to change their meaning a little. This happens in English in words like *goody-goody* and *sing-song*. (Sometimes the second word is in a slightly different form than the first word.) In the Hottentot language of Africa, *go* means "see"; *go-go* means "to look at carefully." *Khoe-b* is a "man" or Hottentot; what he does is *khoe-khoe*, "speaks Hottentot." In another African language, Ewe, *wo* means "to do"; *wo-wo* is already "done," but *ma-womawo* is "not to do."

In Southeast Asia, Malay and Bahasa Indonesian double words to make more of something. So ask for *buku* if you want one book, but *bukubuku* if you want more than one. Your cheeks are *pipi* (pronounced *pee-pee*) and your teeth are *gigi* (*gee-gee*) in Indonesian. The color yellow is *kuning* in Malay, but if something is tinted yellow, you say it with a bit of a stutter: *kekuningkuningan*. In Khmer of Cambodia, *kmeing* means "child," *kmeing-kmeing* means "children." *Chap* means "fast," *chap-chap* means "very quickly."

AGGLUTINATIVE LANGUAGES: STUCK LIKE GLUE

Linguists sometimes classify languages by how many pieces their words have. (Some other ways languages can be classified are listed in the Glossary under "Typological Classification.") "Agglutinative" languages "glue" a lot of pieces together to make words. The Bantu languages, including Swahili, are agglutinative. To say "I love you" in Swahili, you say *ni-na-ku-penda*. This means "I-now-you-love." The verb *-penda* (love) has everything needed in the sentence attached to it.

Many American Indian languages also glue together long words. An Eskimo can say "I wish I had something which would do for a fishing line" in one word: *aulisautissarsiniarpunga*. Which way would you rather say it—in twelve words or in one?

The Nootka Indian language of Canada also builds long words. From *inikw* (fire), they build *inikw-<u>ihl</u>*, which means "fire <u>in the</u>

house." *Inikw-ihl-'minih* is "fires in the house"; *inikw-ihl-'minih-'is* means "little fires in the house." *Inikw-ihl-'minih-'is-ita* means "several little fires were burning in the house." So instead of adding extra words to add ideas, agglutinative languages add affixes to a root word or combine root words.

Are these languages just stringing separate words together and saying them fast, as if you said "several-little-fires-were-burning-in-the-house" without stopping? No; people who speak these languages say that the pieces by themselves don't make sense. In English, *little* and *burning* by themselves have meaning. But in agglutinative languages, the whole long word (like *inikwihl-'minih'isita*) communicates one idea to the listeners.

The Americas and Africa don't have a monopoly on agglutinative languages. Many natives of Australia and nearby Papua New Guinea glue together long words. Australian aboriginal Tiwis say "I kept on eating" as *ngi-rru-unthing-apu-kani*, which literally means "I-past-for some time-eat-repeatedly." In the Kiwai language of Papua New Guinea, *ai-ni-mi-bi-du-mo-iauri-ama-ri-go* means "they three will certainly see us two."

The Basque, Finnish, Hungarian, and Turkish languages of Europe and Asia also build long words. Finnish goes from *kirja* (book) to *kirjassa* (in the book) to *kirjassani* (in my book). In related Hungarian, *hajó* is "ship," *hajók*, "ships," and *hajókban*, "in the ships." Surely no one deserves the Turkish word *sev-il-dir-eme-mek*, "to be impossible to be made to be loved"!

ISOLATING LANGUAGES: ONE-PIECE WORDS

At the other end of the scale from the agglutinative languages are "isolating" languages. These languages don't use any affixes. Their words don't change, no matter how they're used in a sentence, and they're usually only one syllable. Vietnamese and Chinese are isolating languages. There are also a few isolating languages in Africa.

Most Chinese words are roots that can work as noun, verb, adjective, or adverb. *Dà* can mean "large," "greatly," or "enlarge." *Shang* is the idea "above." As a noun it means the "above one," or "ruler." Or it can be an adjective: *shàng biàn* is the "above side," or "top." In *shang mǎ*, "to above (mount) a horse," *shang* works as a verb. But in *lù shang*, "on the street," *shang* is a preposition!

Chinese and Vietnamese nouns are not singular or plural, like *dog* and *dogs*. They're unchanging like the English word *sheep*. Vietnamese *em*, for instance, means "a brother," "brothers," "the brother," or "the brothers." If you want to know whether there's one or many of something you have to add other words, as you do in English when you say, "one sheep," "two sheep," "many sheep."

Verbs in Chinese and Vietnamese don't change either. So Chinese *lai*, which gives the idea of going, can mean "go," "went," "going," "goes," and so on. *When* the person goes, or went, is shown by some other word. So a Chinese person says "he this day go" for "he goes," and "you next day go" for "you will go." In English, you add a word in the same way for the future tense: "you *will* go."

Most Chinese words are only one syllable. But because syllables can end only in certain sounds, Chinese has fewer syllables than English. Most syllables have many meanings. For instance, *fu* can mean "father," "rich," "wife," or "belly." To show that you mean father, you can add *qin*, which means "kinsman." *Fu qin* clearly means "father." These are two words used together to make the meaning clear.

Many Chinese words are used as combinations like this. Some sets of words are quite picturesque. "Fire mountain" means "volcano." "One coat day" means weather that's a little cold. You might freeze to death, though, on a "seven coat day"!

Special counting words, which tell what kind of thing you are counting, also make things clearer. For instance, *kou* (mouth) is used for counting things with a round opening, like pots or wells. *Ba* (handle) is used for knives, spoons, and other things with handles. Vietnamese also uses counting words. *Con* is used for counting animals. So *sáu con mèo* means "six cats," or literally "six animal cats," and *hai con voi* means "two elephants," or "two animal elephants."

Word order is important in an isolating language. If you are just saying "man kill duck," it is very important that you don't change the order and say "duck kill man," which is something altogether different! In inflected languages, though, word order is much less important.

INFLECTED LANGUAGES: CHANGING THE PIECES

Inflected languages use affixes to show how a word is used in a sentence. English uses some inflections, like the *-ed* in *loved*, which shows that *loved* is a past tense verb. The *'s* in *Mary's* shows that the word is possessive, "belonging to Mary."

Other languages use many more inflections than English. Russian, German, Latin, and other highly inflected languages change the endings of nouns depending on how they're used in a sentence. If you wrote the sentence "Peter sees Paul" in Latin, you could write the words in any order and the meaning would not change. *Petrus Paulum videt, Paulum videt Petrus,* and *videt Paulum Petrus,* are all correct. This is because the *-us* ending on *Petrus* means that Peter is the one who did the action, the subject of the sentence. *-Um* on *Paulum* shows that Paul received the action; he is the object of the sentence.

Verbs also change in inflected languages according to how they're used. In English you say "I run," but "he run<u>s</u>." The *-s* shows that *he* is running, not *I*. But you also say "we run" and "they run," without the *-s*. So the pronoun has to be used; just saying "run" is not clear enough.

In some languages you can leave the pronoun out, since the ending on the verb tells who is acting. In Spanish, *yo corro* means "I run," but *corro* will do just as well, since the *-o* means "I" am running. *Corre,* on the other hand, can mean "you run," "he runs," "she runs," or "it runs," so you may have to use a pronoun if it's not clear who you're talking about.

Most languages get simpler in structure as time passes. Latin was much more inflected than Spanish is today. Old English was also more inflected than modern English. For instance, "to find" was *findan,* "he found" was *fand,* "they found" was *fundon,* and "was found" was *funden.* As Old English came in close contact with the Vikings' Old Norse, which was similar but with different grammar,

TABLE 7
PUTTING TOGETHER THE PIECES: LANGUAGE TYPES
Each type of language has its own way of putting together pieces of words. Compare the words for "man" in the inflected German language, the agglutinative Swahili language, and the isolating Mandarin Chinese language.

Language	"man"	"man's"	(to a) "man"	"men"	(to) "men"
German	Mann	Mannes	Manne	Männer	Männern
Swahili	←———— mtu ————→			←——— watu ———→	
Chinese	←———————————— nán rén ————————————→				

Old English became simpler. That way people speaking different languages could understand each other more easily. Many irregular English words that don't follow normal patterns come from Old English inflections. Rather than *finded*, we use a word almost like the Old English *fand*: modern English *found*.

Semitic languages like Arabic and Hebrew use prefixes, suffixes, and infixes. Most words in these languages are built from three letters. For instance in Arabic, the root *d-r-s* means "to study." "He studied" is *darasa*. "I studied" is *darast*, with a suffix. "I study," in the present, takes a prefix: *adrus*. Another prefix, *ma-*, makes a verb a place name: *madrasa* means "school." If you double the *r*, you get *darras*, "to make someone study," or "to teach." From that you can make *mudarrisa*, "teacher."

What type of language is English: isolating, agglutinative, or inflected? English has lost most of the inflectional endings of Old English. A few persist, though, as in *look/looked*, and *house/houses*. Many words are unchanging, and word order tells us how words are used in a sentence, as in isolating languages. Some English words, like *unlikeliness* and *disarmament*, look as if they came from an agglutinative language. Like many languages, English is a combination of types. Just as our words come from a hodgepodge of languages, so they're put together in a hodgepodge of ways.

> If a people have no word for something,
> either it does not matter to them or
> it matters too much to talk about.
>
> Edgar Z. Friedenberg

8

CAMELS AND KANGAROOS, COUSINS AND KINGS: A WORD FOR EVERYTHING

When you learn another language, you start by learning words. When you have learned everything else about the language, you will still be learning words! There are at least a million words in English, and about two thousand are added each year, while other words drop out of use. Most people, though, use fewer than 100,000 words. The words of a language are called its "vocabulary."

CAMELS AND SNOW

Each language has its own words, but they don't always describe the same things. Languages are affected by where their speakers live. Eskimos are surrounded by snow, and what type of snow it is makes a big difference in their lives. So, Eskimo languages have at least a hundred words for ice and snow. One word means falling snow, others mean soft snow, hard-packed snow, melting snow, and icy snow. One Eskimo word for "summer" means "season of inferior sledding"!

Arabs living far to the south have one word, *thalj*, for both "snow" and "ice." Desert nomads depend greatly on camels, however, so Arabic has many words that you would translate "camel." The most common is *jamal*, which comes from the same Semitic word as the English word *camel* does. Arabic has other words for male and female camels, camels at certain ages, at different stages of pregnancy, and giving milk for different lengths of time. Different names describe a camel's breed and color. Rather than saying "one-year-old female camel" or "two-year-old male camel," Arabic-speakers use particular words to differentiate camels in each year of their lives until they're full-grown, and when they grow old.

Farther north, the reindeer herders of Lapland (Scandinavia) have dozens of words in their Saami language to describe reindeer of different colors and ages.

In English culture, horses were once important as the main means of transportation and power, and they still are important among those who breed, ride, and race them. So English has many words for different kinds of horses, like *filly, gelding, roan, pony, pinto, palomino, colt, bronco, appaloosa, stallion, thoroughbred, cob, mare, mustang,* and many more.

To Italians, food seems to be important. They are said to have over 500 names for different kinds of noodles. These include *spaghetti*, which literally means "little strings," and *vermicelli*, which means "little worms"!

In the Australian countryside there must be a lot of holes, because the aboriginal language Pintupi has ten different words that could be translated "hole." *Yarla* is a hole in an object; *pirti*, a hole in the ground; *kartalpa*, a small hole in the ground; *yulpilpa*, a hole ants live in; *pulpa*, a rabbit hole; *mutara*, a special hole in a spear. *Pirnki, nyarrkalpa, makarnpa,* and *katarta* are other types of holes. Some Australian languages also have many words meaning "sand."

On the other hand, the Hopi Indian language has only one word for anything that flies and is not a bird. So insects, airplanes, and pilots are all called *masa'ytaka* (flier). But while English has only one word for water, Hopi has two: *pāhe*, meaning water in nature, and *kēyi*, water in a container. What does this tell you about what is important in traditional Hopi culture? Airplanes probably didn't enter much into their daily lives. But living in a dry area of the southwestern United States, water (in nature where you find it and in containers where you keep it for use) must have always been important to them.

Besides a people's land and culture, their religion can also influence their words. An Arab talking about the future says *Inshallah*, which means "If God wills." The Russian word for "thank you," *spasibo*, comes from two words that mean "God save." *Good-bye* comes from "God be with you." Vietnamese days of the week start with "the Lord's day." Monday is called "the second," Tuesday is "the third," all the way to Saturday, "the seventh." The name for Saturday in Hebrew is *Shabbat*, which means "Sabbath," the day of rest commanded in the Ten Commandments in the Bible.

FAMILY TIES

You may have a father, mother, sister, brother, aunt, uncle, cousins, and grandparents. Each language has words for family relationships important to the people who speak it.

Some use fewer relationship words than English. In Italian, *nipote* means a fairly distant relative: niece, nephew, grandson, or granddaughter. An uncle is more important, though; in many Italian dialects he is called *barba* (beard). Your uncle is the "bearded one," your big, strong protector. (This is not the standard Italian word for uncle, which is *zio*. Some Italian dialects are so different from each other that they are almost different languages.)

In English your "uncle" can be your father's brother, mother's brother, father's sister's husband, or mother's sister's husband. You have about the same relationship to all of them. In Arabic, though, there is a different word for your father's brother, *'amm*, and for your mother's brother, *xaal*. This is because these uncles have different roles in the family. In Arab cultures, the father's brothers are responsible for his family if anything happens to him, and they usually are involved in major family decisions. For example, an Arab boy's *'amm* helps decide what career he should follow and who he should marry. The mother's brothers, on the other hand, are usually less involved in the family.

Each cousin is also distinguished in Arabic. *Ibn 'amm* means "father's brother's son" (the person a girl is most likely to marry in some Arab cultures), while *bint xaala* means "mother's sister's daughter." To call someone your cousin in Arabic you have to know exactly how he or she is related to you!

Words for "aunt" and "uncle" in Vietnamese also show which side of the family is more important. There are separate words for your father's older brother and his wife, his younger brother and his wife, and his sister. Then there are words for your mother's sister, her brother (older or younger), and her brother's wife. The father's brothers, who will carry on the family name, are considered the most important relatives.

In the Far East, age is very important, and people older than you must always be respected. In Chinese, Thai, Burmese, Tibetan, Japanese, Korean, Malay, and the Tamil and Telugu languages of South India, different words are used for "older brother" and "younger brother." In some of those languages the difference between brother and sister isn't important at all. Only the age is important. In Malay, *saudara* means both "older brother" and "older sister." In Khmer, *baang* means "older brother or sister" and *pqoun* means "younger brother or sister."

Vietnamese also distinguishes between older and younger brothers and sisters. Your big brother is *anh*, big sister is *chi*, and little brother or sister is *em*. These words are also used to mean "I" or "you." To say "I'll give it to you" to your big brother, you say *em* will give it to *anh*, or "little brother (or sister) will give it to big brother." If your big brother wants to say the same thing, he says *anh* will give it to *em*, or "big brother will give it to little brother." If you are speaking to your parents, you call yourself *cou*. The same words are used for "you" and "I" in talking to people outside the family. If you are talking with an older boy, you call him *anh*, meaning "you." But if you are talking to a younger boy or girl, you say *em*. You would call an older girl *chi*. For someone your own age, you might simply use names: "I give it to you" becomes "Kong gives it to Dei." A wife even calls her husband "big brother," while he calls her "little sister." Speaking to older people, of your grandparents' generation, you use more respectful words for "you": the words that literally mean "grandfather" (*ông*) and "grandmother" (*bà*). These words show honor for people who are older than you are. If you do not use the right words to address people, they may be offended and call you ignorant or disrespectful. In Vietnamese (as well as Khmer), you always think of yourself in terms of your relationship with someone else: male/female, older/younger, close/distant. In English and related languages we think of ourselves more as separate, independent individuals; I am *I* and you are *you*, whatever our relationship is.

In Bolivia, speakers of the Chiquito language look at family members a little differently. In their culture, the relationship between a sister and a brother is not quite the same as the relationship between a brother and a brother, so they use different words. If a *girl* says "my brother" she uses *ichibausi*. A *boy* calls his brother *tsaruki*. The same thing happens with parents. A Chiquito boy calls his father *ijai* and his mother *ipaki*. But his sister calls dad *ishupu* and mom *ipapa*! What would you call your brother in Chiquito? Your answer depends on whether you're a boy or a girl. What would you call your brother in Vietnamese? That depends on whether he's older or younger than you are.

To the Japanese, it is important how close you are to the person you are talking about. So in Japanese you use different words for your own relatives and for someone else's. You would call your own mother *haha*. You would call someone else's mother *okaasan*. Your older brother is *ani*; your friend's older brother is *oniisan*. Your younger brother is *ototo*, someone else's younger brother is *ototosan*. The words for other people's relatives end in *-san*, which makes them polite words for someone at a distance.

RESPECTFULLY YOURS

In the United States, as in the rest of the world, we speak a little differently to people depending on their position. If you were speaking to the President of the United States, you would probably speak more formally and carefully than if you were speaking to your little sister. Everyone speaks differently in different circumstances: at home among friends; talking to strangers, older people, or children; talking to the teacher at school or the boss at work; or giving a speech. You might say "wouldn'tcha, Jim?" to your friend; "wouldn't you, Mr. Smith?" to your teacher; "would you not, ladies and gentlemen?" in a formal speech. In some parts of the United States, when you speak to someone of your parents' generation or older, especially if the person is a stranger, it is considered polite to address them as "sir" or "ma'am."

However in most cultures in the Far East, a person's position in society is so important that you use completely different forms of the language depending on whether you think the other person is more important or less important than you are.

In these cultures, you must show respect to people in a higher position than yours. Special words in Korean, Japanese, Vietnamese, Lao, Burmese, and Javanese honor a stranger, boss, or upper-class person. Other words show closeness to friends, family members, and children. For instance, in Japanese you might say *katta*, "I bought." But if you were talking about your teacher buying something, you would use *o kai ni natta*, which means "honorable buying did." If you asked your friend for a drink of water you would use *mizu* for "water." But if you asked your father for a drink you would be more polite and say *omizu*.

Suffixes on people's names also show respect in Japanese. You could call your teacher, Mr. Smith, Smith-*sensei*. (*Sensei* means "one who was born earlier" and is used for teachers, doctors, political leaders, and others.) Your father's boss might be Jones-*sama*; his friend, Johnson-*san* (that's a little less respectful); your favorite little brother, Johnny-*chan*. The endings show different levels of politeness and respect.

Khmer-speakers use different words for "you" to talk to equals, less important people, more important people, children, relatives, servants, priests, or royalty, as well as different words for men and women. So a Cambodian has to know a person's status before he speaks! This is also true in Javanese, a language of Indonesia. In Javanese almost everything you say shows whether the person you are speaking to is more important (richer, more educated, older, with a better job) than you are or less important, and how well you know them. To ask, "Are you going to eat rice?" you would have to first think about who you're talking to. If it is a government official or someone else important you would say, *Menapa pandjenengan badé dahar sekul?* If it is someone less important, but who you don't know well, you'd say, *Napa sampéjan adjeng neda sekul?* But if you're talking to your friend, or if the government official were talking to you, *Apa kowé arep mangan sega?* would be appropriate. Even the words meaning "to eat"—*dahar, neda,* and *mangan*—change depending on who you're speaking to!

Certainly in these languages you must think before you speak. There are many levels of Korean society. These have developed during a long history of Confucianist philosophy, which teaches a high degree of respect for elders and those in authority. Everyone from the king to the peasant traditionally had a well-defined place. These levels are reflected in the Korean language. A Korean has to decide which of six endings to put on each verb: the intimate *-na,* the familiar *-e,* plain *-ta,* polite *-oyo* or *-so,* or deferential *-supnita.* (Educated speakers today prefer not to use the first two endings, not wanting to show disrespect to anyone.) The speaker has to analyze his or her relationship with the hearer: Are they of equal status? If so, how close are they in age? If they are within two years of the same age, then what is their relationship (classmates, husband-wife, teacher-pupil, customer-salesperson . . .)? All these things are so important in Korean culture that they determine how people talk to each other.

ME AND YOU

Most languages don't have a whole system of words to show respect, but many use different words for "you." In English the word *you* covers male or female, friend or stranger, one person or many (though some dialects have plural words like *y'all*). Many Indo-European languages have two words for "you." In German you call your friend or someone in your family *du,* while a stranger or someone you want to show respect to is *Sie.* In Spanish your friend is *tú,* while others are *usted.* Your classmate in French class is *tu;* the teacher is *vous*. Your Russian friend is *ti*, anyone else is *bi*. In these cultures relationships and respect are so important that they are reinforced by everyday language.

In modern France many people are beginning to use the familiar *tu* for everyone and to drop the use of formal *vous*. This probably means that their culture is becoming less conscious of the differences between people, and perhaps more relaxed about beginning relationships, as most Americans are. Right now, though, it is difficult for French people to know which form to use with strangers, since some people expect *tu* for everyone and others still think *tu* is disrespectful. This type of tension is common when cultures, and the languages that reflect them, are making major changes.

In Hindu India, society is divided into thousands of groups called "castes," divided by occupations, religious practices, and tribes. A person's caste is determined from birth and cannot change. Each group is clearly "above" or "below" other groups. Although this system is not kept as strongly as it used to be, this consciouness of people's places is still reflected in Indian languages. Hindi and Bengali have three "you's": a polite one for superiors, an informal one for equals, and one for "inferiors" and children.

Old English had different words for "you, one person," "you, two people," and "you, three or more people." In Middle English, the words for "you, one person," became *thou* and *thee*, used in speaking to a friend or someone below the speaker on the social scale. (The two words were used as different parts of sentences, in the same way that we still use *I* and *me*.) The two-person form was dropped, and the plural form became *ye* and *you*, which were used in more formal situations to show respect. In the 1600s a religious group called the Quakers, or Society of Friends, began to call everyone *thou* and *thee* to show that they believed everyone was completely equal. Other speakers of English, though, soon dropped *thee* and *thou* and took the formal *you* as a general word for "you" instead. In the King James Version of the Bible, translated in 1611, the familiar *thee* and *thou* were used in speaking to God in prayer, to show God's nearness; *ye* and *you* were used to address people. Some

Christians still use *thee* and *thou* to refer to God, but as terms of respect and reverence rather than familiarity. Language is always changing!

In English you use different pronouns for "he" and "she," but all the other pronouns (*I, you, we, they,* etc.) can refer to either boys or girls. Arabs, though, use several words for "you": a girl is *anti*, a boy, *anta*. A group of people are *antum*. *Antumaa* is not used so often; it means "the two of you."

Finnish, Hungarian, Chinese, and Khmer (Cambodian), on the other hand, don't even separate "he" and "she." They use the same pronoun for "he," "she," or "it." So a Finn can't say "she walked into the room." He has to say "the girl walked into the room," or "it walked into the room." This is no more confusing than saying "they" in English whether you're talking about boys or girls. In fact, French, Spanish, and other languages have a "they" for males and another "they" for females! The male "they" is used for mixed groups.

In English, "we" has two meanings: "the person I'm talking to and I," or "someone else (who may not be around) and I." Vietnamese and some American Indian languages use two different words for those two meanings. In Malay, *kita* means "you and I," while *kami* means "someone else and I." Hawaiian has four words for we: *kaua,* "you and I," *maua,* "someone else and I," *kakou,* "all of you and I," and *makou,* "some other people and I."

NAMING NAMES

In English, most people have three names: their own first (or "given") and middle names, and a last name, their family name. When a woman gets married she traditionally takes her husband's last name, and often uses her father's family name (her maiden name) as her middle name. Children usually take their father's family name as their own. Other languages and cultures name people differently.

In Vietnamese, your family name comes first. Your middle name is usually Thị if you're a girl and Van if you're a boy. Your personal name comes last. A girl whose father's family name is Lê might be called Lê Thị Dêi. A woman does not change her name when she gets married, but her children usually take their father's family name rather than hers.

In Arabic, your own name is first, then your father's name, then your grandfather's name, and then sometimes a family name. Layla daughter of Ahmad son of Faysal would be called Layla Ahmad Faysal. In some Arab countries people are commonly called by their father's names, like Ibn Sa'ud, "son of Sa'ud." In other Arab countries, parents are called by their oldest son's names, like Abu Husayn, "father of Husayn," and Umm Husayn, "mother of Husayn." The first son may have many older sisters, but the parents never use a daughter's name; it's clear who is the most important child in the family.

Russians call their children by a given name, then "son of" (-*vich*) or "daughter of" (-*vna*) the father, then the family name (which has an -*a* added to it for a girl). Natasha daughter of Peter of the Dolgov family would be Natasha Petrovna Dolgova, while her brother Ivan would be Ivan Petrovich Dolgov. Many languages use family names which originally meant "son of" someone. In English we have names like Robertson and Johnson. The Scots use the prefixes *Mac* and *Mc*; MacIan would be "son of Ian." Irish uses *O'* (O'Hara, son of Hara). The prefix *Fitz* on some English names comes from the Norman variation of the French *fils* (son), so Fitzhugh means "Hugh's son." Polish uses a suffix, -*ski*, and Greek uses -*poulos*, both meaning "son of."

In the Burmese language of Southeast Asia, each person has two given names (like a first and middle name in English). They usually do not use a family name or father's name at all. The wife keeps her own name when she is married. Prefixes are added to the front of each name to show the person's age and sex: *ma* (sister) for a girl or young woman, *daw* (aunt) for an older woman, *maung* (brother) or *ko* (older brother) for a boy or young man, and *U* (pronounced *oo*) for an older man. A younger boy would address an older boy named Htun as Ko Htun, but an older man would call the same boy Maung Htun. The prefix *U* actually means "uncle," so the Burmese diplomat U Thant (secretary general of the United Nations, 1962–1972) was actually "Uncle Thant"; Thant was his first name. He was called Maung Thant as a young man.

In Korean and Chinese, the father's family name comes first, then the person's own first name. A woman does not change her name when she gets married. So a girl named Myung, whose family name is Kim, would be called Kim Myung.

In Malayalam and other languages of India, a person goes by his own first name and then his father's first name. A family name is rarely used. A girl who gets married goes by her first name followed by her husband's first name. So when Lakshmi daughter of Ram marries Biju, her name changes from Lakshmi Ram to Lakshmi Biju. It's as if Sally daughter of Don married Jeremy, and changed her name from Sally Don to Sally Jeremy.

ONE, TWO, MANY

Numbers must be numbers, in any language, right? Wrong! Many Australian aboriginal languages and some African "click" languages have only a few number words, like "all," "many," "few," "one," and "two." They don't need exact numbers in their everyday lives.

The English number system is based on tens. Eighty-five, for instance, is eight tens and five ones. Most counting systems use tens, probably because we have ten fingers. Our word *digit* for "number" also means "finger" and comes from the Latin word *digitus* meaning "finger" or "toe." In some systems, twenty is used, perhaps because we have twenty fingers and toes. Welsh and French use twenties as well as tens. Welsh forty is *deugain*, "two twenties." French ninety-one is *quatre-vingt-onze*, or "four-twenty-eleven" (4 x 20 + 11). The Hawaiian language counts by forties; 965 would be "two four-hundreds, four forties and five" ((2 x 400) + (4 x 40) + 5).

In the Khmer language of Cambodia, "six" is "five-one," "seven" is "five-two," "eight" is "five-three" and "nine" is "five-four." There is a different word for "ten," then "eleven" is "ten-

TABLE 8
NUMERALS IN DIFFERENT LANGUAGES

European*	Arabic	Devanagari (Hindi)	Chinese/ Japanese**	Khmer (Cambodian)	Burmese	Mayan Hieroglyphs
0	•	०	〇	០	၀	🝰
1	١	१	一	១	၁	•
2	٢	२	二	២	၂	••
3	٣	३	三	៣	၃	•••
4	٤	४	四	៤	၄	••••
5	٥	५	五	៥	၅	───
6	٦	६	六	៦	၆	•⎯
7	٧	७	七	៧	၇	••⎯
8	٨	८	八	៨	၈	•••⎯
9	٩	९	九	៩	၉	••••⎯
10	١٠	१०	十	១០	၁၀	⎯⎯
11	١١	११	十一	១១	၁၁	•⎯⎯
20	٢٠	२०	二十 (=2○)	២០	၂၀	🝰 with •
21	٢١	२१	二十一 (=2→)	២១	၂၁	🝰 with ••
100	١٠٠	१००	百 (→○○)	១០០	၁၀၀	🝰

*The numbers used in English and many other languages are usually referred to as "Arabic numerals," or "Hindu-Arabic numerals." They were invented in India, brought to Arabia, then the Moors brought them to Europe in about the eighth century.

**This is traditional usage, where each number is multiplied by the number after it: 21 = (2×10) + 1. More modern usage, in parentheses, uses a place value system. Japanese characters are shown here; Chinese characters are almost the same.

one," "twelve" is "ten-two," and so on up to "sixteen," which is "ten-five-one." Many American Indian languages also name their numbers based on the word for "five." The African Yoruba language approaches numbers from a different direction, calling 199 "two hundred minus one" rather than "one hundred ninety-nine."

The ancient Sumerians, Babylonians, and Assyrians counted by twelves rather than by tens. This system was probably based on astronomy; they studied the twelve constellations called the zodiac which mark the passing of the year. Mathematically, twelve is an easier system to use than ten, since twelve can be divided evenly by more numbers (2,3,4,6) than ten (which can only be divided evenly by 2 and 5). This counting system gave us our twelve-month year, twenty-four (2 x 12) hours in a day, sixty (5 x 12) minutes in an hour and sixty seconds in a minute, as well as twelve things in a *dozen* (which comes from the Latin *duo*, "two," plus *decem*, "ten") and twelve *inches* (from the Latin *uncia*, "one-twelfth") in a foot.

In English we form the words for the "teen" numbers, from thirteen to nineteen, differently than we form the twenties, thirties, or larger numbers. *Thirteen* is really *three-ten*, with the ones first and then the tens, unlike *twenty-three*, where the tens are first and then the ones. Many languages have a special sequence for the numbers between ten and twenty, like the Spanish *once, doce, trece, catorce* (eleven, twelve, thirteen, fourteen), which are different than *veinte y uno, veinte y dos, veinte y tres, veinte y cuatro* (twenty and one, twenty and two, twenty and three, twenty and four) and so on. In agglutinative Basque, though, the numbers are added after ten, so that *hama* (ten) can be changed to *hama-hiru* (ten-three, or thirteen), *hama-lau* (ten-four, or fourteen), *hama-bost* (ten-five, or fifteen) and so on.

CAN I BORROW A WORD, PLEASE?

Many cultures have words for things they use that other cultures don't. English has borrowed some of those words as English-speakers have seen those things. You may eat *curry* from the Tamil language of India, *okra* or *yams* from African languages, *goulash* from Hungarian, or *pizza* from Italian. Germany gave America *pretzels*; the Mexicans brought *tacos* and *enchiladas*. The Japanese wear the *kimono*. The *sombrero* came from the Spanish language of Mexico. *Pants* came from the Old Italian *pantalone*. *Skirt* came from the Old Norse (Viking) word *skyrta*, which originally meant a *shirt*!

Animal names are often borrowed. Explorers in North America ran into the moose, woodchuck, and (most unpleasantly!) the skunk. They borrowed the Indian names (*moos, wuchak,* and *segankw*) for those animals. The *cockatoo*'s name is from a Polynesian language, and South American Indians gave us *jaguar*.

No one is quite sure where the word *kangaroo* came from. Kangaroos are not called "kangaroo" in any known Australian language; they are called *wallaby* or *wallaroo*. In 1770 Captain James Cook, when he was exploring in Australia, wrote down as many aborigine (native Australian) words as he could, including the word *kangaroo*. He did not realize that there were hundreds of different aboriginal languages. Later explorers tried to use his words, and found that the aborigines of other areas didn't recognize any of them. In fact, they took the word *kangaroo* to be an English word for any kind of animal, and called the settlers' sheep and cows *kangaroos!* Explorers returning to the area where Captain Cook first landed could not find any tribe there that used the word, either. One theory is that Captain Cook saw a kangaroo and asked his guide "What's that?" The guide said *kangaroo,* meaning "I don't understand you." Another possibility is that *kangaroo* may have been the animal's name in some Australian dialect which has since died out.

Scholars say most of the words of Albanian, a European language, are borrowed from Romance, Turkish, Greek, and Slavic languages. As we saw in chapter 4, languages often borrow words from their powerful neighbors.

Many words change meanings when they are borrowed. The Karok Indians of northern California were visited by a trapper named McKay in the 1800s. They took his name, *mákkay,* to mean "white man." They added it to other words, too. For example, *mákkay* combined with *váas* (deerskin blanket) and *yukúkku* (moccasin) makes

ENGLISH: A GENEROUS LANGUAGE

American inventions, ideas, clothes, and customs have traveled to many parts of the world, carrying their English names with them. Germans use *das Knowhow* when they work for *der Boss* or *das Management,* they eat *das Sandwich,* and play with *das Baby.* Swedes watch *den TV:n* and take pictures with *den kameran.* Koreans travel by *taxi* and *bus.* On *le weekend,* the French play *volley* and *basket.* Russian *biznesmeny* (businessmen) play *golf,* while Mexicans get a *jonrón* (home run) playing *beisbol.* Arabs wear *shorrt* and *zheenis,* which the French call *shorts* and *jeans.* Russians wear *shorte,* Swedes wear *den T-shirten* (while eating *den hamburgaren*), and a Spanish-speaker puts on a *suéter* (sweater). A *sumato* (smart) and *apputodeito* (up-to-date) Japanese businessman knows how to use *masu komi* (mass communications), the *cm* (commercial), and *wa-pro* (word processing). The most popular English word may be *okay!* which people around the world use with a smile.

makayvas-yukúkku, "white man-material-moccasins." You call them "tennis shoes"!

Other languages have also borrowed words from English, though you may have to think for a moment to understand them! What do you think the Japanese *chokoréeto, herikóputaa,* and *ákusento* mean? ("Chocolate," "helicopter," and "accent.") How about Swahili *kalenda* or *steki*? ("Calendar," "steak.")

ARE YOU NICE?

Meanings of words change over time. A word's history is called its "etymology." The English word *nice* came from a Latin word, *nescium,* which meant "not knowing, ignorant." In Old French, around the twelfth century, it came to mean "silly." Middle English borrowed it in the thirteenth century with the meaning "foolish." Later it came to mean "shy," then "hard to please," and eventually "accurate" (as in "a nice distinction"). About 250 years ago it came to mean "pleasant," as we use it today. French no longer uses the word *nice*, though there is a city in France named Nice!

School came originally from a Greek word, *scholē*, meaning "leisure" or "free time." Learning, of course, is what you do when you have free time and don't have to work!

Are you *diseased*? This word used to mean lacking ease: "uncomfortable." *Ease* came from a French word, *aise*, meaning "elbow-room." So if you're feeling cramped, without room to move, you could say you're *diseased*.

The name of one disease, *malaria*, came from the Italian for "bad air," because people thought the disease came from the air. It actually is carried by mosquitoes. Do you think you could get *malaria* in Buenos Aires, a city whose name is Spanish for "good air"?

IDIOMS

Each language has "idioms," expressions which mean something different from their literal meanings. When you say to someone "you're pulling my leg," you don't actually mean that she has her hands wrapped around your leg and is tugging on it! A Spaniard would be confused to hear that you're "pulling his leg" or "putting him on." He would say you're "taking his hair." The French say "to buy someone's head," meaning "to laugh at someone." An American student might "cut class" (with scissors?) or "play hookey" (what game is that?). Italian boys "pickle the school," while Russians "hobo the school." A Chinese girl "hides from school" and a Spanish señorita "plays the calf." If a Russian student doesn't study quite enough, he "gets a troika." A *troika* is a sled pulled by three horses, and in Russian schools a "three" means a grade of "C" ("five" is an "A").

In some dialects of French, a sweetheart is called *mon petit choux* (my little cabbage), while a Spaniard calls his beloved *mi corazón* (my heart) or *mi sangre* (my blood).

Some idioms are "euphemisms," ways to avoid saying something

SHIELDS AND SPEARS

One Korean idiom, *mo sun* (shield and spear), recalls a whole story. Long ago a weapons-maker made shields. He went out in the square and shouted, "Shields no spear can pierce! Shields no spear can pierce!" He sold many shields. Then he began making spears. He advertised them, "Spears that can pierce any shield! Spears that can pierce any shield!" and sold lots of spears. So "shield and spear" means "utter nonsense, impossible."

embarrassing. In Britain if you're going to the restroom, you can say you're going "to spend a penny." A German who is "in different conditions" is pregnant.

In French, if you're terrified of someone you "have a blue fear" of them; in English, of course, a coward is "yellow." In English, if you have other things to try, you "have other fish to fry." In French you "have other cats to whip."

Some idioms are the same from language to language. In Spanish if you make a fool of yourself you "put the foot in," *meter la pata*, like the English "put your foot in it." In Swedish *pricken över i:et*, "dot the i," means "to give something a finishing touch."

To be *too* picky is in French *chercher les poux dans la paille*, "to look for lice in the straw." But if you're no help at all, a Yiddish-speaker might say to you, *a shainem dank dir im pupik*, "many thanks in your belly button!" (Thanks for nothing.)

The German saying *du trampelst auf meinen Nerven herum;* "you are trampling on my nerves," means "you're getting on my nerves, you're bugging me." In Spanish you might tell that person *véte a freir esparragos*, "go fry asparagus," like the English "go fly a kite." When you get very angry, you *pones el grito en el cielo*, "scream at the sky." If you wanted to say instead, "I've had tough times before; I can handle it," you might use the Iranian Farsi idiom, *man gorge borun didam*, "I'm a wolf that has seen a lot of rain."

In Korean something very rare is "like harvesting beans from a field in a drought," while in Arabic it's "in apricot time," a very short season of the year. Something that happens very fast in Korea is "like frying beans with lightning." But if it didn't turn out very well, some Swedes would say *krabbar,* "it crabbed."

In Russian, something might happen *kakda rak nagareeya sfisnyet,* "when the crawfish whistles on the mountain"; not in a million years! Russian "I'll show you where the crawfish spend the winter" means "I'll punish you very severely"!

SAY WHAT YOU MEAN

Some words, like *hum, fizz,* and *gurgle,* sound like what they mean. This is called "onomatopoeia." The Tamil language of India has words like *munumunu* and *tonutonu.* Can you guess what they mean? *Munumunu* is "murmuring and muttering," a bit like English "moan." *Tonutonu* is "the sound of beating drums," or "complaining."

Every language has a wide variety of words. Some are as short as *a* and *I,* others as long as Mary Poppins's favorite, *supercalifragilisticexpialidocious.* The longest word yet discovered in Turkish is *çekoslavakyalılaştıramadıklarımızdanmısınız?* That means, "Are you the people whose nationality we cannot change to Czechoslovakian?" (How often do you think that word is used?) In New Zealand, one hill is named "Taumatawhakatangihangakoauauotamatea(turipukakapikimaungahoronuku)pokaiwhenuakitanatahu." Try saying that three times fast! It means "the place where Tamatea, the man with the big knee who slid, climbed, and swallowed mountains, known as Land-Eater, played on his flute to his loved one."

Some languages have beautifully expressive words and phrases. African Bantu languages have words like *mumagamagama,* "one who loses other people's things," and *muwavi,* "a good-looking woman who can't cook." Do you growl when you're woken up in the mornings? Then you're a *muwandoloci.*

Some expressive words have disappeared from English. If you tell a *hoddypeak* he's full of *fadoodle,* will he *glop* you with *ug*? A *hoddypeak* is a "blockhead," *fadoodle* is "foolishness," to *glop* is "to stare at in wonder or alarm," and *ug* means "fear."

Some words sound delightful, like the Albanian *xhaxhmëxhuxh*, pronounced *jahjmajooj*, which means "little dwarf man." A tongue twister in Bahasa Indonesian, the phrase *ular lari lurus*, means "a snake runs wild." Whatever it is, somebody somewhere has a word for it!

> It is well to remember that grammar
> is common speech formulated.
> W. Somerset Maugham

9

THE BLUEPRINT OF LANGUAGE: GRAMMAR

Do you study grammar in school? The word *grammar* comes from a Greek word, *gramma*, which meant "writing." At first *grammar* referred to the study of literature, then to the study of language. For a long time it meant the study of Latin. That's where the phrase "grammar schools" comes from; Latin was an important subject in basic schools.

When linguists say "grammar," they mean the way a language works. In school when you study grammar you learn how words are put together in standard English. (Remember "standard English" from chapter 2?) That is called "prescriptive grammar": how you "ought" to speak and write to be accepted as an educated person.

Linguists study something different: "descriptive grammar," or "syntax." They try to work out the rules which native speakers automatically use to make sentences. This includes how words are arranged, how they're related to each other, and what form of each word is used. You know the grammar of the dialect you grew up speaking. You use it every time you talk, without even thinking about grammar.

If words are the bricks of language, grammar is the blueprint that shows how to build the house. Without the blueprint, the bricks would be put together any which way and the house would not stand. Without grammar, words would not communicate anything to other people.

WHO TALKS FUNNY?

WORDS IN ORDER

Are[3] the[6] in[5] make[12] sentences[9] order,[8] words[2] not[4] not[11] right[7] sense[13] if[1] do[10]. Could you understand that? Put the words in order by number. Now they communicate something.

In English and most related languages, the subject of the sentence comes first, then the verb and then the object. You say "Anthony caught the ball." "Anthony" is the subject, "caught" is the verb, and "the ball" is the object. "The ball caught Anthony" would mean something altogether different! Centuries ago in Old English, the object often came before the verb: "Anthony the ball caught." In Spanish the verb can come first: "Caught Anthony the ball."

Sometimes poets change word order to focus on an idea or to create rhythm and rhymes. For instance in Longfellow's poem, "Paul Revere's Ride," he says "One, if by land, and two, if by sea; And I on the opposite shore will be." The verb, "be," is at the end, rather than in its usual position in the middle: "I will be on the opposite shore."

In most languages, as in English, the subject comes first. In a few, like Tagalog (of the Philippines) and Welsh, the verb starts the sentence. Japanese, Korean, Tamil, German, and other languages put the verb at the end of the sentence. A Korean might say, "Father yesterday his taxes paid." The Japanese sentence *Kinoo katta mannenhitsu wa teeburu no ue ni arimasu* literally means "Yesterday bought fountain pen as-for table's top on is." In English word order that's "The fountain pen which I bought yesterday is on the table."

Very few of the world's languages put the object of the sentence first, then the subject and the verb. But in the movie *Return of the Jedi,* Yoda uses that pattern: "When nine hundred years you reach, look as good you will not," he says, and "Strong with the Force you are." This unusual word order makes Yoda seem foreign and unique.

Adjectives are words that describe nouns. In English they come before nouns: "the little red hen" (the underlined words are adjectives). In many languages they come after nouns. In Arabic, for instance, "the little red hen" is *iddajaaja issagiira ilhamra,* or "the-hen the-little the-red." In Khmer, "that big red car of mine" would be "car big red of-I that." The Vietnamese for "a thick book" translates, "one volume book thick."

Languages like Rumanian, Danish, and Bulgarian place the word meaning "the" after the noun. For "the boy" they say "boy the." Swedish and Norwegian use "the" twice: *den stygga gosse-n* means "the bad boy-the" (*den* means "the," and *-n* is a shortened form of *den*).

Russian, most Slavic languages, Khmer, and Finnish have no word meaning "the" or "a." So Russian *zhena* means "wife," "a wife," or "the wife." This makes it difficult for Russians learning English; they don't know quite where to put *the*, *a*, or *an*, since they don't use these words at all in their own languages.

English uses little words called "prepositions": *of, in, for,* and so on. These are called prepositions because they're positioned before the noun. Japanese, Hindi, and other languages use postpositions after the noun with the same meanings. Instead of "in school," they say "school in." Eskimo *iglu-mi* means "in the house." *Iglu* is the word English borrowed as "igloo," while *-mi* means "in." Old English had postpositions, but modern English doesn't.

Every language has patterns that make sense to its speakers. See if you can figure out what each of these sentences means before you look at the English:

Korean: "I apple him give."
English: "I give him an apple."

Farsi (Iran): "She the fire uses the stick to stir."
Senoufo (Africa: Ivory Coast and Mali): "The stick, she uses the fire stir."
English: "She uses the stick to stir the fire."

Portuguese: "Tell-me-you have."
English: "You will tell me."

Hopi: "This house negative big, very small."
Vietnamese: "House not big, house this small."
English: "This house is not big, it is small."

German: "I know not, where you this book bought have."

English: "I don't know where you bought this book."

Eskimo: "To-arrive-first-be-able-would-not-said-him-he." (one word)
English: "He said that he would not be able to arrive first."

Khmer (Cambodian): I gave book large him.
English: I gave him the large book.

Speakers of these languages would find English word order just as confusing as their word order sounds to you!

NOUNS AND THEIR FRIENDS

As you saw in chapter 7, in some languages word order isn't very important. Nouns in inflected languages take different forms to show how they are acting in the sentence. These different forms are called "cases." The subject, or do-er, of the sentence has one form or case; the object, or receiver, has a different one. Other endings or forms of the noun may be used for possessive nouns, objects of prepositions, and indirect objects.

Old English had a complicated set of cases. We only use one of them now for nouns other than pronouns. When you add 's to a word, as in "the shark's jaws," you are making what is called the "genitive" case. When you add the genitive ending, 's, to a word, it shows possession. Some Native Americans form the genitive case quite differently. Instead of "the shark's jaws," they would say "his jaws the shark." Arabs say simply "jaws the shark"!

English still has different pronouns for different cases. Instead of writing "the boy brought the boy's toy to the boy," we can write "he brought his toy to him." *He*, *his*, and *him* all refer to the boy, but they are each different pronouns because they are used differently in the sentence. *He* is in the "nominative" or "subjective" case because it is the subject of the sentence. *Him* is in the "accusative" or "objective" case; it is the object of the verb *brought*, telling what the boy brought. *His* is in the "genitive" or "possessive" case. It shows who the toy belongs to. (*Boy's* in the first sentence is also in the genitive case; the *'s* is the case ending.) The other pronouns in English also change this way. For example, we use *I* for the nominative case, *me* for the accusative, and *my* for the genitive.

Many languages use case endings to show how a noun is used in a sentence. German uses four cases: nominative for the subject, accusative for the direct object, dative for the indirect object, and genitive for the possessive. The noun itself usually doesn't change in German, but the article "the" changes: *der Bruder* means "the brother, subject of the sentence"; *den Bruder,* "the brother, object of the sentence"; *dem Bruder,* "to the brother"; and *des Bruders,* "of (or belonging to) the brother."

Russian also inflects nouns for different cases. If a Russian wants to say "the book is good," she uses *kneega* for "book," since it's the subject of the sentence. If she wants to say "I read the book," she uses *kneegoo* for "book," since it's the object of the sentence. In this Russian sentence, each noun is used differently, and so each one has a different ending:

Петя пишет письмо   Сергею пером в комнате   моего брата.
Pyet<u>ya</u> peeshyet peesm<u>o</u> Syerge<u>yoo</u> pyer<u>om</u> v komnat<u>ye</u>   moy<u>ego</u> brat<u>a</u>.
Petya is writing a letter   to Sergei with a pen in the room of my brother.

The different endings for the nouns in this sentence show each one's function; they tell whether the noun is the subject of the sentence or its object and whether it is singular or plural. The endings also depend on whether the noun is masculine, feminine, or neuter (see below), which is why *peesmo* doesn't have the same ending as *kneegoo,* although they're both in the accusative case. Besides the four cases which German uses, Russian has two more: an instrumental case and a prepositional or locative case. Rather than writing "with a pen," as we would say in English, a Russian puts *pyero* (pen) in the instrumental case and says *pyerom*. No preposition (like the English *with*) is needed. The phrase "in the room" does need a preposition, *v* (in), which is followed by *komnata* (room) with the ending for the prepositional case, which makes it *v komnatye*. (As you see, Russian is written with a different alphabet than ours; these words are transliterated into the nearest English sounds.) All these different noun endings may seem complicated to you, but a Russian child learns them by hearing them every day, and has no more trouble with them than you do with saying "he sees" rather than "he see."

Latin had six or seven cases, but its daughters, the Romance languages, have mostly stopped using them. Only Rumanian still uses two cases. Of the Celtic languages, Irish Gaelic still uses five cases, but its sisters Welsh and Breton have given up case systems. Classical Arabic uses three cases, but colloquial dialects leave off the case endings. Hindi, Turkish, Hungarian, Icelandic, Greek, Slovak, Czech, Serbo-Croatian, Russian, and Polish all use endings on nouns to show different parts of the sentence. Finnish uses fifteen cases, while the Georgian language of the Caucasus Mountains (in the former Soviet Union) has the imposing number of twenty-three!

In Japanese, Khmer, and Chinese, though, there are no case endings, or even endings that tell whether a noun is singular or plural. So Japanese *hito* means "man" or "men." On the other hand, Arabic has an ending for two of something, and another for three or more. So "eye" is *'ayn*, two eyes are *'aynayn*, and three eyes are *'ayuun*. In Eskimo, one polar bear is *nanuq*, two polar bears are *nannuk* and more than two polar bears are *nannut*. Old English had the word *wit* for "we two" and *git* for "you two."

A few languages even have special endings for three of something. In Tyattyalla, a native language of Australia, speakers can talk about: *gattimgattimek*, (a boomerang), *gattimgattimul* (a pair of two boomerangs), *gattimgattimurrakullik* (a set of three boomerangs), or *gattimgattimurrak* (more than three boomerangs).

In many languages, nouns have a gender: they are either feminine, masculine, or neuter (with no gender). This is a way of classifying words into categories. Usually it is arbitrary, not related to any masculine or feminine characteristics of a noun. That's why a noun may have different genders in different languages. For example, in French the sun is masculine (*le soleil*), while in German it is feminine (*die Sonne*). Sometimes the gender of a word is built-in. In Spanish, for example, the word for boy (*el muchacho*) is masculine and the word for girl (*la muchacha*) is feminine. In German,

THE TURNIP, SHE GOES...

Mark Twain was quite entertained by the use of gender in the German language. He explained it this way:

> In German, a young lady has no sex, while a turnip has. Think what overwrought reverence that shows for the turnip, and what callous disrespect for the girl. See how it looks in print—I translate this from a conversation in one of the best of the German Sunday-school books:
>
> Gretchen: Wilhelm, where is the turnip?
> Wilhelm: She has gone to the kitchen.
> Gretchen: Where is the accomplished and beautiful English maiden?
> Wilhelm: It has gone to the opera.
>
> To continue with the German genders: a tree is male, its buds are female, its leaves are neuter; horses are sexless, dogs are male, cats are female—Tom-cats included, of course; a person's ... head is male or neuter according to the word selected to signify it, and *not* according to the sex of the individual who wears it,—for in Germany all the women wear either male heads or sexless ones.... The inventor of the language probably got what he knew about a conscience from hearsay.

From *A Tramp Abroad* by Mark Twain. New York: Harper and Brothers, 1906.

---

though, a young girl is *ein Mädchen* and a young woman is *ein Fräulein,* both of which are neuter nouns, neither feminine nor masculine! Old English used to have the same peculiarity: *wifmon* (woman) was a masculine word, and *maegden* (maiden) was neuter. In modern English, none of our words have genders.

In some languages, like Spanish, Portuguese, and Italian, feminine nouns usually end in -*a,* while masculine ones usually end in -*o.* In Spanish *la pluma* (the pen) is feminine, and *el periódico* (the newspaper) is male. Words describing the noun, like articles ("a" or "the") and adjectives, are masculine or feminine, too. In Spanish, "the handsome boy" is *el muchacho hermoso*; "the beautiful girl" is *la muchacha hermosa*. All three words—the article, the noun, and the adjective—have the same gender.

In some Dravidian languages of India there are two genders: a superior one, used for males, gods, and goddesses, and an inferior one used for females and things that aren't alive. So in these languages, a goddess is closer to a man than to a woman, and a girl is more like a rock than like a boy! Would you like to be a girl in a place where these languages are spoken?

In many languages when you tell your parents you're going out with a "friend" you have to say whether the friend is a girl or a boy. In Spanish a girl friend is *amiga*, a boy friend is *amigo*. Italian friends are *amica* or *amico*, German friends are *Freundin* or *Freund*, and French friends are *amie* and *ami*. But if you're going out with a group of friends, you use a plural form, like Spanish *amigas* or *amigos*. *Amigas* is a group of girls, but if there's even one boy in the group, you call them *amigos*, as if they were all boys. Any group with at least one male in it, no matter how many females there are, is called by the masculine plural. The same is true in French, Italian, German, Arabic, and Hebrew. Who do you think has traditionally been most important in those cultures?

Very inflected languages, like Russian and German, have different forms of each noun according to its case, gender, and number (singular or plural). There are more than seventy forms for Russian nouns! Articles and adjectives also change for case, gender, and number in these languages. In the Russian sentence above, for example, *moyego* (my) in *moyego brata* (my brother) has an adjective ending for the masculine genitive case.

VERBS AND THEIR HELPERS

"I race," "he races," "I raced," "they will race." English verbs have only a few forms. There is no real future tense; added words, like "will" or "is going to," show that something will happen in the future.

GRAMMAR: THE BLUEPRINT OF LANGUAGE

Some languages, like Chinese, have only one form for verbs. The Khmer verb *tiw* could mean "go," "goes," "is going," "am going," "went," "have gone," or "has gone." But a verb in Bilin, a language of Africa, can have over 10,000 different forms!

Most languages use endings to show verb tenses, but some African languages add to the beginning of verbs instead. Swahili, an agglutinative language, uses prefixes for the person and tense of a verb. "He wanted" is *a-li-taka*. *A-* means "he" and *-li-* means past tense. *Ni-* means "I" and *-sema* means "say." How would you say "I said" in Swahili? Right: *ni-li-sema*. The prefixes change for negatives. *Si-ku-sema* means "I did not say." *Sema!* without any endings means "Say!"

Verbs show how a culture sees time. One American Indian language uses different forms for the recent past, long-ago past, and the past of myths and legends. The flow of history is evidently important in their culture. They probably think and talk more about their ancestors and beginnings than English-speakers generally do. Some Australian aborigines focus more on the future. They use five different future tenses: two for things that will happen later on today, and three for farther in the future. They have probably learned that the far future is much less predictable than what will happen today!

English verbs do not have many forms, but we use helping words to make time distinctions that many other languages don't make. For instance, we can say *did, has done, has been doing, had done, had been doing, was doing, will have done, will be doing,* and so on. These words distinguish when an action started and finished, and whether it was ongoing or one-time. This might show an interest in exact details of time, when and how things happened, in our culture.

Spanish and some of its relatives have two different verb forms in the past tense to show one of these distinctions. *Pensé,* "I thought," is different than *pensía,* "I was thinking." The first is completed, the second is ongoing. Spanish also has two present tenses, one for what is definitely happening, and one for what is possible (the "subjunctive"). The verb "to say" (*decir*) has different endings in these two sentences: *Lo dice* means "he says it": that's definite.

Temo que lo diga means "I'm afraid he'll say it": that's possible, but not definite. For the future, Spanish has a regular tense and a conditional tense. The conditional is for what might happen depending on something else happening. "*If* a spaceship lands in my yard, *then* I will *call* you." *Call* in that sentence would be in the conditional tense. Many languages, from Polish to Swahili, use different verb forms for what really happened and what might happen.

Japanese has a "tentative" tense, used for actions that aren't certain, definite, or completed. So *yomimashoo* means "I think I will read" or "let's read." Or it could mean "shall we read?" or "I suppose he has read." There's nothing on a Japanese verb to tell you who is acting. *Kau* means "I, you, he, she, we, or they buy." In Japanese culture, humility is very important, and it is rude to mention persons (especially yourself, but you also would not want to embarrass others by focusing attention on them). So pronouns are rarely used, and you have to figure out from the conversation who's doing the buying!

The Fox Indian language has one verb form that means "God forbid that this should happen!" and another that means "What if it did happen! What do I care?"

Basque, the European language with no relatives, has forty different forms for its verbs. Here are a few forms of the verb which means "to carry":

eramatendet: "I carry it."
eramatendezu: "you (familiar) carry it."
eramatenditut: "I carry them."
eramatendituzu: "you (familiar) carry them."
eramatendizut: "I carry it for you."
eramatendigute: "they carry them for us."

In some languages, verbs show direction. In the North American Indian language Karok, *path* means "throw," *páath-roov* means "throw upriver," *páath-raa* means "throw uphill," *paath-rípaa* means "throw across-stream." There are thirty-eight other forms, too! Does this tell you anything about the Karoks' relationship to the land around them? The Karoks lived on the Klamath River in

• •

FIGURE 3
PUZZLE: DECIPHERING A LANGUAGE

Linguists often go into remote areas to study languages that outsiders have never learned before. Besides learning the words of the language, they have to listen carefully to figure out which sounds are important in the language (the phonemes) and what rules are used to put words into sentences (the grammar). By collecting sentences, they work out rules which can be used to make other sentences. Here are some sentences from a real language (Arabic, transliterated into our script). See if you can figure out the meanings of the words and the rules used to put them together so you can make new sentences. (Answers are on the next page.)

Bint raahat ila madrasa.
A girl went to a school.

Hiya raahat ila madrasa.
She went to a school.

Bint raahat ila madrasa kabiira.
A girl went to a big school.

Hiya raahat ila madrasa sagiira ams.
She went to a small school yesterday.

Now, can you translate this into English?

Hiya raahat ila madrasa kabiira ams.

Can you translate this into Arabic?

A girl went to a small school.

In Arabic, where do you think you add an adjective to a noun: before or after the noun?

• •

northwestern California, where they fished for salmon. The river, as well as other landforms, must have been very important in their lives when these words developed.

English-speakers constantly use forms of the verb "to be" (*am, is, are, was, were*). Many languages, like Hawaiian and Balinese, don't have a verb meaning "to be." In Hawaiian, "we are fine, thanks" is *maika'i no makou, mahalo,* literally "fine indeed we, thanks." Some languages, like Russian and Arabic, don't use "to be" in the present tense but use it in the past and future. So you can say "the book was blue" and "the book will be blue," but today, "the book blue."

ANSWERS TO "PUZZLE: DECIPHERING A LANGUAGE" (on previous page)

Hiya raahat ila madrasa kabiira ams.
She went to a big school yesterday.

A girl went to a small school.
Bint raahat ila madrasa sagiira.

In Arabic, an adjective (like *kabiira*, "big," or *sagiira*, "little") comes after a noun (like *madrasa*, "a school").

Translations of other words: *bint*, a girl; *raahat*, went; *ila*, to; *hiya*, she; *ams*, yesterday.

A linguist, of course, would have to have a lot more samples of a language to check the rules he or she works out.

Spanish has two words meaning "to be." *Ser* means to be permanently. It would be used in sentences like "Juana is a girl" and "the book is red." *Estar* means to be temporarily, as in "Juan is in the house" or "he is reading."

The emphasis in Japanese is on whether something is alive or not. There are three words for "to be." *Desu* tells *what* something is: *enpitsu desu*, "it is a pencil." This is used for people or things. But when you are talking about *where* something is, you use *arimasu* if it's a thing: *enpitsu ga arimasu*, "there is a pencil." If you're talking about where a living being—like a person—is, you use *imasu*: *Nyuu Yooku ni imasu*, "he is in New York."

Many languages use verbs for words that in English are adjectives. In Khmer (Cambodian), for instance, the verb *lqaa* means "to be pretty or good"; the verb *sapbaay* means "to be happy."

THIS, THAT, AND THE OTHER

What is the difference between *this* and *that*? *This* is close, and *that* is farther away. In Spanish, there are three words: *este* (near me), *ese* (near you), and *aquel* (far from both of us). Japanese uses *kore*, *sore*, and *are* in the same way. English used to use *yon*, for "that far away," but you don't hear that very often nowadays.

Eskimo languages have about thirty different ways to say *this* and *that.* Some of them mean "that one in there" (perhaps in another room), "that high up there" (like a bird in the sky), and "that unseen" (something you hear or feel).

It is important to the Hopi Indians exactly how a person came to know something. Each of these sentences would use a different word for "that": "I see that it is new." (You can tell from clues, perhaps it is shiny or clean, and from past experience of what new things look like.) "I see that it is red." (You can tell directly, with your eyes.) "I hear that it is new and red." (You know from someone else's experience.)

The word *it* can also have many forms, depending on how a culture looks at objects. The Paiute Indian language has different words for *it* if *it* is visible or not visible. Yana and Navajo Indians have to know the shape of a thing to say *it*. They will say "round thing," for instance, for a stone.

"This and that" are not the same everywhere!

> **The palest ink is better than the most retentive memory.**
> Chinese proverb

10

FROM HIEROGLYPHICS TO ALPHABETS: LANGUAGES IN WRITING

If you have an idea you want to share with your friends, what do you do? You put your idea into words and tell them. But what if your friends are far away, and can't hear you? Or what if you want to be able to remember your idea later? Then you put your words into writing.

Many cultures have developed ways to send messages and remember ideas. Our ancestors left their messages as drawings and carvings on every continent except Antarctica. They range from cave paintings in Europe and Asia to Eskimo ivory carvings. The Incas of Peru kept accounts of their possessions using "quipu," a system of strings and knots. The Yoruba of Africa use cowrie shells to send messages. Two shells together mean agreement, while two shells placed apart mean disagreement to the point of being enemies. Systems like these can only communicate simple messages agreed on beforehand.

Next to a steep trail in New Mexico, Indians have painted a message. It shows a mountain goat standing upright and an upside-down horse. Any traveler can see that a mountain goat can get up this trail, but a horse trying to pass through will be in big trouble! Such pictures, like the Yoruban shells and Incan quipu, can communicate a few ideas. But they do not represent words or sounds, so they are not complete writing systems.

Many civilizations tell stories about the beginnings of their writing systems. According to Chinese legend, the four-eyed emperor Ts'ang Chien invented Chinese characters by looking at the patterns of the stars, marks on the backs of turtles, and tracks of birds. Hindus believe their god Brahma used patterns from seams in the human skull to create their writing system. Ancient Egyptians believed that the bird-headed god, Thoth, invented their system of writing hieroglyphics. The Greeks give a great hero, Cadmus, credit for bringing their letters from Phoenicia.

PICTURE-WORDS

Full writing systems use symbols (for words, syllables, or sounds) which can be combined to make any word in a language. The Sumerians invented the first known writing system some time after 4000 B.C. At first they inscribed pictures on clay tablets. By 3000 B.C. the pictures had developed into a system of wedge-shaped characters we call "cuneiform" (from Latin *cuneus*, "wedge"). The Egyptians, who might or might not have gotten the idea from the Sumerians, began writing with a system of picture characters called "hieroglyphics" somewhere between 3400 and 3100 B.C. In Central America, the ancient Olmecs (about 1200 B.C.), Zapotecs (from about 500 B.C.), Mayas (about 100–800 A.D.), and Aztecs (about 1400–1520 A.D.) also used writing systems with pictures for words. However, none of these systems were as complex or complete as the scripts developed in the eastern hemisphere. The Sumerian and Egyptian writing systems fell out of use before the time of Christ, but the Chinese started using a word-picture script in about 1300 B.C. which is still used today.

All these early writing systems were "logographic" scripts. *Logographic* comes from the Greek *logos* (word) and *graphein* (to write); these scripts use a symbol for each word. To communicate "a man killed four bears," you could draw a picture of a man killing four bears. Each person would draw the picture differently. But in a logographic writing system, you would use symbols for "man" and "kill" (maybe a picture of a spear or bow). Then, rather than drawing four bears, you would write symbols meaning "four" and "bear." Each person would use the same symbols. Writing began like this; one symbol for each word.

Western languages use a few "logograms." If you see the symbol $, you think of the word "dollars." The sign & stands for the word "and," and # is a logogram meaning "number."

The trouble with a logographic system is that if there were one symbol for every word in the language, how would anyone learn to write? For every word you would have to learn a different symbol. Very early, people began combining symbols and using some characters to stand for syllables rather than words.

Can you think of pictures for ideas like "bright" and "good"? The Chinese combined 日 (sun) and 月 (moon) to make 明 (bright). The pictures for "woman," 女, and "child," 子, combined mean "good," 女子. Chinese uses about 214 simple characters called radicals. They are combined in thousands of ways to make words. Learning to read and write Chinese takes many years. Recently, the Chinese have simplified their writing system so more people can learn it.

Have you ever done rebuses? You use pictures that sound like words. "I plan it," for instance, could be written "👁 🪐" (eye planet). So the picture of an eye could come to stand for the sound of "I." At one time in Chinese, the word *yi* could mean either "scorpion" or "easy." So the character meaning "scorpion," 易, came to also mean "easy."

The Egyptians also used one picture to stand for several words that sounded alike. You could do this in English if you wanted to write the word "son." You could use a picture of a sun: ☼. If it wasn't clear whether you meant "sun" or "son," you could add a picture of a boy, 👦☼, to show that you meant a boy son, not the sun in the sky.

Do you remember the word *ma* from chapter 6? In one tone of Chinese it means "mother"; in another, "horse." The Chinese symbol for "mother," since it sounds like "horse," uses the symbol for "horse," 马. It is combined with the symbol for "woman." So the reader sees 妈 ,"woman-*ma* (horse)" and knows the sign means "mother," not "horse."

Chinese script is still logographic. But it's hard to see what the pictures are! Over time, it has changed so that symbols could be written more quickly. The word *rì,* (sun) was first written ☉. Today it is written 日. The symbol for "up," *shàng,* was at first written ⊥. Now it has become 上.

In about 700 B.C., the Egyptians developed a faster way to write hieroglyphics. This shorthand, called "demotic" script (from the Greek *demotikos,* "for the people"), was used for government documents and letters (and later for religious writing also). Demotic writing looks more like curves than like pictures. For instance, the hieroglyphic picture of a whip, 𓌳, first became the in-between "hieratic" (meaning "priestly") character, 𓌳, which became the demotic character ⁄.

The meaning of Egyptian hieroglyphics was eventually forgotten. For over a thousand years, no one could read the many inscriptions on Egyptian tombs and monuments. In 1799, one of Napoleon's engineers in Rosetta, Egypt found a slab of rock covered with characters. Napoleon had men copy and study it. When the British defeated Napoleon, they put a special clause in the treaty saying they would get the "Rosetta Stone." One of Napoleon's generals had taken it home and tried to keep it, but the British eventually got it. It is now in the British Museum.

Why was the Rosetta Stone so special? It had inscriptions carved on it in Egyptian hieroglyphics, demotic script, and Greek, and it said the same thing in each language. Scholars could tell from the Greek that it was cut in 196 B.C. for a statue honoring King Ptolemy Epiphanes. Since scholars could read the ancient Greek, they thought the stone could be used as a key to decipher hieroglyphics and demotic script.

Do you think it would be easy to figure out the Egyptian writing, knowing the message's meaning? It wasn't. There were pieces missing from the stone. Also, Egyptian and Greek don't use words in the same order. Some of the Egyptian symbols stood for words, some for syllables, and some for words that sounded like what they pictured. Some signs told what kind of things they were talking about, like our picture ☼ in the example 𓀀☼ (son). Those signs weren't pronounced; they were extra clues, as we know now. But the people trying to decipher them didn't know if the symbols stood for words, syllables, sounds, or extra information.

Several men tried to work out this puzzle. A French boy named Jean François Champollion decided, when he was eleven years old, that he would be the one to decipher hieroglyphics. First he learned the Coptic language, a descendant of the Egyptian language. Then he spent fifteen years comparing every Egyptian inscription and papyrus (paper made from the papyrus plant) he could find.

First he worked out the names, which were written inside ovals. "Cleopatra" turned out to be written K-L-E-O-P-A-T-R (in hieroglyphic letters) followed by pictures meaning "divine," "female," and "royalty." Since he knew the pronunciation of the names from the Greek, that gave him the sounds of some of the letters, and made it easier to recognize which symbols weren't pronounced. From clues in the names he worked out other words.

By 1822, twenty-three years after the Rosetta Stone was discovered, Champollion had deciphered the hieroglyphics. Many scientists didn't believe he was right, though, until in 1866 another inscription in two languages was discovered. It confirmed what Champollion had said. The demotic script was finally deciphered by a German college student, Heinrich Brugsch, in 1848. At last, the ancient writing could be read!

Some other ancient systems of writing have still not been deciphered. On Easter Island in the South Pacific Ocean, picture writing is inscribed on wooden tablets, with every other line of writing turned upside down. These tablets are recent, with some made perhaps as late as the 1850s, but their secret has been forgotten. On the island of Crete (in what is now southern Greece), inscriptions in a pictographic writing and in a script called Linear A, from as early as the nineteenth century B.C., are still unreadable. (Linear B, a later Cretan script, was deciphered in 1952.) The writing on seals and copper plates of the Indus River Valley also remains a mystery. (The Indus Valley civilization flourished from about 2700 to 1750 B.C. in an area of today's India and Pakistan.) New Champollions are needed to break the codes. Any volunteers?

ARRIVAL OF THE ALPHABET

The Egyptians soon found it was easier to let pictures represent sounds rather than words. So they started using pictures to represent syllables, and sometimes even single consonants. About 1700 B.C., Semitic tribes living in Palestine and Syria started using consonant symbols rather than syllabic symbols. So instead of having different signs for *ta, te, ti, to,* and *tu,* for example, they just used one sign for *t.* You had to guess what the vowels were. (As if you wrote that last sentence, "Y hd t gss wht th vwls wr.") This was the first true "alphabet," a system of symbols which each stood for a sound, rather than a word.

Usually the consonant symbols came from the first letters of words. So the shape that meant "door" came to stand for the sound *d.* This symbol, in Egyptian hieroglyphics, was ▦ . Do you think it looks like a door? It was later written: ⌂. The ancient Middle Eastern tribes made it faster to write and called it *daleth:*△. The Greeks borrowed it as *delta,* and changed it into: Δ. When the Romans borrowed it, and then the English, it became our letter *D.*

The Phoenicians, who were traders and sailors living in what is now Lebanon, developed the Semitic system into a twenty-two-letter alphabet before 1200 B.C. They completely dropped picture symbols and only used symbols for consonants. Being great travelers, they soon spread this easy new system of writing to all their neighbors.

Around 1000 B.C., the Greeks borrowed the Phoenician alphabet. They changed some symbols into vowels. So instead of one symbol which could mean *ta, te, ti, to,* or *tu,* symbols for *t* and *a* could now be put together to make *ta.* The Greeks got rid of other letters, and added new ones to show the sounds which we now write *ph, ps, kh,* and *ks.* They simplified some letters so they could be written more quickly.

Around 800 B.C., the Etruscans of Italy borrowed the Greek alphabet and changed it to suit their language. A century or two later, the Romans took twenty-one of the Etruscan letters and added the letters *g* and *y.* All the western alphabets, including the English alphabet, came from this Roman alphabet. THEGREEKSWROTEALL

INCAPITALLETTERSWITHNOSPACESBETWEENWORDSANDNO PUNCTUATION In the sixth and seventh centuries A.D., scribes developed the small letters: *a, b, c, d,* etc., so that they could write more quickly. The capital letters were kept as fancy decorations at the beginning of sentences.

The Anglo-Saxons living in England wrote in a script called "runes." These were carved on wood, stone, or iron. The modern word *write*, in fact, comes from an Old Norse word, *rita,* which meant "to carve." The missionary St. Patrick brought Christianity, and the Roman alphabet, to Ireland in the fifth century. St. Augustine and Irish missionaries brought Roman letters to England about 200 years later. There were some sounds in Anglo-Saxon that Latin didn't have. So the Anglo-Saxons kept two characters from the runes. One called *thorn,* þ, meant *th*, and one called *wynn* meant *w. Wynn* was eventually changed to *uu,* then to *w. Thorn* became a *y* shape but was still pronounced *th*. So names like "Ye Olde Inn" should be read "The Old Inn." Later *y* came to mean another sound, and *th* was added to Middle English for the old *thorn* sound.

Some letters were originally used a little differently than we use them now. *I, j,* and *y* took some time to settle down to their current use. In the 1400s, *mother* was written *modyr; wife* was written *huswyff. J* started off as a fancy form of *i* in the 1300s; by the 1600s it had its current sound. At first *u* was used as either a vowel or as the consonant now written *v.* Then people began writing *v* at the beginning of words and *u* anywhere else in the word. A letter from Queen Elizabeth to King James VI of Scotland, written sometime between 1582 and 1590, begins: "I haue, right deare brother, receaued your frendly and affectionat letters. . . ." See how *u* was used instead of *v*? But in the 1600s people began using *u* just as a vowel and *v* just as a consonant.

OTHER ALPHABETS

Many languages use some form of the Roman alphabet. Some add marks to letters to represent sounds that Latin did not have. So German has "umlauts" (two dots) over some of its vowels: *ö, ä, ü* (re-

FIGURE 4
THE ABCs IN SPACE AND TIME

The English alphabet and its ancestors are under the line; other alphabets are above the line. All dates are approximate. Arrows show how symbols used in a script changed over time.

						600s Khmer alphabet	800s Japanese hiragana syllabic script		1400–1520 Aztec pictographic script		1821 Cherokee syllabic script
	⋙ → 川 (river)			500 B.C. Zapotec pictographic script	100–800 A.D. Mayan pictographic script	600s Devanagari (Sanskrit-India) alphabet					
☉ → ☽ → 𓃾	1300 B.C. Chinese pictographic script										
(sun, day) Sumerian cuneiform	1200 B.C. Olmec pictographic script		700 B.C. Egyptian demotic	450–300 B.C. Square Hebrew alphabet		400s Arabic alphabet	800s Cyrillic alphabet		1400 Korean Hangul alphabet	1600s Vietnamese alphabet	

			800 B.C. Etruscan alphabet	700 B.C. Roman alphabet	0 A.D.	400s A.D. Roman alphabet arrives in Ireland	600s Roman alphabet arrives in England		1600s English alphabet reaches modern form
4000–3000 B.C. picture-writing develops	1700 B.C. Semitic alphabet (consonants) (might have developed from Egyptian characters)	1200 B.C. Phoenician alphabet (consonants)	𐤀 𐤁 𐤂	𐤀 → A 𐤁 → B 𐤂 → C (C used for g and k sounds, later just k)				small (lower-case) letters develop	
Egyptian hieroglyphics (symbols for pictures and symbols)		1000 B.C. Greek alphabet (consonants and vowels) Α → A Β → B Γ → Γ							

Bull

House

Throne

member these from chapter 5?). To make the sound *ny,* Spanish and Portuguese use a "tilde" on the letter *n* (*ñ*). Portuguese and French have the "cedilla": *ç*. French also has the "acute accent" (*é*) and the "grave accent" (*à, è*), as well as the "circumflex" (*ô*). Italian also uses vowels with accent marks (like *à, é,* and *í*). Scandinavian languages like Norwegian, Danish, and Swedish use *ø, å,* and other symbols. Turkish, Polish, Czech, Rumanian and other alphabets have letters with check marks, accents, and dots over them and hooks under them. All these marks are called "diacritics."

The Vietnamese used to write with modified Chinese characters, adopted when Vietnam was a province of China. In the 1600s, a French missionary named Alexandre de Rhodes noticed that "the people (of Vietnam) spend almost all their lives learning to read." He developed a writing system using the Roman alphabet with special marks (diacritics) for tones and sounds unique to Vietnamese. There are so many different accent marks that the letter *a* can be written eighteen different ways! The use of this alphabet spread slowly. In 1910 the French, who had ruled Vietnam since 1859, made it the official alphabet of the country. That modified Roman alphabet is still used by the Vietnamese (see examples in appendix 1).

Korea also started off using Chinese characters. China dominated Korean government, literature, and religion for much of its history. During that time, Korea used Chinese as its court language. Korean literature was written in the Chinese language until the end of the nineteenth century. More than half of the words of Korean are borrowed from Chinese. Today, though, Korea has its own alphabet. The Korean King Sejong, in the 1400s, had a group of scholars develop an original twenty-eight-letter alphabet, called *Hangul,* to make it easy for all the people to read and write, instead of just scholars. It was not generally accepted until this century. South Koreans still use some Chinese characters for words borrowed from Chinese and to distinguish words that sound alike from each other. Their alphabet gives the sound of the word, while the Chinese characters help to show the word's meaning. The Korean alphabet was such an achievement that Koreans still celebrate October 9 each year as Hangul Day, to honor the invention of their alphabet.

Nearby Cambodia was more influenced by India than by China. Cambodians use a form of a southern Indian alphabet for their Khmer language. The Khmer alphabet seems to be the largest one, with seventy-four letters. The smallest alphabet is evidently the Rotokas alphabet of the Solomon Islands (in the Southwest Pacific Ocean), with only eleven letters!

Two missionaries to the Slavic peoples, St. Cyril and St. Methodius, developed an alphabet for Russian and its relatives in the early Middle Ages (800s). It's based on the Greek alphabet, with some other letters added. The flowery Cyrillic alphabet (named after St. Cyril) is still used by at least thirty languages besides Russian, including Bulgarian, Ukrainian, and Kazakh.

If you look at words written in the Cyrillic alphabet, some letters are familiar, and are pronounced almost like in English: A, K, M, and O, for instance. But watch out; some letters that you think you recognize are really pronounced differently. B is pronounced like English V, H like English N, C like S, and P like R. Some letters, like Π and Φ, look like Greek letters, and others, like Щ and Ж, don't look like English or Greek.

The Semitic traders who brought the alphabet to the Greeks also carried it farther east. The alphabets of Ethiopian Amharic, Burmese, Javanese, Tibetan, Bengali, Tamil, Mongolian, Armenian, and many other languages of India and the Far East look quite different from the Latin alphabet you use. The Burmese alphabet, for instance, is written almost entirely with curves. They say this is because it was first written on palm leaves, which would have torn if the Burmese had used straight lines. But all these alphabets were developed from the same ancient Semitic alphabet.

Arabic and Hebrew are still usually written with only a few vowels. They have special signs that can be written above or below the consonants to show what the other vowels are. The vowel signs are usually used only when the meaning would not be clear without them, or in formal religious writing. Arabic and Hebrew are both written from right to left, not from left to right as English is written. The Arabic alphabet is the second most commonly used alphabet in the world, after the Roman alphabet we use.

Old Persian, the ancient language of Iran, developed its alphabet by order of a king (as Korean did). King Darius, in 522 B.C., wanted to record his coming to power, his crushing of a revolt, and the accomplishments of his first year of rule. So he ordered a script to be developed for the language of his empire. It used the wedge-shaped characters of Sumerian cuneiform to represent syllables. In 637 A.D., Arabs conquered Persia and replaced the Persian religion, Zoroastrianism, with Islam. After that, the Persian, or Farsi, language, was written with the Arabic alphabet. It had to be modified, since Arabic had no *p*, *ch*, or *v* sound. Extra dots were added to Arabic letters to make those sounds.

Another king who affected his alphabet was a king of Madagascar, which is also called the Malagasy Republic. Foreign missionaries who were trying to create a Malagasy alphabet in the nineteenth century couldn't agree on the letters. Some of the missionaries were from French-speaking countries and others were from English-speaking countries, and some letters are pronounced differently in French and English. So the king decreed that the Malagasy consonants would be English, while the vowels would be French!

Some languages use different scripts in different countries. The Kurds, who are mostly Muslims, use a modified Arabic script for their Kurdish language in Iran, Iraq, and Syria. In Russia they use a Cyrillic script, and in Turkey the Kurds use a Roman script like ours.

DIFFERENT KINDS OF SCRIPTS

A few languages still use syllabic scripts, where each symbol represents a syllable rather than a sound. In the American Indian language Cree, there is a symbol for each consonant. Each symbol can be pointed up, down, left, or right depending on what vowel comes after it. Obviously, Cree only has four vowels! The shape of the symbol, combined with its direction, tells you the sound of a syllable.

A Cherokee Indian named Sequoyah invented a syllabic alphabet

LANGUAGES IN WRITING 131

FIGURE 5
WRITING SYSTEMS OF THE WORLD

Each language has its own alphabet. Even the many languages that use the Roman alphabet, as English does, personalize it with special marks and letters. Here are some examples of alphabets that are very different from the Roman one. The words are the equivalent of "how are you?" in each language.

Logographic Script

Chinese 您 好？

Logographic/Syllabic Combination

Japanese お元気ですか.

Syllabic Scripts

Cherokee ᎥᎯᎴ

Amharic (Ethiopia) ኧጎሯሞን ፋሀ

Alphabetic, written left to right

Greek Τι κανετε;

Russian Как вы поживаете?

Korean 안 녕하 십니까?

Burmese ၆၅ ၆ော၁င်း ၁ွာ၁း

Khmer (Cambodia) សុខ សប្បាយ ជា ទេ?

Malayalam (southern India) സുഖമായി ഇരിക്കുന്നോ?

Hindi (India) आप कैसे हैं।

Alphabetic, written right to left

Urdu (Pakistan) آپ کا کیا حال ہے؟

Arabic كيف حالك؟

Farsi (Iran, Afghanistan) حال شما چطور است.

Hebrew מה שלוםך?

for his language. He could not read or write, but he had seen the white man's "talking leaves" (books) and he dreamed of making some for his own people. After twelve years of hard work, he came up with eighty-five symbols. Each symbol stands for a syllable: a consonant plus a vowel. Some of them look like English letters but are pronounced differently. For instance, *G* is said *na,* and *M* is said *lu.* Two letters that look something like *GW* are pronounced *wa 'ya,* which means "wolf." The Cherokee chiefs accepted this system in 1821, and soon the entire tribe could read and write in Cherokee. Nowadays, though, Cherokee children usually use the English language and script. Schools have encouraged them to use English so that they can more easily be a part of American society. In some places programs have been started to help Cherokees speak, read, and write in their original language as well as in English.

Many alphabets of India are descended from Devanagari, which means "writing of the city of the gods." The Devanagari alphabet was originally used for Sanskrit, the great-grandmother of modern Hindi, Nepali, and other Indic languages. Devanagari and its descendants have symbols for consonants with vowel symbols attached to them. A consonant by itself can stand for just a consonant, or a consonant with an *a* sound. A line goes along the top of each word, with the letters attached to it. Some Indian languages have up to 700 characters, each representing a syllable.

Japanese uses a combination of three different writing systems. Some of their characters are borrowed from Chinese. These are pictures that represent words. Sometimes they're pronounced the Japanese way, sometimes the Chinese way. The characters that mean "man," "strength," and "vehicle" are read *hito, chikara,* and *kuruma* in Japanese. But if the three characters are put together, they're read as if they were ancient Chinese: *jin-riki-sha,* which means "rickshaw" (a man-powered vehicle).

Chinese words do not change their endings, but Japanese words do. So the Japanese took some Chinese characters and gave them each the sound of a syllable. They use those characters to write endings on words and to write small words without a Chinese equivalent. So *kakimashita* (wrote) is written with the Chinese character for "write," and the symbols for *ki-ma-shi-ta*. We do the same in English when we write *4*, which is a logogram for the number "four," and change it to *4th*, with two letters to show the ending sound added to "four." Besides Chinese characters and syllabic symbols, the Japanese have a third set of characters, used only at certain times, such as for borrowed foreign words.

Words in Japanese, as in Chinese and Korean, are traditionally written from right to left, going down in columns instead of across the page. All three of these languages are now often written left to right across the page. You could write Japanese without Chinese characters, using just a syllabic script. But there are many words in Japanese that sound alike, like the English *pear* and *pair*. These are called "homophones," from the Greek *homo-* (alike) and *phone* (sound). Just as the different spellings of *pear* and *pair* tell us which one is meant, the Chinese character tells the Japanese reader whether the word pronounced *kami* means "good taste," "hair of the head," "paper," "governor," or "god"! The Japanese word pronounced *ka* has 214 different meanings. Chinese characters are an important way to distinguish Japanese words.

If you speak Japanese you need to learn about 3,000 different characters to read most books. The government is trying to limit the number of characters used now to 1,850, so it won't be quite so difficult to learn to read Japanese!

A language like Japanese, where most syllables are just one consonant and one vowel, can use a syllabic script. But creating a syllabic script for English would be a nightmare. We use many combinations of consonants, both at the beginning and end of syllables. A syllabic script would need separate symbols for *scrunch, stop, quote, quick*, and thousands of other combinations that make syllables in English!

SPELLING

An ideal writing system has one letter for each meaningful sound of a language, and one sound for each letter. For instance, English

FISHY SPELLINGS George Bernard Shaw said that we could write the word *fish* as *ghoti*. The *gh* would be pronounced as in *cough*, the *o* as in *women*, and the *ti* as in *nation*.

What does *kphoxxe* spell? If the *k* sounded like the *k* in *know*, the *ph* like that in *phone*, the *o* made the sound it does in *come*, and the *x* and *e* came from *xylophone* and *me*, then *kphoxxe* would spell *fuzzy*!

Can you make up your own fishy (or fuzzy) spellings?

---

m always has the same sound, and that sound is always written *m*. But most English letters are not like that.

All English vowels have several pronunciations, like the *e*'s in "Gr<u>ee</u>t th<u>e</u> gr<u>ea</u>t b<u>ea</u>r and g<u>e</u>t him som<u>e</u> n<u>e</u>w <u>ea</u>rth." Say the following sentence aloud and notice all the ways *ough* can be pronounced: "Th<u>ough</u> the r<u>ough</u> c<u>ough</u> and hicc<u>ough</u> pl<u>ough</u> me thr<u>ough</u>, I <u>ough</u>t to cross the l<u>ough</u>." (*Lough* is pronounced like *lock* and is an Irish word for "lake.")

How did English get such a hodgepodge of spellings? First of all, twenty-six letters are used for about forty different sounds, so some of the letters have to be combined. Also, after the Norman conquest in 1066 A.D., French scribes began writing the English language with letters they were used to using in French. For instance, they wrote *qu* at the beginning of *queen* rather than *cw*, and put a *c* in words like *circle* and *cell*, which logically should start with *s*.

Printing a language helps standardize its spelling. But many early printers in England were Dutch or other nationalities, and used conventions of their own languages for spelling. They also had to choose from various dialects of English. And, in order to make the printed lines on a page all the same length, they sometimes took out or added letters to words. *E* was a letter that was often added, rather than adding spaces.

English is full of words borrowed from other languages. It often has kept the spelling close to the spelling in those languages as in *canoe, chaos, garage, bizarre,* and *llama.* English has spellings from French, Dutch, Greek, Portuguese, and many other languages.

Changes in spoken English created many homophones (words that sound the same but are spelled differently and have different meanings). Now *know* and *no* sound alike. But in Old English the *k* of *know* and *knight* was pronounced as a *k* rather than being silent. In words like *should* and *would,* the *l*'s were pronounced until the 1500s. Try saying them as they were written then: *shold, wold.*

Sometimes spelling gives clues to relationships between words. For instance, *sign* and *signature* are pronounced differently. But their spelling shows they have related meanings. They both developed from the Latin *signum,* meaning "mark" or "seal." *Medicine* and *medicate* also are spelled similarly, showing their common origin, the Latin *medicus* (doctor).

Many people have suggested new systems of spelling which would be more regular. In one system, called Anglic, the beginning of the Gettysburg Address would look like this: "Forskor and sevn yeerz agoe our faadherz braut forth on this kontinent a nuw naeshon, konseevd in liberti. . . ."

Do you like it? It's quite different from what we're used to. The trouble is, all the English literature of the past would have to be rewritten, or people would have to learn the old spelling in order to read it! Another problem is the same as that of Japanese. We would no longer have a way to tell the difference between homophones like *two/too/to, right/write,* and *hole/whole.* Andrew Jackson once said that it was a mighty poor mind that couldn't think of more than one way to spell a word! But consistent spelling would certainly make it easier to learn to read and to spell.

By about 1600 English spelling had stabilized to about what it is today in England. But Americans weren't satisfied. Benjamin Franklin published a paper in 1768 promoting *A Scheme for a New Alphabet and a Reformed Mode of Spelling.* His plan wasn't adopted, but he influenced Noah Webster. Webster did succeed in getting some American spellings simplified, though not as many as he and Franklin would have liked. Webster's *Blue-Backed Speller* of 1783 was used in the eighteenth and nineteenth centuries to teach millions of children to spell. That helped to standardize American spelling. Webster's *Dictionary of the English Language* in 1828 was the first dictionary to include specifically American usages and spelling. (Its successors are today's Merriam-Webster dictionaries.) American spelling is a little different than British spelling because of these changes. Americans write *honor* while the British write *honour,* American *color* is British *colour,* American *wagon* is British *waggon,* and American *center* is British *centre.*

Traditionally Canada has used some British spellings, like *colour* and *honour,* and some American spellings, like *wagon.* Today, though, standard Canadian spelling is becoming more American, and Canadians more often use *color* and *honor,* although the British spellings are acceptable, too. This is probably because Canada is independent of Britain now and is being influenced more by the nearby United States than by England across the sea.

French also has spellings left over from old pronunciations. For instance in *ils tiennent,* "they hold," the *-s* of *ils* and the *-ent* of *tiennent* are silent, though they used to be pronounced. Irish and Scots Gaelic also follow old spellings, so that a phrase like the Irish Gaelic *mo mháthair,* "my mother," is said *mo vaher.*

Other languages, like Portuguese and Norwegian, are constantly revising their spelling to keep up with current pronunciation. Many nations are simplifying their alphabets much more drastically. The Chinese have experimented with a script similar to ours called *pinyin,* and the people of Japan and India have experimented with the Roman alphabet. In 1928, the Turkish leader Kemal Atatürk decreed that Turkish would be written with a modified Roman alphabet rather than the Arabic alphabet. Simpler scripts are also being developed for many languages of India, with their huge syllabic systems.

Missionaries (like St. Cyril in the eighth century and many Bible translators today) and educators sometimes have to invent alphabets for groups of people who have never had their languages in writing. First they have to determine the phonemes of the language: which sounds actually determine meaning. They have to decide whether to use a syllabic or alphabetic script (usually alphabetic scripts are used today). Then they have to choose letters or symbols for each phoneme. The sound we write as *ch* in English, for example, is written in various Roman alphabets as *c, č, ć, ts,* or *tch*, as ч in the Cyrillic alphabet, as نش in the Arabic alphabet, as च् in the Devanagari alphabet of India, and it could also be written as some other symbol. The alphabet inventor may choose a script on the basis of politics or religion, for instance an Arabic script for a language in a Muslim area, or a Cyrillic script for a language in Russia or Eastern Europe where the surrounding languages are written in Cyrillic. The script may be chosen for nationalistic reasons, to give more unity with the country where it is spoken, as well as for practical reasons. It is, of course, cheaper and easier to print materials in an alphabet already used in the area, and it might make it easier to find teachers who can teach the new reading system. The characteristics of the language might be important, especially if it has tones or many unusual sounds.

A few languages, like Spanish, Korean, and Finnish, come close to having a "perfect" alphabet: one letter for every sound and one sound for every letter. The Finns, for instance, write some letters twice to show that they are held extra long, but otherwise they have one letter for each sound.

On the other end of the scale, if everyone wrote with logograms like the Chinese, you could write something and everyone in the world could understand it! But that's assuming everyone in the world could spend many years studying to learn what all the signs meant.

Our whole civilization depends on writing. What would we do without books, newspapers, magazines, signs, and mail? We can learn from the thoughts and discoveries of people who lived many years ago, or who live many miles away. Writing connects us with each other.

> The man who knows no foreign language
> knows nothing of his mother tongue.
> Goethe

> Juan: "If a person who speaks two languages is bilingual, and a person who speaks three languages is trilingual, what do you call a person who speaks only one language?"
> Layla: "An American."
> Joke shared by people who speak several languages

11

LEARNING LANGUAGES: YOU CAN TALK FUNNY, TOO!

WHY WOULD ANYONE WANT TO TALK FUNNY?

If you speak English, you can be friends with people from the U.S., Canada, Great Britain, Australia, New Zealand, and parts of India and Africa. But what if you want to go to Mexico, and meet people who speak Spanish? What if you're traveling in Germany, and need to find a bathroom? What if one of your parents is transferred to another country, and you find yourself with neighbors who speak Hebrew or Swahili? Or maybe you'd like to get to know a boy or girl who speaks Vietnamese.

Anyone can learn a second language. (And a third, and a fourth, if you like.) With a second language you'll be able to talk with many more people than you can now. You will also learn about the people who speak that language: how they live, think, and act. According to a Turkish proverb, the more languages you know, the more people you are!

By talking to people who speak another language and by reading books in that language, you can learn about new things. Scientists often study German or Russian so they can read the latest scientific papers in those languages. If you enjoy good stories, you can find brand-new ones in another language.

In 1970, several Americans were poisoned by eating a kind of mushroom. No cure was found, and two people died. Finally a chemist heard about it on the radio. He knew that, seven years before, a paper had been published giving a treatment for this kind of poisoning. Why didn't American doctors know about it? The paper was published in several languages . . . but not in English. If more American doctors had been reading journals in other languages, the people who were poisoned might have been saved.

Why don't more Americans learn foreign languages? The United States is a large country where you can travel a long way without meeting anyone who doesn't speak English (though this situation is changing). English is also a popular language in other countries, so that it's possible to get by in many places with only English. So Americans haven't felt the necessity to learn another language, as many other nationalities do. The Netherlands (Holland) is a tiny country, about half the size of South Carolina, surrounded by nations who don't speak Dutch. To do business or travel almost anywhere, Dutch people need other languages. Children in Holland study English, French, and German in school, as well as their own Dutch language. Once they are familiar with those four languages, they can take a fifth language as a "foreign language"!

In Hungary, too, other languages are necessary. In middle school all students have to study either English or German. In high school, besides Hungarian, everyone must study at least two languages, choosing from German, English, and French. Peter, age fifteen, speaks Hungarian, English, and Spanish and wants to learn German, too, so he can work in a bank when he grows up. He says, "If we have only one language, we can't stay alive. I couldn't get a good job without other languages."

Learning one language helps you learn others. Some day if you want to do business in Japan, you'll be glad that you studied Spanish or French in school. Exposure to any other language will help you learn to produce other sounds and put together words in other ways than you do in English. It will help you to think about how your own language works, and recognize that there are different patterns in languages. That will make it easier for you to learn Japanese or any other language. Witold, age thirteen, speaks Polish and English, understands some Russian, and is learning Spanish. He says, "It is easier to learn another language after learning one. Some words are sort of the same, and you understand the system of languages. I want to learn French after I am fluent in Spanish. It will be easy because they are a lot alike."

ARE SOME LANGUAGES BETTER THAN OTHERS?

Do you think a lot of people speak English because it's better than other languages? Maybe it's easier, or more logical? Not at all. People speak English because of politics and trade. People who want to do business with Great Britain or the United States learn English. Countries that have been dominated in the past by the British Empire often use English in their political and educational systems.

All languages can communicate what their speakers want to say. So they're all equally "good." If life changes, and new words are needed, languages borrow or create new words. People speak their languages in different dialects, and some people think their dialects are "bad," while the standard language, the dialect with widest social acceptance, is "good." But any dialect spoken by a group of people is a perfectly good way of communicating. Of course they may need to learn another dialect or language to talk with people of another group. Someone from northern Germany may not be able to understand the everyday dialect of a Swiss German. But they can both use the standard language, High German, to communicate. High German is not better than their dialects. But without some agreed-on standard, German-speakers would soon split up into many small groups who could not talk to each other or read the same books.

WHICH LANGUAGE IS THE HARDEST?

All healthy children learn to speak their native language in the first few years of their lives. No language takes longer for children to learn because it is more difficult. By the time any child is five or six years old, he knows the basics of his language, and can make up an infinite number of sentences.

People used to think that the languages of primitive tribes must be simpler than languages of "advanced" cultures. But that isn't true at all. A famous linguist, Edward Sapir, said, "When it comes to linguistic form, Plato walks with the Macedonian swineherd, Confucius with the head-hunting savage of Assam." (Plato and Confucius were philosophers from the sophisticated societies of ancient Greece and China, while Macedonia and Assam were earlier, simpler, cultures of southern Europe and Northeast India. Their languages, though, were equally complex.) Even tribal languages far from modern civilizations have a rich variety of sounds, words, and expressions. Every language can show all kinds of relationships and ideas. English has borrowed words from some tribal cultures, since it had no words of its own for things like *totem* and *boomerang*.

In some Eskimo languages a noun can have more than a thousand different forms, each with its own shade of meaning. In the Kwakiutl Indian language, to say "this man lies ill," you must be much more exact: "This-visible-man-near me I-know lies-ill-on-his-side-on-the-skins in-the-present-house-near-us." Does that sound simple?

Every language is about equally difficult, overall, to its native speakers. But each language is complicated in some ways and simple in others. The many different endings for nouns in Russian and Finnish are difficult. English has difficult irregularities, using *said* rather than *sayed*, and *went* rather than *goed*, for instance. Chinese has a straightforward word order and no word endings. But it uses tones, which means its sounds take longer for a non-native speaker to learn. (One study, though, found that Chinese babies, by about ten months old, babble in the tones of Chinese, sounding quite different from babies surrounded by English. So tones are learned very early by native speakers!)

All languages are not equally difficult in writing. A language that is spelled according to its sounds, like Spanish or Arabic, is easier to learn to write than an irregularly spelled language, like English or French. It is harder still to learn to write with logograms in Chinese or Japanese.

It's easiest for people to learn a second language somewhat like their first language. If your first language is English, you shouldn't have too much trouble learning Dutch, Spanish, or Italian. The nasalized vowels and irregular spellings of French may give you a little difficulty. German is closely related to English but has kept many grammatical structures that English has dropped, so it's harder for English-speakers to learn than Dutch, Spanish, or Italian would be. Most European languages have many words related to English words.

Languages unrelated to English, like Arabic, Vietnamese, and Chinese, take longer for English-speakers to learn. Those languages are not "harder" than English. Remember, Arab, Vietnamese, and Chinese children all learn their own languages with no problem. It takes them a while to learn English, since their languages are so different from ours.

How can people from many countries communicate with each other? Once all educated Europeans knew Latin, and used it to communicate with each other. Today many people learn English and French, which are understood in many countries. "Artificial" languages have also been invented to help all people communicate. Esperanto is an artificial language based on European languages. Can you understand this sentence: "La inteligenta persono lernas la interlingvon Esperanto rapide kaj facile"? That's Esperanto for "The intelligent person learns the Esperanto language quickly and easily."

Unfortunately Esperanto has no relationship to any Eastern or African languages, so it is just as difficult for those people to learn as any European language. Other languages have been created, like Volapük, Interglossa, Monling, and some numerical codes. Even a Basic English has been developed, using only about 850 words. It combines simple words, using *get in* for "enter," and *small tree* for "bush." But it keeps the irregular spelling of English, and does not communicate difficult ideas very well. None of these languages has particularly caught on. Artificial languages do not have a body of native speakers fighting to keep them alive. They do not have a culture and history behind them, either, which would give them the richness and interest of natural languages.

Why don't you try making up your own language, for fun? You could use it to communicate secrets to your friends, or to your brothers and sisters. Will your secret language be isolating, agglutinative, or inflected? (See chapter 7—isolating is the easiest to make up!) You could use the sounds of English, or add clicks or other sounds from chapter 5. In Esperanto, all nouns end in -*o*, with the plurals ending in -*oj*, while present tense verbs all end in -*as*, past tense verbs in -*is*, future tense verbs in -*os*, and command forms in -*u*. Will you use special endings for your nouns and verbs? Or will you make up different noun classes, with different prefixes, like Swahili does? What kind of writing system will you use for your language? Logographic, syllabic, alphabetic? You could invent your own unique system of writing, like Sequoyah did for the Cherokee language!

HOW CAN YOU LEARN A LANGUAGE?

There are many ways to learn a language. The easiest is to grow up with it! But there are other ways. You could take language classes in school. You might get to travel to another country and learn. Library books and tapes can help. Appendix 1 of this book can give you a start. Ask a friend to teach you some of his or her language. Better yet, if your parents or grandparents speak another language, ask them to always speak to you in it. Even a few words are a beginning.

The biggest step toward learning a language is to really *want* to learn it. Linguists say the person who is most likely to learn a language well is one who wants to become part of the culture where the language is spoken, and who has many opportunities to hear and practice the language. Find those opportunities. If you are studying Spanish, find some Spanish-speaking friends. Ask them to talk to you sometimes, slowly and simply, in Spanish. Listen to them talking to each other. Often people are talking about what they're doing or what's going on around them. So if you know some words, you may be able to figure out what they're saying.

You can use games to start learning a language. "Simon says" is a great one, if you have a friend or teacher who speaks a foreign language to lead it. The leader should give directions in the language and act them out at the same time so everyone understands what he or she is saying. You follow the directions, too, if the leader said "Simon says." You can give Simon a name from the language you're studying, like *Paco dice* for a Spanish game or *Layla taqul* for an Arabic game.

Some board games like Monopoly are available in other languages. You could get a friend to translate your own favorite game into his or her language. Card games like Uno can easily be played using the names of colors and numbers in another language.

You can also learn words that are used in your favorite sport, and practice them when you're playing. Better yet, join in a game where most of the players are speaking another language, and you'll catch on quickly!

Find pictures you like from books and magazines and discuss them with a friend in another language. You can ask questions in English like "What's in the picture?" "What are the people doing?" "What might happen next?" "What colors are in the picture?" "How many cats are there?" and listen to the answers in the foreign language. Listening to or reading a story while you look at pictures in a book is also a fun way to learn a language. When you have studied for a while, try to read simple, interesting books in the language.

Your library or bookstore may have books and tapes of stories and songs in other languages. You can learn a lot from songs if you play and sing them over and over. Some good tapes are listed in the back of this book.

Listen carefully to how native speakers pronounce words and put them together. Imitate them as closely as you can. Remember, no language is exactly like English! But your mouth is made just like everyone else's; you can pronounce any sound exactly as if any language were your first language. The younger you are, the easier it is to learn a new set of sounds.

Every time you learn a new word or phrase, practice it as much as you can. Say it to anyone who understands your second language, and listen for it when other people are talking.

As you learn words for things in your house, you can write the names on index cards and tape them to the objects. So if you are learning Spanish, you can put a sign on a table saying *mesa*, and every time you see the table you will remember *mesa*. However you do it, your goal should be to think in the language, so that when you look at the table you won't think, *table—oh, that's* mesa *in Spanish*. Instead, you will see the table and just think *mesa*.

Notice patterns in the language. Spanish *la casa roja*, "the house red" shows that adjectives come after nouns in Spanish. That means if you want to talk about "the white house," you'd better say *la casa blanca* (not *la blanca casa*, a word-for-word translation from English).

If people laugh at you at first, laugh right along with them. After all, you probably do sound funny! It is said that a person has to murder a language before learning to speak it well. You will make thousands of mistakes, so you might as well start making them. Making mistakes means you're learning!

A man learning Arabic once told his friends, "My stomach hurts when my father eats rice." He meant, of course, that his *father's* stomach hurt. But his friends had a good laugh, and so did the man, when he realized what he'd said. They all became better friends, and the man's father didn't have to eat any rice!

So: listen to a language, practice what you know, and listen some more. Ask your friends and teacher for help. Don't be afraid to make mistakes!

You can also help your friends and classmates who need to learn English. Jolanta, age eleven, came to an American school speaking only Polish and a few words of English ("yes," "no," and "my name is . . ."). She says, "People laughed at me at first because I knew no English. But two girls helped me. When the teacher used hard words, they would explain to me in easier words. That helped a lot." Now, two years later, Jolanta is helping her mother learn English.

She says her mother always gets A's on her English tests, thanks to Jolanta and her brother! Now Jolanta is studying a third language, French, so she can talk to her French friends, too.

Fifteen-year-old Ildi, from Hungary, had a hard time learning English, too. She says, "I looked at words in my textbooks and I didn't understand anything. I had to look up every word in the dictionary. But my brother and another boy who spoke Hungarian translated for me and helped me. The second year was much easier. . . . If you want to learn a language, it's easier if you're around people who speak it all the time. You can have lots of fun and friends if you know other languages."

DON'T MOST PEOPLE SPEAK JUST ONE LANGUAGE?

Probably over half the people in the world speak more than one language. Most Africans speak at least three languages. For instance, children in Tanzania, a country in eastern Africa, speak one of eleven different languages at home. In school they learn Swahili, the trade language of their country. That way they can understand the teacher and talk to each other. Many of them learn English later on, especially if they want to do business with people from other countries.

In a city in the Italian Alps called Sauris, most people speak three languages. They use Italian, since they are inside the country of Italy, for church, school, government, and talking with outsiders. Friulian, the language of their area, is used for talking among themselves, and with people who live nearby. German, the language of Austria less than fifteen miles away, is often used between close friends. So most Saurians grow up trilingual.

In many villages of India, people speak languages that cannot be understood even a hundred miles away. Imagine that the people of New York and the people of Philadelphia could not understand each other. A newspaper published in Philadelphia could not be read in New York. Truckloads of food or factory goods could not be exchanged between them. How would they work it out? Many people in each place would need to learn another language. In India people learn standard Hindi or English. Then villages can trade with each other, and villagers can read messages, books, and newspapers from other places.

Indian children not only learn several languages, they often learn several alphabets! Malayalam-speakers in southern India, for example, learn their own Malayalam (pronounced Mah-lay-AHL-uhm) alphabet, which has fifty-six letters, including fourteen vowel signs which can be attached to any letter. They also learn Hindi, which has a totally different alphabet of fifty-nine symbols. On top of that, they study English, and learn the Roman alphabet which English uses!

In South America, many speakers of American Indian languages are also bilingual, since they have to use Spanish or Portuguese to communicate with people outside their tribe.

In 1990, according to the U.S. Census, about thirteen percent of Americans spoke a language other than English at home. More than half of them spoke Spanish—about seven percent of all Americans. The United States has no official language named in its Constitution, as many countries do. However, people who come from other countries and want to be naturalized as U.S. citizens have to pass a test that shows they can speak, read, and write English. American schools, and most aspects of American life, encourage immigrants to quickly learn English.

It is difficult for people who don't speak English to get along in America. Children who don't speak English may feel embarrassed that they don't understand their classes, or they may be teased and made to feel stupid. To make it easier for them, some states now have bilingual education programs, where the children study partly in English and partly in their native language. Others have English as a Second Language programs, to teach children English rather than expecting them to pick it up from their classes. Some states also provide government services in other languages. California, for instance, employs thousands of Spanish-speakers to help non-English-speakers use the court system and other government services.

Some people do not want other languages besides English to be used by American schools or by the American government. An organization called U.S. English promotes the idea that English should be the only official language in the United States. They believe that the English language binds the United States together. They also believe that making schools and government services bilingual will make people less likely to learn English, since they won't need it so badly. They think there should be programs in the schools to help kids learn English, but not programs which also help them maintain their first languages. At least eighteen states have now passed laws declaring English as their official language. On the other hand, at least three states have passed laws making their governments multilingual. What do you think? Should English be made the official language of the United States? Do you think it would make a difference in whether or not people learn English, or in the unity of the country?

LEARNING FROM LANGUAGES

Each language, no matter how many relatives it has, is unique. It has its own sounds, words, and ways to put words together. Every language can teach us about human beings: their history, how they live, how they think. Over two hundred years ago the American scholar Samuel Johnson said, "I am always sorry when any language is lost, because languages are the pedigrees of nations."

Language can make a difference in how people see the world. You may see an "orange" ball. But a person whose language has no word for "orange" might call the ball "red," and think of it as pretty much the same color as a ball you would call "red." An aborigine with no word for "four" would think of four things as "many," while you would see a group of four. Hopi Indians don't talk about "two days" and "three days"; they talk about "second day" and "third day." They understand time differently than English-speakers do.

In American culture an adult teaches a child, "this is a tree," or "this is a book." But in some tribes of Papua New Guinea, children are taught, "we call this a tree," or "we call this a book." The child learns from the start that there are other ways of naming things, and is ready to discover later that a tree can also be called an *árbol* (Spanish) or *cây* (Vietnamese).

There will always be languages you don't understand. Some people, when they hear something they don't understand, say, "It's Greek to me." Shakespeare used that phrase in the play *Julius Caesar* (Act 1, Scene 2), but it comes from before his time. Monks used to write notes in religious manuscripts. When they came across something in the Greek language, they would write in Latin, *Graecum est, non legitur.* That meant, "It is Greek, it is not read." At first that was used because some Greek texts were heresy, against the church's teachings. Later it meant that the monks couldn't understand Greek. The French, by the way, when they run into something they don't understand, say *c'est du chinois*, "it's Chinese!"

Mark Twain, in his book *The Innocents Abroad*, shows us how to have fun trying to speak someone else's language. He says about his trip to France, "We never did succeed in making anybody understand just exactly what we wanted, and neither did we ever succeed in comprehending just exactly what they said in reply—but then they always pointed—they always did that, and we bowed politely and said, 'Merci, Monsieur.'" In Russia, he says, "I talked to the Russians a good deal, just to be friendly, and they talked to me from the same motive; I am sure that both enjoyed the conversation, but never a word of it either of us understood."

Like Mark Twain, we can enjoy others, whatever language they speak. And the more you learn of their languages, the better you'll understand and enjoy people!

Here's what some people who speak several languages say about it:

Rory, who is fourteen, learned Arabic from his Palestinian mother and English from his British father. Now he is studying French and German on his own, because he likes languages and because he wants more choice of jobs when he grows up. He says, "I enjoy it. When I go to England, my brother and I can talk to each other in Arabic and no one understands us. . . . If you only spoke one language, it would be difficult to get around in the world."

Fourteen-year-old Tesdaniya is from Ethiopia. She speaks Amharic, Arabic, and English. She says, "It helps me make friends with people. And it makes you feel smart. Some of my friends can't speak Amharic, and they ask me to translate what other people say."

Steve, age twelve, has lived in twelve countries. He learned Norwegian from his father and Finnish from his mother. Now he speaks English, too. He says, "I like it. It's easy. I like talking with people. It would be boring to only speak one language, because you wouldn't understand other people or know what to say to them."

So what are you waiting for? Start learning a language!

TABLE 9
CRITICAL LANGUAGES

The U.S. government thinks language learning is important. In 1985 the Department of Education published a list of 169 "critical" languages. They said that knowledge of these languages would help scientific research or the security and economy of the United States. The languages they chose were:

Achinese (Indonesia), Acholi (Uganda), Afrikaans (South Africa, Namibia), Akan (Ghana), Albanian, Amharic (Ethiopia), Arabic, Armenian (Armenia, Middle East), Assamese (India), Aymara (Bolivia, Peru), Azerbaijani (Azerbaijan, Iran)

Bahasa Indonesian, Balinese (Indonesia), Baluchi (Pakistan), Bamileke (Cameroon), Bashkir (Russia), Basa or Kru (Africa), Belorussian (Belarus), Bemba (Zambia), Bengali (Bangladesh, India), Berber (Morocco, Algeria), Bhojpuri (India, Nepal), Bikol (Philippines), Bulgarian, Burmese (Myanmar), Buryat (Russia, Mongolia, China)

Cambodian or Khmer, Catalan (Spain), Chinese, Chuvash (Russia), Ciokwe (Angola, Zambia, Zaire), Czech

Danish, Dari (Afghanistan), Dinka (Sudan), Dutch

Efik (Nigeria), Eskimo, Estonian, Ewe-Fon (Ghana, Togo, Benin)

Fijian, Finnish, French, Fulani (Nigeria, Cameroon, Niger)

Gã (Ghana, Togo), Ganda (Uganda), Gbaya (Central African Republic), Georgian (Georgia, former Soviet Union), German, Greek, Guaraní (Paraguay, Brazil), Gujarati (India, Pakistan)

Haitian Creole, Hausa (Nigeria), Hebrew (Israel), Hindi (India), Hmong (China, Vietnam, Thailand, Laos), Hungarian

Iban (Indonesia, Malaysia), Icelandic, Igbo (Nigeria), Ilocano (Philippines), Irish Gaelic, Italian

Japanese, Javanese (Indonesia)

Kamba (Kenya), Kannada (India), Kanuri (Nigeria), Kashmiri (India), Kazakh (Kazakhstan, China), Kikuyu (Kenya), Kirghiz (Kyrgyzstan), Kongo (Zaire, Congo, Angola), Korean, Kpelle (Liberia, Guinea), Krio (creole language of Sierra Leone), Kumauni (India), Kurdish (Turkey, Iraq, Iran, Syria)

Lahnda (India, Pakistan), Lamani (India), Latvian, Lithuanian, Luba (Zaire)

Macedonian, Madurese (Indonesia), Maithili (India, Nepal), Malagasy (Madagascar), Malayalam (India), Manchu (China), Mandekan or Bambara (Mali), Manipuri (India), Marathi (India), Maya (Mexico, Guatemala, Belize), Mende (Liberia, Sierra Leone), Minangkabau (Indonesia), Mixtec (Mexico), Mongolian, Mordvin (Russia), More (Burkina Faso), Mundari-Ho (India)

Nahuatl (Mexico), Neo-Melanesian or Tok Pisin (Papua New Guinea), Nepali, Newari (Nepal), Ngala or Losengo (Mozambique, Malawi), Norwegian, Nyanja (Malawi, Zambia)

Oriya (India), Oromo (Ethiopia)

Papiamento (Netherlands Antilles), Pashto (Afghanistan, Pakistan), Persian or Farsi (Iran), Polish, Polynesian, Portuguese, Punjabi (India, Pakistan)

Quechua (Peru, Bolivia, Ecuador)

Rappang or Buginese (Indonesia, Malaysia), Romanian, Romany (Gypsies), Rundi (Burundi), Russian, Rwanda

Sango (Central African Republic), Santali (India), Serbo-Croatian (Yugoslavia, Croatia, Bosnia-Herzegovina), Shona (Zimbabwe), Sindhi (Pakistan, India), Sinhala (Sri Lanka), Slovak, Slovene, Somali, Songhai (Mali, Niger), Sotho (Lesotho, South Africa), Spanish, Sundanese (Indonesia), Swahili (Kenya, Tanzania), Swedish

Tagalog (Philippines), Tajik, Tamil (India, Sri Lanka), Tatar (Russia), Telugu (India), Temen (Sierra Leone), Thai-Lao (Thailand, Laos, China, Vietnam), Tibetan (China), Tigrinya (Ethiopia, Eritrea), Tiv (Nigeria), Toba Batak (Indonesia), Tsonga (Mozambique, South Africa), Tungus (Siberia), Turkish, Turkmen, Tuvinian (Russia)

Uighur (China), Ukrainian, Urdu (Pakistan, India), Uzbek

Vietnamese, Visayan or Cebuano (Philippines)

Wolof (Senegal)

Yakut (Russia), Yao (Malawi, Tanzania), Yiddish (U.S., Israel), Yoruba (Nigeria), Yucatec (Mexico)

Zapotec (Mexico), Zulu-Xhosa (South Africa).

(Notes: Many of these languages can be spelled in different ways. Most of them are spoken in other countries near the ones listed. Berber, Bamileke, Bikol, Eskimo, Polynesian, and Tungus are families of languages rather than single languages.)

APPENDIX 1

HOW TO SAY IT: GREETINGS AND WORDS IN MANY LANGUAGES

To give you a start on learning other languages, here are some basic words in many different languages. Some languages, like Arabic, Khmer (Cambodian), and Russian, use different alphabets than English does. When English-speakers write words from these languages, we can use "transliterations." These represent foreign words, spelled out in the closest letters in our own alphabet. Other languages, like French, German, and Spanish, are spelled in the same alphabet as ours, sometimes using extra marks. Whether they use the same alphabet or not, each language has its own sounds and many have sounds we do not have at all in English. To give you an idea of how to pronounce the words, approximate pronunciations (in one representative dialect of each language) are given in parentheses after each word. Remember, these pronunciations are not exact. The languages which are totally unrelated to English, like Cheyenne, Navajo, Chinese, Arabic, and Khmer, are the most likely to sound completely different than English. If you know someone who speaks one of these languages, get him or her to say the words to you, so you can get the right pronunciation. Have fun!

PRONUNCIATION KEY

The pronunciations in parentheses use the following letters from English to give the approximate pronunciations on the right:

a	as in sat
ah	like a in father
apostrophe (')	glottal stop, like the sound in the middle of *uh-oh*
aw	as in law
ay	as in day
e	as in set
ee	as in see
eh (at end of syllable)	like *e* in set

i	as in s<u>i</u>t
igh	as in h<u>igh</u>
ih (at end of syllable)	like *i* in s<u>i</u>t
kh	raspy sound in the back of your throat, like Scottish and German *ch*
n(g)	say an *ng* sound without the final *guh*, like the first *ng* in si<u>ng</u>ing
o	as in h<u>o</u>t
oh	as in <u>oh</u>, or like *oe* in t<u>oe</u>
oo	as in t<u>oo</u>
ow	as in h<u>ow</u>
oy	as in b<u>oy</u>
(r) following vowel	vowel is umlauted; say it almost like the *u* in p<u>u</u>t or f<u>u</u>r, but with rounded lips; don't pronounce the *r*
rr	rolled (flapped or trilled) *r*
u	as in p<u>u</u>t
uh	like *u* in c<u>u</u>t
zh	the sound made by *s* in mea<u>s</u>ure; like a *j* sound without the initial *d*
syllables in **CAPITAL LETTERS**	stressed; said louder than the rest of the word

See chapter 5 for descriptions of different sounds.

ARABIC

These are transliterations from Arabic script. A sound made by squeezing the back of the throat is written as *9*; *hh* stands for a raspy, heavily breathed *h* sound; *rr* is rolled.

Hello ("Peace upon you," or "Greetings")	Assalaamu 9alaykum, or Marrhhaba	(a-ssa-**LAM**-oo 9ah-**LAY**-koom; **MAHRR**-hhah-bah)
Good-bye	Ma9 assalaama	(mah9 ah-sa-**LA**-mah)
Please ("From your excess")	Min fadhlak	(min **FUHD**-luhk)
Thank you	Shukran	(**SHOO**-krahn)
You're welcome	9afwan	(**9AHF**-wahn)
Yes	Aywa, or Na9am	(**IGH**-wah, **NAH**-9ahm)

GREETINGS AND WORDS IN MANY LANGUAGES

No	Laa	(la)
I don't understand	Ma 'afham	(ma '**AF**-huhm)
Excuse me	9afwan	(**9AHF**-wahn)
House	Bayt	(bayt)
Play	Yila9ab	(**YIL**-ah-9ahb)
Today ("The day")	Ilyawm	(il-**YOHM**)
Days Sun.–Sat. (*Yawm* means "day"; Sunday through Thursday are literally days "one" through "five"; Friday is "the day of meeting" [for prayer]; Saturday is "the sabbath [rest] day")	Yawm il'ahhad, Yawm il'ithnayn, Yawm ilthalaatha, Yawm il'arba9a, Yawm ilkhamees, Yawm iljuma9a, Yawm issabt	(yohm il-'**AH**-hhahd, yohm il-'ith-**NAYN**, yohm ith-thuh-**LA**-thuh, yohm il-'**AHR**-bah-9ah, yohm il-khuh-**MEES**, yohm il-**JOOM**-ah-9ah, yohm iss-**SEBT**
Numbers 1–10	Waahhid, Ithnayn, Thalaatha, 'Arba9a, Khamsa, Sitta, Saba9a, Thamaanya, Tisa9a, 9ashara	(**WAH**-hhid, ith-**NAYN**, thuh-**LA**-thuh, '**AHR**-bah-9ah, **KHUHM**-suh, **SIT**-tuh, **SUHB**-ah-9ah, thuh-**MAN**-ee-yuh, **TISS**-ah-9ah, **9AHSH**-ah-rah

BASQUE

G is made by not quite touching your tongue to the roof of your mouth, like a soft gargling sound. *TX* is pronounced like *ch* in *cheese*. These pronunciations are from the Viscayan dialect.

Hello	Kaizo	(**KIGH**-soh)
Good day	Egunon	(ay-goo-**NOHN**)
Good-bye	Abur	(ah-**GOOR**)
Please	Mezedez	(may-**SAYD**-ayss)
Thank you	Ezkarikasko	(ess-kahr-ee-**KASS**-koh)
You're welcome	Ongi etorri	(**OHN**-gee ay-**TOHRR**-ee)
Yes	Bai	(bigh)
No	Ez	(ess)

156 WHO TALKS FUNNY?

I don't understand	Ez deet konprenizen (The root *konpren* was probably borrowed from Spanish)	(ess deet kohn-**PREN**-ee-ssen)
The house	Etxea	(ay-**CHAY**-ah)
My house	Nik etxea	(neek ay-**CHAY**-ah)
Today	Egin	(**AY**-gin)
Numbers 1–7	Bat, Bi, Hiru, Lau, Bost, Zes, Zaspi	(baht, bee, **EE**-roo, low, bosst, sess, **SESS**-pee)

CHEYENNE (North American Indian Language)

Every vowel is pronounced; double vowels are lengthened. An accent mark (é) means to give the syllable high stress. A dot over a vowel (ė) is a whisper mark, meaning that syllable is said softly. An apostrophe (') stands for a glottal stop, like in the middle of *uh-oh*.

Hello	Haáhe	(hah-**AH**-hay)
Good day	Pave-ésheeva	(pah-vay-**AY**-shay-vah)
I'm leaving	Na-ase	(nah-ah-say)
I'll see you again	Nė-sta-vȧ-hóse-vóomȧtse	(nay-stah-vah-**HOH**-say-**VOH**-maht-say)
Come again	Ne'evȧ-hósė-ho'ėhneo'o	(nay-'ay-vah-**HOH**-say-hoh-'eh-nay-oh-'oh)
Thank you	Hahoo	(hah-hoh)
Yes	Héehe'e (once used by women only, now used by both sexes), or Haáhe (used by men)	(**HAY**-hay-'ay, hah-**AH**-hay)
No	Hova'ȧhane	(hoh-vah-'ah-hah-nay)
Now	Hetsetseha	(hay-tsay-tsay-hah)
House	Mȧheo'o	(mah-hay-oh-'oh)
He's playing	E-évoo'soo'e	(ay-**AY**-voh'-soh-'ay)
Today	Hetsetséha-ésheeva	(hay-tsay-**TSAY**-hah-**AY**-shay-vah)

Days Sun.–Sat. (Sunday means "big holy day," Monday is "first day," Tuesday is "second day," and so on to Saturday, which means "little holy day"; Monday is also called e-éne-ma'heoné-esheeve, which means "holy day is finished")	Má'xe-ma'heóne-ésheeva, No'ka-ésheeva, Néxa-ésheeva, Na'ha-ésheeva, Neva-ésheeva, Nóhona-ésheeva, Tshéshke'e-ma'heóne-ésheeva	(**MAH**'-khay-mah'-hay-**OH**-nay-**AY**-shay-vah, noh'-kah-**AY**-shay-vah, **NAY**-khah-**AY**-shay-vah, nah'-hah-**AY**-shay-vah, nay-vah-**AY**-shay-vah, **NOH**-hoh-nah-**AY**-shay-vah, tshaysh-kay'-ay-mah'-hay-**OH**-nay-**AY**-shay-vah)
Numbers 1–10: Of things (i.e. one horse, two horses)	Na'èstse, Néshe, Na'he, Neve, Nóho, Naasóhto, Nésohto, Na'nóhto, Sóohto, Máhtóhtoha	(nah'-ayst-say, **NAY**-shay, nah'-hay, nay-vay, **NOH**-hoh, naah-**SOH**-toh, **NAY**-soh-toh, nah'-**NOH**-toh, **SOH**-toh, mah-**TOH**-toh-hah)
Numbers 1–10: For counting, or of time	No'ka, Néxa, Na'ha, Neva, Nóhona, Naa-sóhtoha, Nésòhtoha, Na'nóhtoha, Sóoh-toha, Máhtóhtoha	(noh'-kah, **NAY**-khah, nah'-hah, nay-vah, **NOH**-hoh-nah, naah-**SOH**-toh-hah, **NAY**-soh-toh-hah, nah'-**NOH**-toh-hah, **SOH**-toh-hah, mah-**TOH**-toh-hah)

CHINESE (CANTONESE)

Tones are important but are not marked here, because there is not a simple system to show them. Most of these letters are pronounced differently than in English. *K* and *t* at the end of syllables are not aspirated (air is not blown out when you say them), and are difficult for an English-speaker to hear. *Ng* is pronounced like the *ng* in *sing*, so *ngoh* is like *Ringo* without the *ri*. Cantonese is written with the same logograms as Mandarin Chinese; following are approximations of the sounds.

Hello	Jou sahn	(joh sahn)
Good-bye	Joigin	(joy-geen)

Please	Mh-goi	(mm-**GOY**)
Thank you	Dojeh	(**TOY**-tyeh)
You're welcome	Mh-hou haak-hei	(mm-**HOH** hahk-hee)
Yes	Hai	(**HAH**-ee)
No	Mh-hai	(mm-hah-ee)
I don't understand	Ngoh mh-mihng-baahk	(ngoh mm-**MING**-bahk)
Excuse me	Deui-mh-jyuh	(**TOO**-mm-**TYE**(**R**))
House	Ngok	(ngohk)
Play	Fan	(fahn)
Today	Kam yǎt	(kahm yaht)
Days Sun.–Sat. (Tones are marked for *yǎt* and *yāt* since these are different words distinguished only by their tones.)	Laihbaai yǎt, Laihbaai yāt, Laihbaai yih, Laihbaai saam, Laihbaai sei, Laihbaai ngh, Laihbaai luhk	(lay-bigh yaht, lay-bigh yat, lay-bigh yee, lay-bigh sahm, lay-bigh see, lay-bigh n(g), lay-bigh lohk)
Numbers 1–10 (Be careful with "nine," *gau*, which said on a different tone means "dog"!)	Yāt, Yih, Saam, Sei, Ngh, Luhk, Chat, Baat, Gau, Sahp	(yat, yee, sahm, see, n(g), lohk, chat, baht, gow, sahp)

CHINESE (MANDARIN)

Tones: ā = tone[1], high level tone; á = tone[2], medium tone going higher; ǎ = tone[3], low tone going down and then up; à = tone[4], high tone going down quickly; a = neutral tone, depends on the tone before it. Mandarin Chinese is written with logograms. The following is one system of putting Chinese into Roman letters, called Pin yin.

Hello ("How are you?")	Ní hǎo?	(nee how)
Good-bye ("See you again")	Zài jiàn	(tzigh jehn)
Please	Qǐng	(ching)
Thank you	Xièxiè	(shyeh shyeh)
You're welcome	Bú kèqi	(boo ke(r)-chee)
Yes ("That's right")	Duìle	(dway-luh)

No	Bù	(boo)
I don't understand	Wǒ bù dǒng	(woh boo don(g))
Excuse me ("I'm sorry")	Duì bù qǐ	(dway boo chee)
House	Wūzi	(oo-dzuh)
Play	Wán	(wahn)
Today	Jīntiān	(jin-tyen)
Days Sun.–Sat. (Notice that Monday is day "one," followed by numbers below)	Xīngqī rì, Xīngqī yī, Xīngqī èr, Xīngqī sān, Xīngqī sì, Xīngqī wǔ, Xīngqī liù	(shin(g)-chee rr, shin(g)-chee ee, shin(g)-chee ahr, shin(g)-chee sahn, shin(g)-chee ssuh, shin(g)-chee oo, shin(g)-chee lyoo)
Numbers 1–10	Yī, Èr, Sān, Sì, Wǔ, Liù, Qī, Bā, Jiǔ, Shí	(ee, ahr, sahn, ssuh, oo, lyoo, chee, bah, jee-oh, she(r))

DUTCH

K and *g* are strongly aspirated, almost as if they were followed by an *h* sound. *Kh* is a raspy sound in the back of your throat.

Hello	Hallo, or Dag	(ha-**LOH**, dahkh)
Good morning	Goedemorgen	(goo-deh-**MOHR**-gen)
Good afternoon	Goedemiddag	(goo-deh-**MID**-dahkh)
Good-bye	Tot ziens, or Dag	(toht seenss, dahkh)
Please	Alstublieft	(ahl-stoo-**BLEEFT**)
Thank you	Dank U	(dahnk oo)
You're welcome ("No thanks," "There is nothing to thank for")	Niets te danken	(neets teh **DAHNK**-en)
Yes	Ja	(yah)
No	Nee	(nay)
I don't understand	Ik begrijp het niet	(ik beh-**GRIGHP** het neet)

Excuse me	Neemt U me niet kwalijk, or Pardon	(naymt oo meh neet **KVAH**-lek, pahr-**DOHN**)
House	Huis	(howss)
Play	Spelen	(**SPAY**-len)
Today	Vandaag	(van-**DAHKH**)
Days Sun.–Sat.	Zondag, Maandag, Dinsdag, Woensdag, Donderdag, Vrijdag, Zaterdag	(**ZOHN**-dahkh, **MAN**-dahkh, **DINSS**-dahkh, **VOONSS**-dahkh, **DOHN**-derr-dahkh, **VRAY**-dahkh, **ZA**-terr-dahkh)
Numbers 1–10	Een, Twee, Drie, Vier, Vijf, Zes, Zeven, Acht, Negen, Tien	(ayn, tvay, dree, veer, vighff, zess, **ZAY**-ven, ahkht, **NAY**-gen, teen)

FRENCH

The pronunciation *u(r)* is pronounced almost like the *u* in *put*. *R* is pronounced in the back of the throat, with a brief gargling sound.

Hello	Bonjour	(bohn(g)-zhoor)
Good-bye	Au revoir	(ohr-vwahr)
Please	S'il vous plaît	(seel voo play)
Thank you	Merci	(mayr-see)
You're welcome	Il n'y a pas de quoi, or De rien	(eel nee ah pah du(r) kwah, du(r) ree-yan(g))
Yes	Oui	(wee)
No	Non	(nohn(g))
I don't understand	Je ne comprends pas	(zhu(r) nu(r) kohm-prahn(g) pah)
Excuse me	Excusez-moi	(ek-skyoo-zay-mwah)
House	Maison	(may-zohn(g))
Play	Jouer	(zhoo-ay)
Today	Hier	(ee-ayr)
Days Sun.–Sat.	Dimanche, Lundi, Mardi, Mercredi, Jeudi, Vendredi, Samedi	(dee-man(g)sh, luhn(g)-dee, mahr-dee, mayr-kreh-dee, zhu(r)-dee, vahn(g)-dru(r)-dee, sahm-dee)

Numbers 1–10	Un, Deux, Trois, Quatre, Cinq, Six, Sept, Huit, Neuf, Dix	(uhn(g), du(r), trwah, katr, sangk, seess, set, weet, nu(r)f, deess)

GERMAN

Some Germans use a rolled *r*, others pronounce *r* far back in the throat, like French *r*.

Hello	Guten Tag	(goo-ten **TAHK**)
Good-bye	Auf Wiedersehen	(owf **VEE**-dayr-zayn)
Please	Bitte	(**BIT**-tuh)
Thank you	Danke	(**DAHN**-kuh)
You're welcome	Bitte sehr	(**BIT**-tuh zayr)
Yes	Ja	(yah)
No	Nein	(nighn)
I don't understand	Ich verstehe nicht	(ikh fer-**SHTAY**-uh nikht)
Excuse me	Entschuldigen Sie	(ent-**SHOOL**-dih-gen zee)
House	Haus	(howss)
Play	Spiel	(shpeel)
Today	Heute	(**HOY**-tuh)
Days Sun.–Sat.	Sonntag, Montag, Dienstag, Mittwoch, Donnerstag, Freitag, Samstag (or Sonnabend in some areas)	(**ZOHN**-tahk, **MOHN**-tahk, **DEENSS**-tahk, **MIT**-vawkh, **DON**-errss-tahk, **FRIGH**-tahk, **ZAHMSS**-tahk or **ZOHN**-ah-bent)
Numbers 1–10	Eins, Zwei, Drei, Vier, Fünf, Sechs, Sieben, Acht, Neun, Zehn	(ighntz, tzvigh, drigh, feer, fu(r)nf, zeks, **ZEE**-ben, ahkht, noyn, tsayn)

HAITIAN CREOLE

This is a creole from a pidgin based on French. Notice how the words sound like French words.

Hello	Bonjou! or Bonswa! or Alò!	(bohn-joo, bohn-swah, ah-loh)

Good-bye	Orevwa! or Babay! or Tchaw!	(oh-ray-vwah, bah-bigh, tchaw)
Please	Souple, or Tan pri	(soo-play, tahn pree)
Thank you	Mèsi, or Granmèsi	(may-see, grahn-may-see)
Yes	Wi, or Anhan	(wee, ahn-hahn)
No	Non	(nohn)
Do you understand?	Tande?	(tahn-day)
Excuse me	Eskize m	(ays-kee-zaym)
House	Kay	(kay)
Play	Jwe	(zhway)
Today	Jodi	(zhoh-dee)
Numbers 1–10	Youn, De, Twa, Kat, Senk, Sis, Sèt, Wit, Nèf, Dis	(yoon, day, twah, kaht, saynk, seess, set, weet, nef, deess)

HEBREW

Hebrew is written with its own alphabet, from right to left. These are transliterations and approximate pronunciations. *KH* stands for a raspy sound in the back of your throat. Apostrophes (') do not represent glottal stops.

Hello ("Peace")	Shalom	(shah-**LOHM**)
Good-bye ("Peace")	Shalom	(shah-**LOHM**)
Please	Bvak'sha	(beh-vah-kah-**SHAH**)
Thank you	Toda	(toh-**DAH**)
You're welcome ("It's nothing")	Al lo davaar	(ahl loh dah-**VAHR**)
Yes ("So it is")	Ken	(ken)
No	Lo	(loh)
I don't understand	Ani lo meveen	(ah-nee loh meh-**VEEN**)
Excuse me	Slicha	(slee-**KHAH**)
House	Bayit	(**BIGH**-yeet)
Play	L'sachek	(leh sah-**KHEK**)
Today ("The day")	Hayom	(hah-**YOHM**)

GREETINGS AND WORDS IN MANY LANGUAGES   163

Days Sun.–Sat. ("First day" through "Sixth day," then "Sabbath")	Yom Rishon, Yom Sheni, Yom Shlishi, Yom R'vi'i, Yom Chamishi, Yom Shishi, Shabbat	(**YOHM** ree-**SHOHN**, **YOHM** shay-**NEE**, **YOHM** shlee-**SHEE**, **YOHM** reh-vee-**EE**, **YOHM** khah-mee-**SHEE**, **YOHM** shee-**SHEE**, shah-**BAHT**)
Numbers 1–10 (These are masculine forms; the feminine forms are slightly different. The number *two* also has a different form, *shnay*, when used with a noun rather than alone.)	Echad, Shnayim, Shlosha, Arbaa, Chamisha, Shisha, Shivaa, Shemona, Teisha, Asara	(eh-**KHAD**, **SHNAH**-yeem, sheh-lo-**SHAH**, ahr-**BAH**, khah-mee-**SHAH**, shee-**SHAH**, **SHEH**-vah, shmo-**NAH**, tay-**SHAH**, ah-sah-**RAH**)

HINDI AND URDU (India and Pakistan)

These are transliterations from the Hindi script, called Devanagari; see chapter 10. Urdu is very similar, but uses a modified Arabic script. When two options are given, the second is the one Urdu-speakers prefer. Other listed words are the same for Hindi and Urdu, though sometimes with slightly different pronunciations. *Gh* is an aspirated *g* sound, made with a puff of breath as English *k* is.

Hello	Namaste, or Salam	(nah-mahss-**TEH**, sa-**LAM**)
Good-bye	Namaste, or Khuda haafiz	(nah-mahss-**TEH**, **KHOO**-da HAH-fizz)
Please	Meherbani	(meh-her-**BAH**-nee)
Thank you	Dhanyavad, or Shukria	(**DAN**-yah-wahd, **SHOOK**-ree-ah)
You're welcome	Koii baat nahi	(koy baht na-**HEEN**(**G**))
Yes (The Jii before the answer makes it more respectful, in both Hindi and Urdu)	Jii han, or Han	(jee hahn(g))
No	Jii nahi, or Nahi	(jee na-**HEEN**(**G**))

I (man or boy) don't understand (in Hindi)	Mai nahi samaja hu	(ma na-**HEEN**(**G**) **SAM**-jah hoo)
I (woman or girl) don't understand (in Hindi)	Mai nahi samajhti hu	(ma na-**HEEN**(**G**) sah-**MAHJ**-tee hoo)
I don't understand (in Urdu)	Mujc samaj nchi	(moo-**JAY** sah-**MAHJ** nah-**HEEN**(**G**))
Excuse me ("Forgive me")	Maaf kiijiye	(mahf **KEEJ**-iy-eh)
House	Ghar	(gher)
Play	Khel	(kayl)
Today	Aaj	(ahdj)
Days Sun.–Sat. (in Hindi)	Etwar or Ravivar, Somvar, Mangalvar, Budwar, Guruvar, Shukravar, Shanivar	(**ET**-wahr or **RAH**-vee-vahr, **SOHM**-vahr, **MANG**-ahl-vahr, **BOOD**-wahr, **GOO**-roo-vahr, **SHOOK**-er-vahr, **SHAN**-ee-vahr)
Days Sun.–Sat. (in Urdu)	Etvar, Peer, Mangal, Budh, Jumerat, Jumma, Hafta	(et-**VAHR**, peer, **MUHN**-guhl, bood, joom-**MAYR**-aht, **JOOM**-mah, **HUHFF**-tah)
Numbers 1–10	Ek, Do, Teen, Char, Panch, Chei, Saath, Aath, No, Das	(ek, doh, teen, chahr, pahnch, chay, saht*, aht*, noh, dess) (*make a puff of breath with the t's on the end of *saht* and *aht*.)

ITALIAN

R's are trilled. Consonants written double are pronounced longer than single consonants.

Hello	Ciao	(**CHAH**-oh)
Good day	Buon giorno	(bwohn **JOHRR**-noh)
Good-bye	Arrivederci	(ahrr-rree-vay-**DAYRR**-chee)

Please	Per favore	(payrr fah-**VOH**-rray)
Thank you	Grazie	(**GRRAH**-tsee-ay)
You're welcome	Prego	(**PRRAY**-goh)
Yes	Sì	(see)
No	No	(noh)
I don't understand	Non capisco	(nohn kah-**PEESS**-koh)
Excuse me	Scusi	(**SKOO**-zee)
House	Casa	(**CAH**-zah)
Play	Giocare	(joh-**CAH**-rray)
Today	Oggi	(**OHJJ**-ee)
Days Sun.–Sat.	Domenica, Lunedì, Martedì, Mercoledì, Giovedì, Venerdì, Sabato	(doh-**MAY**-nee-kah, loo-nay-**DEE**, mahrr-tay-**DEE**, mayrr-koh-lay-**DEE**, joh-vay-**DEE**, vay-nayrr-**DEE**, **SAH**-bah-toh)
Numbers 1–10	Uno, Due, Tre, Quattro, Cinque, Sei, Sette, Otto, Nove, Dieci	(**OO**-noh, **DOO**-ay, trray, **KWAHT**-trroh, **CHEEN**-kway, **SAY**-ee, **SAYT**-tay, **OHT**-toh, **NOH**-vay, **DYAY**-chee)

JAPANESE

These are transliterations from Japanese script. See chapter 10 for examples of the script. Double letters are held longer than single letters. A line over a vowel (ō) means that it is held longer than a single vowel. *R* is a short flap of the tongue against the roof of the mouth, almost like English *d*. Stress is about the same on all syllables.

Hello (on telephone)	Moshi moshi	(moh-shee moh-shee)
Good morning	Ohayō gozaimasu	(oh-high-yoh goh-zigh-mahss)
Good afternoon	Konnichi wa	(kohn-nee-chee wah)
Good evening	Komban wa	(kohm-bahn wah)
Good night	Oyasumi nasai	(oh-yah-soom-ee nah-sigh)
Good-bye ("If it must be so")	Sayōnara	(sigh-yoh-nah-rah)

Please	Dozo	(doh-zoh)
Thank you (There are many other ways to say "thank you" in Japanese; some of them mean "I do a rudeness," "I will receive," and "I have been a bother to you")	Arigatō	(ah-ree-gah-toh)
You're welcome	Dō itashimashite	(doh ee-tah-shee-mah-shee-teh)
Yes	Hai	(high)
No	Iie	(ee-yeh)
I don't understand	Wakarimasen	(wah-kah-ree-mah-ssen)
Excuse me	Gomen nasai	(goh-men nah-sigh)
House	Uchi	(oo-chee)
Play	Asobi	(ah-soh-bee)
Today	Kyo	(kyoh)
Days Sun.–Sat.	Nichi-yōbi, Getsu-yōbi, Ka-yōbi, Sui-yōbi, Moku-yōbi, Kin-yōbi, Do-yōbi	(nee-chee-yoh-bee, geh-tsoo-yoh-bee, kah-yoh-bee, soo-ee-yoh-bee, moh-koo-yoh-bee, kin-yoh-bee, doh-yoh-bee)
Numbers 1–10	Ichi, Ni, San, Shi, Roku, Shichi, Hachi, Ku, Ju	(ee-chee, nee, sahn, shee, roh-koo, shee-chee, hah-chee, koo, joo)

(If you have a Japanese friend, ask him to show you the numbers with his hands; the Japanese count by first closing the fingers one at a time, then opening them back up again, rather than opening the fingers one at a time and then using the other hand, as English-speakers usually do.)

KHMER (CAMBODIAN)

These are transliterations from the Khmer alphabet. Khmer has many vowels which English does not have, so the pronunciations are not very

GREETINGS AND WORDS IN MANY LANGUAGES

close. There are also many levels of language in Khmer. These phrases are in a fairly polite style. *Tng* at the beginning of a word is pronounced as all one sound, like *tongue* without the vowel sound.

English	Khmer	Pronunciation
Hello, sir! (*Cumriep* means "tell," *sue* means "ask," *look* is a polite "you" for a man)	Cumriep sue look	(choom-**RYEP** soo look)
Hello, madam!	Cumriep sue look-srey	(choom-**RYEP** soo look-sray)
Good-bye (Response to "good-bye" is "yes," *baat* or *caah*, as below)	Cumriep lie, or Soum lie haey	(choom-**RYEP** lee-ah, sohm lee-ah hay)
Please, or Excuse me	Soum-tooh	(sohm-toh)
Thanks very much	Qaa-kun craen nah	(aw-koon chah-rahn **NAH**)
You're welcome	Min-qey tee	(man-igh tay)
Yes (man speaking)	Baat	(baht)
Yes (woman speaking)	Caah	(chah)
No (man speaking)	Baat tee	(baht tay)
No (woman speaking)	Caah tee	(chah tay)
I don't understand ("I can't understand")	Kñom sdap min baan tee	(knyohm sdahp man bahn tay)
House	Pteah	(pah-tyeh)
Play	Leng	(layng)
Today	Tngay-nih	(tngigh-nee)
Days Sun.–Sat.	Tngay-qaatit, Tngay-can, Tngay-qangkie, Tngay-put, Tngay-prohoeh, Tngay-sok, Tngay-saw	(tngigh-ah-tit, tngigh-chahn, tngigh-ang-kee-ah, tngigh-put, tngigh-proh-hoh, tngigh-sohk, tngigh-sow)
Numbers 1–10 (Notice "six" is "five-one," and so on)	Muey, Pii, Bey, Buen, Pram, Prammuey, Prampil, Prambey, Prambuen, Dap	(mway, pee, bigh, bohn, prowm, prawm-way, prawm-peel, prawm-bigh, prawm-bohn, dahp)

KOREAN

These are transliterations from the Korean Hangul alphabet; see illustration in chapter 10. Most Korean consonants sound softer than English ones. For instance, Korean *s* sounds more like the second *s* in *sunset* than like the first. There are many levels of Korean speech; the following words are used in formal speech.

Hello	Annyong hasimnika	(ahn-**YOHNG** hah-**SHEEM**-nee-kah)
Good-bye (person staying, "Hoping for a safe return")	Annyonghi kasipsiyo	(ahn-yohng-hee kah-sheep-shee-yoh)
Good-bye (person leaving, "Safely stay peaceful")	Annyonghi kesipsiyo	(ahn-yohng-hee kay-sheep-shee-yoh)
Please (There are many different words for "please," depending on the situation.)	Chom	(chohm)
Thank you	Kamsa hamnida	(kahm-sah **HAHM**-nee-dah)
You're welcome	Chonmaneyo	(**CHOHN**-mahn-ay-yoh)
Yes	Ye, or more informally, Neh	(yeh, neh)
No	Anio	(**AH**-nee-yoh)
I don't understand	Morumnida	(moh-**ROOM**-nee-dah)
Excuse me	Sile hamnida	(sheel-**LAY HAHM**-nee-dah)
House	Jip	(jip)
Play	Nolda	(**NOOL**-dah)
Today	Onul	(oh-**NOOL**)
Days Sun.–Sat.	Ilyoil, Walyoil, Hwayoil, Suyoil, Mokyoil, Kumyoil, Toyoil	(**EEL**-yoh-il, **WAHL**-yoh-il, **HWAH**-yoh-il, **SOO**-yoh-il, **MOH**-kyoh-il, **KOOM**-yoh-il, **TOH**-yoh-il)

Numbers 1–10	Hana, Tul, Set, Net, Tasot, Yasot, Ilgop, Yatul, Ahop, Yul	(HAH-nah, tool, set, net, TAH-soht, YAH-soht, IL-gohp, YAH-dool, AH-hohp, yul)

NAVAJO

Raise the tone of your voice on syllables with an ' (accent) mark. A mark under a vowel (ą) means to say the vowel through your nose. An apostrophe (') stands for a glottal stop, the sound in the middle of *uh-oh*. Vowels written twice are held longer than vowels written once.

Hello	Yá'át'ééh	(yah-'aht-'ay)
Good-bye	Hágoónee'	(hah-goh-nay')
Please	T'áá shǫǫdí	(t-'ah shohn(g)-dih)
Thank you	'Ahéhee'	('ah-heh-hay')
You're welcome	T'áá'áko	(t-'aah-'ah-koh)
Yes	'Aoo'	('oh')
No	Dooda	(doh-dah)
House	Kin	(kin)
We play	Neiiné	(neh-iih-neh)
Today (now until the end of the day)	Díí jí	(diih jih)
Today (the part that's over)	Jı̨į́ dą́ą́	(jiin(g) dahn(g))
Days Sun.–Sat.	Damóo, Damóo biiskání, Damóodóó naakijı̨, Damóodóó tágíjı̨, Damóodóó dı̨'íjı̨, Damóodóó 'ashdla'a jı̨, Damóo yázhí.	(dah-moh, dah-moh biih-skah-nih, dah-moh-doh naah-kih-jin(g), dah-moh-doh ta-gih-jin(g), dah-moh-doh din(g)-'ih-jin(g), dah-moh-doh 'ahsh-dlah-'ah jin(g), dah-moh yahz-hih)
Numbers 1–10	Łáa'ii, Naaki, Táá', Dı̨į́, 'Ashdla', Hastą́ą́, Tsosts'id, Tseebíí, Náhástéí, Neeznáá.	(thlaah-'iih, naah-kih, taah', diin(g), 'ahsh-dlah', hahss-taahn(g), tsohstss-'id, tsay-biih, nah-hah-steh-ih, nayz-naah)

NEW GUINEA PIDGIN

Vowels written as single vowels are pure vowels, not diphthongs, so the *o* in *nogat*, for instance, would be pronounced without the *oo* sound we put at the end of *no* in English.

Hello	Gude gude	(**GOO**-day **GOO**-day)
Good morning	Moning	(**MOH**-ning)
Good afternoon	Apinun	(ap-ih-**NOON**)
Good-bye	Gutbai	(goot-bigh)
See you later	Lukim yu bihain	(**LOOK**-im yoo bee-**HIGHN**)
Please	Plis	(pleess)
Thank you	Tenkyu	(**TENK**-yoo)
You're welcome	Tenkyu tru	(**TENK**-yoo troo)
Yes	Yes, or Yesa	(**YESS**-ah)
No	Nogat	(noh-**GAT**)
I don't understand	Mi no klia gut	(mee noh **KLEE**-ah goot)
I don't know	Mi no save	(mee noh **SAH**-vay)
What is that?	Em wanem samting?	(em **WAHN**-em **SAM**-ting)
Where are you going?	Yu go we?	(yoo goh way)
Hurry	Yu hariap	(yoo hahr-ee-**AHP**)
All right, Okay	Orait	(oh-right)
Close the door	Pasim dua	(**PASS**-im **DOO**-ah)
Sit down	Sindaun	(**SIN**-down)
House	Haus	(howss)
Play	Pilai	(pih-**LIGH**)
Today	Tude	(too-**DAY**)
Days Sun.–Sat.	Sande, Mande, Tunde, Trinde, Fonde, Fraide, Sarere	(**SAHN**-day, **MAHN**-day, **TOON**-day, **TREEN**-day, **FOHN**-day, **FRIGH**-day, **SAH**-ray-ray)
Numbers 1–10 (All the numbers can have *-pela* added before objects, i.e., *Wan, Tu,* but *Wanpela haus, Tupela haus*)	Wan, Tu, Tri, Foa, Faiv, Sikis, Seven, Et, Nain, Ten	(wahn, too, tree, **FOH**-ah, fighv, **SIK**-iss, **SEV**-en, et, nighn, ten)

GREETINGS AND WORDS IN MANY LANGUAGES 171

NORWEGIAN

R is slightly rolled.

Hello	Hallo	(hah-**LOO**)
Good morning	God morgen	(goo **MOHRR**-gen)
Good day	God dag	(goo dahg)
Good afternoon	God kveld	(goo kvel)
Good-bye	Adjø	(ah-**DYU(R)**)
Please	Vær så god	(vayrr soh **GOO**)
Thank you	Takk	(tahk)
You're welcome	Ingen årsak	(**ING**-en **OORR**-sahk)
Yes	Ja	(yah)
No	Nei	(nay)
I don't understand	Jeg forstår ikke	(yay fohrr-**STOHRR IK**-keh)
Excuse me	Unnskyld meg	(**U(R)N**-shool may)
House	Hus	(hooss)
Play	Lek	(lek)
Today	I dag	(ee **DAHG**)
Days Sun.–Sat.	Søndag, Mandag, Tirsdag, Onsdag, Torsdag, Fredag, Lørdag	(**SU(R)N**-dahg, **MAHN**-dahg, **TEERRSS**-dahg, **OONSS**-dahg, **TOORRSS**-dahg, **FRRAY**-dahg, **LU(R)R**-dahg)
Numbers 1–10	En, To, Tre, Fire, Fem, Seks, Syv, Åtte, Ni, Ti	(ayn, too, trray, **FEERR**-eh, fem, seks, syu(r)v, **OHT**-teh, nee, tee)

POLISH

Accented consonants like ś and ć are softened, as if they were followed by a very short *y* sound; *ł* sounds like English *w*, *w* sounds like English *v* or *f*, and *r* is trilled. The following phrases are written in the Polish alphabet, which is adapted from the Roman alphabet.

Hello ("Good day")	Dzień dobry	(djen **DOH**-brreh)
Good-bye	Do widzenia	(doh vee-**DZAY**-nyah)
Please	Proszę	(**PRROH**-shen(g))

Thank you	Dziękuję	(djen(g)-**KOO**-yeh)
You're welcome	Proszę bardzo	(**PRROH**-sheh **BAHRR**-dzoh)
Yes	Tak	(tahk)
No	Nie	(nyeh)
I don't understand	Nie rozumiem	(nyeh rroh-**ZOO**-myaym)
Excuse me	Przepraszam	(pshay-**PRRAH**-shahm)
House	Dom	(dohm)
Play	Grać	(grrahch)
Today	Dzisiaj	(**DJEE**-shigh)
Days Sun.–Sat.	Niedziela, Poniedziałek, Wtorek, Środa, Czwartek, Piątek, Sobota	(nyay-**DJEH**-lah, pohn-yay-**DJAH**-wayk, **FTOH**-rrayk, **SHRROH**-dah, **CHFAHRR**-tayk, **PYOHN**(**G**)-tayk, soh-**BOH**-tah)
Numbers 1–10	Jeden, Dwa, Trzy, Cztery, Pięć, Sześć, Siedem, Osiem, Dziewięć, Dziesięć	(**YEH**-den, dvah, trrih, **CHTAY**-rreh, pyen(g)tsh, shesh, **SHEH**-dem, **OH**-shaym, **DJAY**-vyen(g)tsh, **DJAY**-shen(g)tsh)

RUSSIAN

Russian is written with the Cyrillic alphabet. These are transliterations into the closest letters in our alphabet. The ' sign means that the consonant before it is softened. It sounds as if it is followed by a very brief *y* sound. *Zh* is pronounced like a *j* without the beginning *d* sound. Unstressed vowels are not pronounced clearly.

Hello	Zdravstvuytye	(**ZDRAH**-stvwee-tyeh)
Good morning	Dobroye ootro	(do-bray-eh **OO**-tro)
Good afternoon or Good day	Dobriy dyen'	(do-bray dyen)
Good-bye	Do sveedaneeyah	(doss-vee-**DAHN**-yah)

Please	Pojalooysta	(po-ZHOW-loo-stah)
Thank you	Spaseebo	(spah-SEE-bah)
You're welcome	Nye za shto	(NYEH zah shtuh)
Yes	Da	(dah)
No	Nyet	(nyet)
I don't understand	Ya nye poneemayoo	(yah nyeh po-nee-MAH-yoo)
Excuse me	Prosteetye	(prah-STEE-tyyh)
House	Dom	(dohm)
Today	Syegodnya	(seh-VOHD-nee-ya)
Play	Igrat'	(ee-GRAHT)
Days Sun.–Sat.	Voskryesyehn'ye, ponyedyel'neek, vtorneek, sryeda, chyetvyerg, pyatneetsa, soobbota	(vess-kreess-YEN-yah, pahn-yee-DYEL-nyeek, VTOR-neek, sreh-DAH, chet-VYAYRK, PYAHT-neet-sah, soo-BOH-tah)
Numbers 1–10	Odeen, Dva, Tree, Chetirye, Pyaht', Shyest', Syem', Vosyem', Dyevyat', Dyesyat'	(ah-DEEN, dvah, tree, chee-TEER-yah, pyaht, shest, syem, VOHS-yem, DYEH-vyet, DYEH-syaht)

SOMALI

Pronunciations: *gh* stands for a gargling sound; *hh* stands for a raspy, heavily breathed *h* sound; *9* stands for a sound made by squeezing the back of the throat, *q* is a *k* sound made far back in the throat. Somali is written in the Roman script shown here.

Hello	See tahay	(SAY tah-ay)
Good-bye	Nabadgelyo	(nah-bahd-GEL-yoh)
Please	Fadlan	(FUH-dluhn)
Thank you	Mahadsanid	(mah-hahd-SUHN-id)
You're welcome	Soo-dhawow	(SOH-dah-WOH)
I don't understand	Ma-fahmin	(ma-fuh-MIN)
Excuse me	I-cafi	(ee-9AHF-ee)
Yes	Haa	(hah)
No	Maya	(MIGH-ah)

House	Aqal	(**AH**-kuhl)
Play	Dheel-dheel	(del-del)
Today	Maanta	(**MAHN**-tuh)
Days Sun.–Sat. (Notice how similar these are to the names of the days in Arabic; the Somali names were probably borrowed from Arabic)	Axad, Isniin, Talaado, Arbaco, Khamiis, Jimce, Sabti	(a-**HHUHD**, iss-**NAYN**, tuh-**LAHD**-oh, ahr-**BA9**-oh, kha-**MEESS**, jim-ah-9ee, **SUHBT**-ee)
Numbers 1–10	Hal (southern dialect) or Kow (northern dialect), Laba, Saddex, Afar, Shan, Lix, Tadoba, Syddeed, Sagaal, Toban	(hahl or kow, **LAH**-bah, **SUHD**-dihh, **AH**-fahr, shuhn, lihh, tah-**DOH**-bah, sih-**DED**, sah-**GHAHL**, **TUH**-bahn)

SPANISH

R is rolled. It is a brief flap, almost like a *d*, when only one *r* is written in the Spanish word; a longer roll, like the sound kids make playing cars, when two *r*'s are written. *B* and *v* make the same sound, about halfway between the English sounds of *b* and *v*. Different dialects of Spanish are spoken in Spain and Latin America. *Z* sounds like the *th* of *thin* in the Castilian Spanish of Spain, but is pronounced *s* in Latin American Spanish. Spanish *y* is usually pronounced almost like English *y* in yawn, but in some areas of Latin America it is pronounced like a soft *j*, or *zh*.

Hello	Hola	(**OH**-lah)
Good day	Buenos días	(**BWAY**-nohss **DEE**-ahss)
Good-bye	Adiós	(ah-dee-**OHSS**)
Please	Por favor	(pohrr fah-**BOHRR**)
Thank you	Gracias	(**GRRAH**-see-ahss)
You're welcome	De nada	(day **NAH**-dah)
Yes	Sí	(see)
No	No	(noh)
I don't understand	No comprendo	(noh kohm-**PRRAYN**-doh)

Excuse me	Perdóneme	(payrr-**DOH**-nay-may)
House	Casa	(**KAH**-sah)
Play	Jugar	(hoo-**GAHRR**)
Today	Hoy	(oy)
Days Sun.–Sat.	Domingo, Lunes, Martes, Miércoles, Jueves, Viernes, Sábado	(doh-**MEENG**-go, **LOO**-nayss, **MAHRR**-tayss, mee-**AYRR**-koh-layss, **WHAY**-bayss, **BYAYR**-nayss, **SAH**-bah-doh)
Numbers 1–10	Uno, Dos, Tres, Cuatro, Cinco, Seis, Siete, Ocho, Nueve, Diez	(**OO**-noh, dohss, trrayss, **KWAH**-trroh, **SEEN**-koh, sayss, **SYAY**-tay, **OH**-choh, **NWAY**-bay, dyayss)

SWAHILI

Nn is an *n* sound held long, like the *n*'s in *men knew*.

Hello ("Problems?")	Jambo, or Hu jambo	(**JAHM**-boh, hoo **JAHM**-boh)
Answer ("No problems")	Jambo, or Si jambo	(**JAHM**-boh, see **JAHM**-boh)
Good-bye	Kwaheri	(kwah-**HAYRR**-ee)
Please	Tafadhali	(tah-fah-**DAHL**-ee)
Thank you	Asante	(ah-**SAHN**-tay)
You're welcome ("It's nothing")	Si kitu	(see **KEE**-toh)
Yes ("It is so")	Ndiyo	(**NDEE**-yoh)
No	Hapana, or La	(hah-**PAHN**-ah, lah)
I don't understand	Sifahamu	(see-fah-**HAHM**-oo)
Excuse me	Polesana	(poh-lay-**SAH**-nah)
Sorry	Samahani	(sah-mah-**HAH**-nee)
House	Nyumba	(**NYOOM**-bah)
Play	Cheza	(**CHEZ**-ah)
Today	Leo	(**LAY**-oh)

WHO TALKS FUNNY?

Days Sun.–Sat.	Jumapili, Jumatatu, Jumanne, Jumatano, Alhamisi, Ijumaa, Jumamosi	(joo-mah-PEEL-ee, joo-mah-TAH-too, joo-mah-NAH-nee, joo-mah-TAH-noh, ahl-hahm-EE-see, ee-JOOM-ah, joo-mah-MOH-see)
Numbers 1–10	Moja, Mbili, Tatu, Nne, Tano, Sita, Saba, Nane, Tisa, Kumi	(MOH-jah, MBEE-lee, TAH-too, nnay, TAH-noh, SEE-tah, SAH-bah, NAH-nay, TEE-sah, KOO-mee)

SWEDISH

R is slightly rolled in most parts of the country. Two dots over a letter (like ö) means that it is umlauted; say it as if an r comes after it, but without pronouncing the r.

Hello	God dag	(goo DAH)
Good morning	God morgon	(goo MOHR-on)
Good afternoon	God middag	(goo MID-dahg)
Good-bye	Adjö	(AH-ye(r))
Please	Varsågod	(VAHR-shoh-GOOD)
Thank you	Tack	(tahk)
You're welcome	Ingen orsak	(ING-gyen OOR-shahk)
Yes	Ja	(yah)
No	Nej	(nay)
I don't understand	Jag förstår inte	(yah fur-SHTOHR IN-tuh)
Excuse me	Förlåt, or Ursäkta	(fur-LOHT, OOR-sek-tah)
House	Hus	(hooss)
Play	Leka	(LEE-kah)
Today	I dag	(ee dah)
Days Sun.–Sat.	Söndag, Måndag, Tisdag, Onsdag, Torsdag, Fredag, Lördag	(SU(R)N-dah, MAWN-dah, TISS-dah, OONSS-dah, TOOSH-dah, FRAY-dah, LUR-dah)

Numbers 1–10	Ett, Två, Tre, Fyra, Fem, Sex, Sju, Åtta, Nio, Tio	(et, tvoh, tray, **FEER**-ah, fem, seks, shoo, **OHT**-tah, **NEE**-yoh, **TEE**-yoh)

TAGALOG (Philippines)

Tagalog, the national language of the Philippines, is also called Filipino or Pilipino. It is written with a Roman alphabet, as below. Tagalog is a Malayo-Polynesian language which includes many words borrowed from Spanish—like the days Monday-Saturday—since the Philippines were ruled by Spain from the 1560s until 1898. *Ng*, even at the beginning of a word, is one sound, like the sound at the end of *sing*. (Try saying *singer* without the *si*.)

Hello	Mabuhay	(mah-**BOO**-high)
Good morning	Magandang umaga	(mah-guhn-**DAHNG** oo-**MAH**-gah)
Good afternoon	Magandang hapon	(mah-guhn-**DAHNG** **HAH**-pohn)
Good evening, Good night	Magandang gabi	(mah-guhn-**DAHNG** ga-**BEE**)
Good-bye	Paalaam na po	(pa-**AH**-lam na poh)
Please	Paki	(pa-**KEE**)
Thank you	Salamat sa iyo	(sa-**LAH**-mat sah **EE**-yoh)
You're welcome	Walang anuman	(**WAH**-lahng ah-noo-**MAHN**)
Yes	Oo	(oh-oh)
No	Hindi	(hin-**DIH**)
I don't understand	Hindi ko naintindihan	(hin-**DIH** koh na-**IN**-tin-dih-**HAHN**)
Excuse me	Ipagpaumanhin	(ee-**PAHG**-**PAH**-**OO**-man-**HIN**)
House	Bahay	(**BAH**-high)
Play	Laro	(lah-**ROH**)
Today	Ngayon	(ngigh-**OHN**)

WHO TALKS FUNNY?

Days Sun.–Sat.	Linggo, Lunes, Martes, Miyerkoles, Huwebes, Biyernes, Sabado	(**LING**-goh, **LOON**-ess, **MAHRT**-ess, **MEE**-**YAYR**-koh-less, **HOO**-**WAY**-bess, **BEE**-**YAYR**-ness, **SAH**-bah-doh)
Numbers 1–10	Isa, Dalawa, Tatlo, Apat, Lima, Anim, Pito, Walo, Siyam, Sampu	(ee-**SAH**, dah-lah-**WAH**, **TAT**-loh, **AH**-paht, **LEE**-mah, **AH**-neem, **PEE**-toh, **WAH**-loh, shee-**YAM**, **SAM**-poh)

VIETNAMESE

Listen for tones if you have a friend read you these words: *á* is a rising tone, a high voice goes higher; *ả* is a high tone going lower; *ā* is a low tone going higher; *a* is a middle tone; *à* is a low tone going lower; *ạ* is a low tone.

Hello (to man)	Chào ông	(chow ohm)
Hello (to woman)	Chào cô	(chow koh)
Good-bye	Lời chào xin cào-biệt	(loy chow sin cow-byet)
Please	Xin	(sin)
Thank you (to girl)	Cám ơn cô	(cam un(g) koh)
Thank you (to man)	Cám ơn ông	(cam un(g) ohm)
You're welcome ("I'm sorry, I can't [accept your thanks]")	Không dám	(khohn(g) dyam)
Yes (A polite acknowledgment, meaning "obeying")	Vâng	(yuhng)
No	Không	(khohn(g))
I don't understand	Tôi không hiêû	(toy khohn(g) hay-oh)
Excuse me	Xin lỗi ông	(sin loy uhm)
House	Cái nhà	(kigh nyah)
Play	Choi	(choh-ee)
Today ("Day this")	Hôm nay	(hohm nigh)

GREETINGS AND WORDS IN MANY LANGUAGES   179

Days Sun.–Sat. (Sunday is "the Lord's day," Monday "the second day," Tuesday "the third day," and so forth)	Chủ nhật, Thứ hai, Thứ ba, Thứ tư, Thứ năm, Thứ sáu, Thứ bảy	(choh nyet, too high, too bah, too tu(r), too nuhm, too sow, too bigh)
Numbers 1–10	Mòt, Hai, Ba, Bốn, Năm, Sáu, Bảy, Tám, Chín, Mười	(moht, high, bah, bohn(g), nuhm, sow, bay, tahm, chin, moo-ee)

YIDDISH

These are transliterations from the Hebrew alphabet. Compare these words to German, the language Yiddish developed from, and to Hebrew, which gave it many words.

Hello	Sholem aleichem	(**SHAW**-lem a-**LAY**-khem)
Reply	Aleichem sholem	(a-**LAY**-khem **SHAW**-lem)
Good-bye ("Be healthy," or "Go in health")	Seid gezund, or Gai gezunterhayt	(zight geh-**ZINT**, gay geh-**ZINT**-er-hayt)
Please	Seid azoy gut	(**ZIGHT** ah-zoy **GOOT**)
Thank you	A dank	(ah **DAHNK**)
You're welcome	Nito far vos	(nee-**TAW** fuhr **VAWS**)
Yes	Ye	(yaw)
No	Nit, nayn	(nit, nighn)
I don't understand	Ich vishtain nit	(eekh fahr-**SHTAY** nit)
Excuse me	Seit moichel	(zight **MOY**-khel)
House	Hois	(hoyz)
Play	Schpielen	(**SHPEEL**-en)
Today	Haint	(hint)
Days Sun.–Sat.	Suntog, Montog, Diensttog, Mitvoch, Donnerschtog, Freitog, Schabbes	(**ZOON**-tik, **MAWN**-tik, **DEENSS**-tik, **MIGHT**-vawkh, **DAW**-nersh-tik, **FRIGH**-tik, **SHAH**-biss)

180 WHO TALKS FUNNY?

Numbers 1–10   Ain Or Ains, Tsvai,   (ighn or ighntz,
                  Drei, Fir, Finf, Zeks,   tsvigh, drigh, feer,
                  Zibn or Sibben, Akht,   finnif, zeks, **ZIB**-in,
                  Nein, Tsehn   akht, nighn, tsen)

APPENDIX 2
LANGUAGE LEARNING AND LANGUAGE ACQUISITION

Language "acquisition" means "picking up" a language, by hearing it rather than by studying it. A child "acquires" his or her first language(s). This is usually thought of as a different process than language "learning," being taught a language later in life. A language is most easily learned in a "second language" situation, where the student is living in a culture where the language is usually spoken. A "foreign language" situation means the student is learning a language in a place where it is not generally spoken.

Here are methods of language teaching, from traditional to experimental:

Grammar-Translation. Memorizing lists of words, inflections, and grammatical rules, for mental discipline as well as knowledge. Emphasizes reading, writing, and translating, not speaking. This method was commonly used in the nineteenth century and is still used to teach Latin and ancient Greek.

Direct Method. Teacher uses only the foreign language in class, with pictures and props, and does not explain grammar or do any translating. The emphasis is on speaking. The goal is to teach the student to think in the language rather than mentally translate. The teacher corrects the students' grammar when they speak. This method needs large amounts of class time and a very fluent teacher. It may be frustrating for adults who are used to analyzing and explanations.

Reading Method. Uses reading with controlled-vocabulary readers, practice in pronunciation and reading aloud, and minimal grammar study, to teach students to read in the language without looking up many words.

Audio-lingual Approach. Method based on techniques developed by the military in World War II. Emphasizes speaking and listening, then reading and writing. Students memorize dialogues for various situations. Pattern practice involves repeating basic grammatical patterns and substituting other words in the patterns. For instance, the teacher says in the language, "Where is the girl?" The class repeats, "Where is the girl?" Then the teacher says, "boy." The class substitutes, "Where is the boy?"

This system teaches the sounds and some grammar of the language. It views language as a system of habits formed by much repetition.

Cognitive Approach. In an attempt to use what the student knows about languages, this approach gives explanations and descriptions of language structures, then exercises which practice these structures. Views language as a combination of rule-learning and habit-formation.

Natural Approach. Developed by Stephen D. Krashen and Tracy D. Terrell in the 1980s, this approach tries to copy the way children acquire their first language. Students are given "comprehensible input" in the language, hearing speech in a context they are interested in and understand. They are encouraged to listen for some time before they begin to speak in the language. Pictures, games, motions (of the students and the teacher), and props are used. Explanations are given when requested. Reading interesting material in the language is encouraged. Classes are intended to be low-pressure and interesting to reduce the student's "affective filter" (low motivation, high anxiety, low self-esteem), which keeps him from learning the language well. A related approach is J. Asher's "Total Physical Response" method, in which the teacher tells the class (in the language) what to do while doing it himself, and the class copies his actions.

Other recent methods focus on the learner's overcoming mental barriers, reducing anxiety, and increasing self-confidence. These include Caleb Gattegno's "Silent Way," Charles A. Curran's "Counseling-Learning/Community Language Learning," and Georgi Lozanov's "Suggestopedia."

GLOSSARY

ACCENT. 1) Extra stress on a particular syllable in a word. 2) The way a non-native speaker pronounces a language, usually using sounds from his or her native language. 3) The way a certain dialect of a language is pronounced.

ADJECTIVE. A word, such as *yellow* or *several*, which describes a noun.

ADVERB. A word, such as *carefully* or *downward*, that describes a verb, adjective, or another adverb.

AFFIX. A piece of a word which must be attached to a root word, such as *-s* in *walks*. Also called a "bound morpheme." *See* MORPHEME.

AFFRICATE. Combination of a stop and a fricative: for instance, *ch*, which is a combination of the stop *t* and the fricative *sh*; or *j*, which is a combination of the stop *d* and the fricative *zh*. *See also* STOP, FRICATIVE.

AGGLUTINATIVE LANGUAGE. Language like Turkish or Eskimo in which root words and affixes are combined without being changed. *See also* TYPOLOGICAL CLASSIFICATION.

ALPHABETIC SCRIPT. A writing system in which each symbol stands for a sound.

ANGLO-SAXON. *See* OLD ENGLISH.

APPLIED LINGUISTICS. Ways linguistics is used in other fields. The most common use of linguistics is in improving the teaching and learning of foreign languages.

ARTICLE. A word or affix which makes a noun definite (referring to something specific) or indefinite (referring to any member of the group defined by the noun). In English, *the* is a definite article; *a* and *an* are indefinite articles. *The man* is a specific man; *a man* is any man.

ARTIFICIAL LANGUAGE. A language invented by someone, rather than developed naturally. An artificial language starts out with no native speakers, though parents who study it could speak it to their children, making them native speakers. Esperanto and Volapük are artificial languages.

ASPIRATION. Pronouncing a sound with a puff of air. The letters *p*, *t*, and *k* are aspirated at the beginning of words in English, but not always at the end of words. Linguists write an aspirated consonant with a raised *h*, like *p^h*.

BILINGUAL. Knowing two languages.

BORROWING. Transfer of words, sounds, or structures from one language to another language. The words may be somewhat changed in the process. For instance, Arabic has borrowed the word *computer* from English, but the Arabs pronounce it "kohm-byoo-terr."

CASE. The function or use of a noun in a sentence; how it is related to the other words in the sentence. For instance, the subject of a sentence is in the subjective, or nominative, case.

COGNATES. Related words in different languages which have similar meanings, sounds, and/or spellings. For instance, Spanish *fuerza* and English *force* are cognates.

COLLOQUIAL. Form of language used in everyday conversation.

COMPARATIVE LINGUISTICS. *See* HISTORICAL LINGUISTICS.

CONSONANT. A sound in which the airstream is constricted or slowed in some way. The English sounds written as *b, d, f, g,* and *h* are examples of consonants.

CREOLE LANGUAGE. A pidgin language which is now spoken as the first language of a group of people, so that it has become a complete language. *See* PIDGIN LANGUAGE.

CUNEIFORM. The ancient Sumerian writing system using wedge-shaped characters inscribed on clay tablets.

DEAD LANGUAGE. A language which is no longer spoken by anyone as a first language.

DEMOTIC SCRIPT. A shortened version of Egyptian hieroglyphics, developed for government documents and letters, and later also used for religious writing.

DESCRIPTIVE GRAMMAR. The rules and patterns which native speakers automatically use to make sentences in a language or dialect. This includes how words are arranged, how they are related to each other, and what form of each word is used.

DIACRITICAL MARK, or DIACRITIC. A mark added to the basic form of a letter which changes the pronunciation of the letter, like the curve called a "tilde" over an *n* which gives it the sound *ny*: ñ.

DIALECT GEOGRAPHY, or LINGUISTIC GEOGRAPHY. The development of linguistic maps showing where features of different dialects are used; for instance, in which towns the word *bogle* is used to mean "scarecrow," compared to where *flay-crow* is used.

DIALECT. A variety of a language spoken in a certain area (regional or geographic dialect) or by a certain group of people (social dialect).

DIALECTOLOGY. The study of dialects. *See* DIALECT GEOGRAPHY, SOCIAL DIALECTOLOGY.

DIGLOSSIA. The use of two different dialects or levels of a language, one for formal and one for informal situations. For instance, Arab countries are diglossic, with classical or modern standard Arabic used in books, on television, and for formal occasions, while local colloquial dialects are used in everyday speech.

DIPHTHONG. A combination of two vowel sounds into one sound; the tongue moves in pronouncing it, rather than staying in one place as it does for a pure vowel sound. The vowel sounds in *out, ray,* and *boy* are examples of English diphthongs.

DUAL. A grammatical form used in some languages to show that there are two of something. For instance, the Arabic *kalbayn* is a dual noun; it means "two dogs." Some languages also have dual forms of verbs, used when two people are doing something. *See also* SINGULAR, PLURAL.

ETYMOLOGY. The history of the words of a language, including when they were first used, where they came from, and how their forms and meanings have changed. Also, the history of a single word, as in "The etymology of *nice* is given in chapter 8."

EUPHEMISM. A more socially acceptable substitute for an offensive word. *See also* SWEARING, TABOO.

FIRST LANGUAGE, MOTHER TONGUE, or NATIVE LANGUAGE. The language people learn when they are growing up—usually their parents' language.

FRICATIVE. A consonant sound made by slowing the breath, like the sounds written in English as *s, f, th, sh,* and *v.*

GENDER. Classification of a noun as feminine, masculine, or neuter (with no gender). It may be related to the meaning of the noun; for instance the Spanish word *amiga,* meaning a female friend, is in the feminine gender. Or it may be arbitrary; for instance the Spanish word *mesa* (table), is also feminine.

GLOTTAL STOP. A quick closing of the throat, like the sound in the middle of *uh-oh* and the sound in the middle of the Cockney pronunciation of *bottle* (bo'el).

GLOTTALIZED CONSONANT. A consonant pronounced with the back of the throat closed, as if the speaker were holding his or her breath.

GRAMMAR (or SYNTAX). The ways that morphemes, words, and phrases are combined into sentences, and how words, phrases, clauses, and sentences are related to each other in a language. "Grammar" may also include morphology, or may be used to mean a complete description of a language. *See* DESCRIPTIVE GRAMMAR, PRESCRIPTIVE GRAMMAR.

GREAT VOWEL SHIFT. A change in the pronunciation of English vowels in the 1400s and 1500s. Most vowels began to be pronounced farther forward in the mouth.

HIEROGLYPHICS. A system of writing using mostly characters which are pictures. Usually refers to the ancient Egyptian script. *Hieroglyphics* comes from the Greek *hieros,* meaning "holy," and *glyphein,* "to carve," since the hieroglyphics were originally used only for religious texts, and the Greeks thought Egyptian hieroglyphics were a mystical priestly writing.

HISTORICAL AND COMPARATIVE LINGUISTICS. The study of how languages have changed through history and how they are related to one another. Some methods used by historical linguists are the "comparative method," "internal reconstruction," and "lexicostatistics." In the comparative method, similar words in several languages are used to figure out what a word in the parent language may have been. Linguists look for "cognate sets" with shared patterns of letters, like English *blood,* Swedish *blod,* Dutch *bloed,* and German *Blut.* These words all start with *bl-,* have similar vowels, and end with similar sounds (*d* or *t*). This implies that they originally developed from the same word. Internal reconstruction means that words in one language are compared with each other to figure out what the parent language was like, sometimes assuming that irregular words were once regular. Lexicostatistics means counting corresponding words and unrelated words in two languages in order to estimate when the two languages became different from their parent language.

HOMONYMS. Words that sound alike and are spelled alike, but have different meanings, such as *right* (correct) and *right* (direction opposite to left). They may come from the same source or may have different etymologies (word histories).

HOMOPHONES. Words that sound alike but have different meanings and spellings, such as *right* and *write.* Homophones usually have different etymologies and usually were not originally pronounced the same.

IDIOM. Phrase which means something different than its literal meaning. For instance, "dead end" does not actually mean something died.

IMMIGRANTS. People who leave their native country and move to a new country permanently.

INDO-EUROPEAN LANGUAGES. A huge family of languages, believed to be descended from one language called Indo-European. It includes most of the European languages and many languages of India and surrounding areas.

INFIX. An affix added inside a word. *See also* AFFIX, PREFIX, SUFFIX.

INFLECTED, or INFLECTIONAL, LANGUAGE. Language like Latin or Greek in which affixes are added to or combined with root words. *See also* TYPOLOGICAL CLASSIFICATION.

ISOLATE. A language with no known related languages. Korean, Japanese, and Basque are the most widely spoken language isolates.

ISOLATING LANGUAGE. Language like Chinese or Vietnamese in which few affixes are added to root words. *See also* TYPOLOGICAL CLASSIFICATION.

JARGON. Technical or specialized words and phrases used by people in a particular occupation or with a common interest, like the jargon of basketball players or the jargon of electrical engineers.

LINGUA FRANCA. A language used as a common means of communication in an area where a number of different languages are spoken. For instance, Swahili is a lingua franca in areas of East Africa where many different languages are spoken. Those who need to speak with people of other tribes, for business or travel, learn Swahili. Lingua franca literally means "French language" in Italian.

LANGUAGE FAMILY. A group of languages which developed from one language at some time in history. For examples, see table 2: Major Language Families. *See also* HISTORICAL LINGUISTICS.

LINGUISTICS. The study of language.

LINGUISTS. People who study linguistics. Some well-known linguists are Jean François Champollion, Noam Chomsky, Edward Sapir, and Ferdinand de Saussure.

LOGOGRAPHIC SCRIPT. A writing system in which each symbol stands for a word.

MIDDLE ENGLISH. The language of the English people from about 1066 to 1476 A.D. (Some scholars would say it extended to about 1600 A.D.; languages change gradually, at different rates in different areas.)

MORPHEME. The smallest part of a word that has meaning. For instance, *cats* is made of two morphemes: *cat*, which represents an animal, and *-s*, which means a plural, more than one. A "free morpheme," like *cat*, can stand alone. A "bound morpheme," like *-s*, must be attached to another morpheme. *See also* AFFIX, PREFIX, SUFFIX.

MORPHOLOGY. The study of morphemes and how they are combined.

MOTHER TONGUE. *See* FIRST LANGUAGE.

MULTILINGUAL. Able to use several languages.

NATIVE LANGUAGE. *See* FIRST LANGUAGE.

NOUN. A type of word which represents a person, place, thing, animal, or idea, such as *boy* or *growth*.

OFFICIAL LANGUAGE. A language recognized by a country's government and usually used for official business and education in that country. A country may have any number of official languages.

OLD ENGLISH, or ANGLO-SAXON. The language of the English people from about the fifth century until about 1066 A.D.

PHONEMES. Sounds that distinguish one word from another in a language. If a phoneme is substituted for another phoneme in a word, the meaning of the word changes. The two phonemes are called a minimal pair. For instance, in English /b/ and /p/ are a minimal pair, since bat and pat have different meanings. If a sound is part of a minimal pair, linguists say it is a phoneme of the language. Phonemes are usually marked by two slashes: /p/. There are two possible pronunciations, or allophones, of /p/ used in English: [p] and [p^h]. The first sounds like the beginning of *pat,* while the second sounds like the end of *tip.* Since there is no word in English that changes meaning depending on whether it starts with [p] or [p^h], [p] and [p^h] are not a minimal pair, and therefore are not phonemes in English.

PHONEMICS. The study of phonemes.

PHONETICS. The study of how sounds are produced, sent, and received. A phonetic description of a sound is marked with brackets: [p], [p^h]. *See also* PHONEME.

PHONOLOGY. The study of the sounds used in language. *See* PHONETICS, PHONEMICS.

PIDGIN LANGUAGE. A combination of several languages in a simplified form, used by a group of people who do not speak a common language. *See also* CREOLE LANGUAGE.

PITCH. The musical tone of the voice.

PLURAL. A grammatical form used to show that there is more than one of something. For instance, *dogs* is a plural noun; it shows that there is more than one dog. Verbs can also be in the plural, when a language has special forms to refer to more than one person doing something. *See also* DUAL, SINGULAR.

POSTPOSITION. A type of word which has the meaning of a preposition, but follows a noun rather than coming before it. A language that uses postpositions would say the equivalent of "me by" rather than "by me." *See also* PREPOSITION.

PREFIX. An affix which is attached to the beginning of a word, such as the *pre-* in *prehistoric. See* AFFIX.

PREPOSITION. A word that comes before a noun or noun phrase and tells the relationship between a noun or pronoun and another word. For instance, *over, by,* and *from* are English prepositions.

PRESCRIPTIVE GRAMMAR. The patterns of a language that are taught as the "proper" way to speak and write. These are patterns used by educated speakers of the standard form of the language (such as standard English). *See also* GRAMMAR.

PRONOUN. A word which can replace a noun or noun phrase. For instance the pronoun *she* can be used instead of *Sally, the girl, the woman* or *that girl*.

PSYCHOLINGUISTICS. The study of how language is related to the human mind. Psycholinguists study how children acquire language, what parts of the brain are involved in using language, and what disorders can cause language difficulties.

RETROFLEX. A sound in which the tongue is curled backwards to the roof of the mouth. Some Indian languages have retroflexed *t, d, l,* and *n*.

ROMANCE LANGUAGE. A language descended from Latin, the language of Rome. The Romance languages are Catalan, Dalmatian, French, Italian, Portuguese, Provençal, Rhaeto-Romance, Romansch, Rumanian, Sardinian, and Spanish.

ROOT. A base morpheme to which affixes can be added. For instance, *grow* is a root to which the affix *-ing* can be added to make *growing*. See also MORPHEME, AFFIX.

SEMANTICS. The study of meaning: how words and sentences communicate ideas.

SHIBBOLETH. A word or custom that distinguishes one group of people from others.

SINGULAR. A grammatical form used to show that there is only one of something. For instance, *dog* is a singular noun; it shows that there is only one dog. There can also be singular forms of verbs, when they refer to only one person doing something. For instance, *runs* in *he runs* is singular; *run* in *they run* is plural. See also DUAL, PLURAL.

SLANG. Very informal language using new and lively words and expressions which generally disappear from use after a short time.

SOCIAL DIALECTOLOGY. The study of how speech differs between people with different levels of education and social status, and of different ages, races, and genders.

SOCIOLINGUISTICS. The study of how people use language; especially, how they use language differently in different situations and with different types of people. Includes the study of social dialects.

STANDARD LANGUAGE. A dialect of a language which educated speakers normally use, especially in writing and in formal situations. The standard language may be defined and regulated by an organization like the French Academy, or simply agreed on by most educated speakers, like standard English. It may be an artificial compromise between various spoken dialects, or it may be the dialect of a prestigious group within a society.

STOP. A consonant sound where the breath is stopped at some point, like the sounds written in English as *p, t, d, g, b,* and *k*.

STRESS. To say a syllable more forcefully or more loudly than other syllables. A stressed syllable is also called an accented syllable.

SUFFIX. An affix which is attached to the end of a word, such as the *-ly* in *carefully.* See AFFIX.

SWEARING. The use of words that most people in a society think are bad, rude, immoral, or irreverent. *See also* EUPHEMISM, TABOO.

SYLLABIC SCRIPT. A writing system in which each symbol stands for a syllable.

SYLLABLE. A part of a word which contains only one vowel sound.

SYNTAX. *See* GRAMMAR.

TABOO. Forbidden. Taboo words are those which most people in a culture think it shameful to say. From the Tongan word *tabu. See also* SWEARING, EUPHEMISM.

TENSE. A form of a verb that tells when an action occurs and whether it is continuing or not. For instance, *he ran* is in the past tense; *he is running* is in the present progressive tense.

TONAL LANGUAGE. A language in which tones help determine the meanings of words. *See* TONE.

TONE. The musical note on which a syllable is pronounced, relative to the syllables before or after it. For instance, a high tone means that the syllable is pronounced on a higher note than the other syllables.

TRANSLATION. Rendering the meaning of words from one language into another. This can be word-for-word, where each word is exactly translated, or more often phrase-for-phrase or sentence-for-sentence, where the meaning of each phrase or sentence is given in the other language. Translation out loud while a foreign language is being spoken is called "interpreting."

TRANSLITERATION. A system of substituting letters from one alphabet for equivalent or similar letters from another alphabet.

TRILINGUAL. Knowing three languages.

TYPOLOGICAL CLASSIFICATION. Classifying languages by their characteristics rather than by their history. The most commonly used and probably the simplest system is the one proposed by von Schlegel and explained in chapter 7 of this book. This theory divides languages into isolating, inflectional, and agglutinative. (*See* ISOLATING LANGUAGE, INFLECTIONAL LANGUAGE, AGGLUTINATIVE LANGUAGE.) Many languages do not fit clearly into one of these categories, so linguists have come up with many other ways of classifying languages. Some divide languages into analytic, synthetic, and polysynthetic, according to how many ideas are communicated by an average word. Languages can also be classified by the types of sounds they use (e.g., "tonal language" or "click language") or by word order (e.g., English is an "SVO language," whose normal word order is Subject, then Verb, then Object).

UMLAUT. The change of a vowel so that it sounds more like the vowel that begins the next syllable. Sometimes the following vowel has been dropped from the word, but the umlauted vowel continues to be pronounced as it was when the following vowel was there. Umlauted vowels are often marked with a double dot above them, like *ü*, and are pronounced almost as if they were followed by an *r* sound.

VERB. A type of word which represents an action or a state of being, such as *run* or *is*.

VOCABULARY. The words of a language.

VOICED. A sound in which the vocal chords in the speaker's throat vibrate, like *z, d, b*, and *g*.

VOICELESS. A sound in which the vocal chords in the speaker's throat do not vibrate, like *s, t, p*, and *k*.

VOWEL. A sound in which the airstream coming out of the throat is not stopped or slowed. *A, e, i, o, u*, and *y*, in various combinations, are used to represent the vowel sounds of English.

WRITING SYSTEM. A system of representing a language as marks on a surface. Full writing systems use symbols for words, syllables, or sounds. The symbols can be combined to make any word in a language.

FURTHER RESOURCES: WANT TO TALK FUNNY?

Do you want to learn more about languages? Look in your library under the 400s for books about language and specific languages. Books on specific countries sometimes give a few words of the languages of those countries. Also look in the travel section of bookstores for language books. Here are some good ones to start with.

GENERAL BOOKS ON LANGUAGES, WRITING, AND ENGLISH

BERLITZ, CHARLES. *Native Tongues.* New York: Grosset & Dunlap, 1982. Short fun facts about many languages; chapters include "Language Incidents That Changed History," "Same Sounds—Different Meanings," "Do Animals Have a Language?" and "Counting—Fingers, Toes, and Computers." Ages 12 and up.

EPSTEIN, SAM, and BERYL EPSTEIN. *What's Behind the Word?* New York: Scholastic Book Services, 1967. History of English language. Ages 8–12.

HACKWELL, JOHN W. *Signs, Letters, Words: Archaeology Discovers Writing.* New York: Charles Scribner's Sons, 1987. The history of writing. Ages 13 and up.

HALSEY, WILLIAM D., editorial director. *Macmillan Dictionary for Children.* New York: Macmillan, 1982. The introduction to this dictionary contains an interesting history of languages. The development of each letter is shown in the text, and many word histories are given throughout.

KATZNER, KENNETH. *The Languages of the World.* London: Routledge & Kegan Paul, 1986. Samples of writing in many languages with a short description of each language. Ages 12 and up.

KENNICUT, WALLY. *Alphabet Roots.* Waxhaw, N.C.: Summer Institute of Linguistics, 1989. A booklet of stories about many alphabets, with comments on Bible translation. Ages 8 and up.

OGG, OSCAR. *The 26 Letters.* New York: Thomas Y. Crowell, 1971. The history of the alphabet. Ages 10 and up.

PEI, MARIO. *The Story of Language.* New York: New American Library,

1965. Every aspect of languages, with examples from around the world; chapters include "The Saga of Place Names," "Cant and Jargon," "Language and the Family," and "The Translation Problem." Ages 14 and up.

SARNOFF, JANE, and REYNOLD RUFFINS. *Words: A Book about the Origins of Everyday Words and Phrases.* New York: Charles Scribner's Sons, 1981. Ages 10–14.

VAUGHAN, MARCIA K. *Wombat Stew.* Morristown, N.J.: Silver Burdett, 1984. A silly picture story with many Australian words. Ages 4 and up.

BOOKS ON SPECIFIC LANGUAGES

DUNHAM, MEREDITH. *Numbers: How Do You Say It?* New York: Lothrop, Lee & Shepard Books, 1987. Number words in English, French, Spanish, and Italian, and how to pronounce them. Ages 4 and up. Also in this series: *Shapes: How Do You Say It?, Picnic: How Do You Say It?* and *Colors: How Do You Say It?*

EKOOMIAK, NORMEE. *Arctic Memories.* New York: Henry Holt, 1990. Written in English and the Eskimo language Inuktitut. Ages 9 and up.

ELLIS, D. L. *Just Enough Dutch: How to Get by and Be Easily Understood.* Basic phrase book. Lincolnwood, Ill.: Passport Books, 1983. Ages 10 and up. Also in this series: *Just Enough French, German, Greek, Italian, Portuguese, Serbo-Croat,* and *Spanish.*

FEELINGS, MURIEL L. *Jambo Means Hello: Swahili Alphabet Book.* New York: E.P. Dutton, 1974. A Swahili word and cultural description for each letter of the alphabet. Ages 5 and up.

GIBLIN, JAMES CROSS. *The Riddle of the Rosetta Stone.* New York: Harper Collins, 1990. The deciphering of the Rosetta Stone and the culture and history of ancient Egypt. Ages 10–12.

GOLDSTEIN, PEGGY. *Long Is a Dragon in Chinese: Chinese Writing for Children.* San Francisco: China Books, 1990. Introduction to seventy-five Chinese characters. Ages 5–13.

HALL, GERALDINE. *Kee's Home: A Beginning Navajo/English Reader.* Flagstaff: Northland Press, 1971. Basic words and sentences in Navajo, with information on how to pronounce the language. Ages 8 and up.

HASKINS, JIM. *Count Your Way through the Arab World.* Minneapolis: Carolrhoda Books, 1991. The numbers in Arabic from one to ten, with related cultural information and pictures for each number. Ages 6–10. Series also includes Africa, Canada, China, Japan, Korea, Mexico, and Russia.

HIRATE, SUSAN H., and NORIKO KAWAURA. *Nihongo Daisuki! Japanese Language Activities for Children.* Honolulu: Bess Press, 1990. Teaches Japanese using games and songs (with lyrics and music, no tape). Ages 5–12.

KERSHUL, KRISTINE. *French in Ten Minutes a Day.* Menlo Park, Calif.: Sunset Publishing, 1988. A basic workbook, geared for travelers, with flashcards, a menu guide, and stickers to put on household items. Ages 14 and up. Also in this series: Chinese, German, Hebrew, Italian, Japanese, Norwegian, Russian, and Spanish, plus English for Spanish-speakers.

SCOTT, JOSEPH, and LENORE SCOTT. *Egyptian Hieroglyphs for Everyone.* New York: T. Y. Crowell, 1968. How to read hieroglyphics. Ages 13 and up.

Usborne, a British publisher whose books are distributed in the U.S. by EDC Publishing, Tulsa, Okla., has beautifully illustrated language books including the following:

Beginner's Italian Dictionary. Picture dictionary with everyday words and phrases, including a grammar guide and phrase explainer. Ages 11 and up. Also in German, French, and Spanish.

Children's Wordfinder in German. Picture dictionary with over 3,000 words. Ages 7–11. Also in French.

Essential German. Language guide for teenage travelers, including words, phrases, and slang. Also French and Spanish.

The First Thousand Words in Hebrew (also in French, German, Italian, Russian, and Spanish), 1979–1985; *Round the World in Spanish* (also French); and *The Animal Picture Word Book in French.* These books connect words with pictures and include pronunciation guides. Ages 2–13.

The Word Detective in French. Shows the parts of speech with examples connected to pictures. Ages 5–12. Also in German. 1983.

TAPES

BERLITZ PUBLICATIONS. *Berlitz, Jr. French.* New York: Aladdin Books, 1989. Book and tape with simple phrases taking Teddy the bear through the day. Ages 4–9. Also in this series: German, Italian, Spanish.

BURNINGHAM, ROBIN. *Hawaiian Word Book.* Honolulu: Bess Press, 1982. Basic vocabulary, pronunciation, and culture, illustrated book and tape. All ages. Also in this series: *Japanese Word Book* (by Yuko Green, 1989), and *Chinese Word Book* (by Jiang An, 1990).

CRIMINALE, ULRIKE. *Springboard to French.* Guilford, Conn.: Jeffrey Norton Publishers, 1988. Uses games like "Simon Says" and directions like

"Stand up" to teach comprehension. Enough repetition to make learning easy. Based on Total Physical Response method of language learning. Includes manual and two cassettes. Ages 3–12. Also available in German and Spanish.

CROWN PUBLISHERS. *Living Languages* courses in many languages, including *Children's Living French, Children's Living Spanish,* and *Children's Living German*. New York: Crown Publishers. Books and tapes. Children's series include dialogues, songs, poems, and fairy tales, all in the new language, for ages 5–12. These are more complete courses than the other tapes listed here, which are introductory. Other Living Languages courses, including French, German, Hebrew, Italian, Japanese, and Spanish, as well as English for speakers of various other languages, are available for ages 12 and up.

KOBO, YOSHIAKI. *Japanese for Children*. Lincolnwood, Ill.: National Textbook Company, 1987. Book and tape.

SONG TAPES

PENTON OVERSEAS. *Lyric Language: French*. Carlsbad, Calif.: Penton Overseas, 1991. "Family Circus" characters and songs like "At the Zoo" and "Happy Birthday," with lines sung alternately in French and English. Highly recommended for language introduction. Songbook and cassette. All ages. Series also includes German, Italian, Spanish, and Swedish. Videos also available.

TEACH ME TAPES. *Teach Me French*. Minneapolis: Teach Me Tapes, 1985. French and English children's songs like "Mary Had a Little Lamb" and "Alouette," sung in both French and English with French narration. Includes cassette and coloring book with all words. All ages. Teacher's guides are also available. Series also includes *Teach Me German, Hebrew, Italian, Japanese, Russian,* and *Spanish,* and the more advanced *Teach Me More French, German, Japanese,* and *Spanish*.

STORY TAPES

AUDIO-FORUM. *Storybridges to French for Children*. Guilford, Conn.: Jeffrey Norton Publishers, 1988. Includes the stories "Goldilocks and the Three Bears," "The Turtle's Music," "Peter and the Wolf," and others told in English with French words, phrases, and songs. Easy to follow. Ages 4–10. The series also includes *Storybridges to Spanish* and *Storybridges to German*.

PASSPORT BOOKS. *"Once Upon a Time"* series. Lincolnwood, Ill.: Passport

Books, 1989. Folktales like "The Little Red Hen" in French, German, or Spanish (no English explanations) to read in a storybook while listening to them on tape. Series includes *Il Etait Une Fois* (French stories), *Es War Einmal* (German stories), and *Habia Una Vez* (Spanish stories). For more advanced language learners, with some background in the language. Ages 8–12.

INDEPENDENT STUDY LANGUAGE COURSES

INTERNATIONAL LINGUISTICS CORPORATION. *The Learnables*. Kansas City, Mo.: International Linguistics Corporation. Courses in Chinese, Czech, English, French, German, Hebrew, Japanese, Russian, and Spanish. Student listens to a native speaker of the language on audio tape while looking at corresponding pictures; teaches student to understand spoken language. Later levels teach reading and grammar. Ages 7 and up.

SWEET, DR. WALDO E. *Artes Latinae*. Wauconda, Ill.: Bolchazy-Carducci Publishers. (Originally published by Encyclopaedia Britannica Educational Corporation.) Complete course in Latin language, culture, and history, with self-programmed texts, graded readers, audio cassettes, tests. Ages 7 and up.

See also *Living Languages* courses, page 195.

The U.S. government publishes self-study programs for many languages (ranging from Albanian to Yoruba), which are available through Audio Language and Knowledge Institute, New York, N.Y. They also carry the *Language/30* series for travelers, from Educational Services, which give a quick introduction (two cassettes and book) to each of 34 languages.

BIBLIOGRAPHY

GENERAL REFERENCE BOOKS

BODMER, FREDERICK. *The Loom of Language.* 1944. Reprint. New York: W. W. Norton & Company, 1985.

BREWSTER, E. T., and E. S. BREWSTER. *Language Acquisition Made Practical.* Colorado Springs, Colo.: Lingua House, 1976.

BRYSON, BILL. *Mother Tongue.* London: Hamish Hamilton, 1990.

COMRIE, BERNARD, ed. *The World's Major Languages.* New York: Oxford University Press, 1987.

COULMES, FLORIAN. *The Writing Systems of the World.* Oxford: Basil Blackwell, 1989.

COWAN, GEORGE M. *The Word That Kindles.* Huntington Beach, Calif.: Wycliffe Bible Translators, 1979.

CRYSTAL, DAVID. *The Cambridge Encyclopedia of Language.* Cambridge: Cambridge University Press, 1987.

DIRINGER, DAVID. *The Alphabet: A Key to the History of Mankind.* New York: Philosophical Library, 1948.

DOBSON, E. J. *English Pronunciation 1500–1700.* London: Oxford at the Clarendon Press, 1968.

EDWARDS, A. D. *Language in Culture and Class.* London: Heinemann Educational Books, 1976.

ELGIN, SUZETTE HADEN. *What Is Linguistics?* Englewood Cliffs, N.J.: Prentice-Hall, 1979.

FALK, JULIA S. *Linguistics and Language.* Glenview, Ill.: Scott, Foresman and Co., 1978.

FAMIGHETTI, ROBERT, ed. *The World Almanac and Book of Facts: 1994.* Mahwah, N.J.: Funk and Wagnalls, 1993.

FERGUSON, CHARLES A., and SHIRLEY BRICE HEATH, eds. *Language in the USA.* Cambridge: Cambridge University Press, 1981.

FRIEDRICH, JOHANNES. *Extinct Languages.* Translated by Frank Gaynor. New York: Philosophical Library, 1957.

GRIMES, BARBARA F., ed. *Ethnologue: Languages of the World.* 12th ed. Dallas: Summer Institute of Linguistics, 1992.

HARDING, EDITH, and P. RILEY. *The Bilingual Family: A Handbook for Parents.* Cambridge: Cambridge University Press, 1986.

HENDRICKSON, ROBERT. *American Talk: The Words and Ways of American Dialects.* New York: Viking Penguin, 1986.

JOHNSTONE, PATRICK. *Operation World.* Grand Rapids, Mich.: Zondervan, 1993.

JOST, DAVID A., ed. *Word Mysteries and Histories.* Boston: Houghton Mifflin Co., 1986.

KRASHEN, STEPHEN D. *Inquiries & Insights.* Hayward, Calif.: Alemany Press, 1985.

KRASHEN, STEPHEN D., and TRACY D. TERRELL. *The Natural Approach: Language Acquisition in the Classroom.* San Francisco: Alemany Press, 1983.

KUCERA, H. "The Mathematics of Language." In *American Heritage Dictionary.* 2d ed. Boston: Houghton Mifflin, 1982.

LANGACKER, RONALD W. *Language and Its Structure.* New York: Harcourt Brace Jovanovich, 1973.

"Languages of the World." In *The New Encyclopaedia Britannica: Macropaedia.* Vol. 22. Chicago: Encyclopaedia Britannica, 1986.

LEHMANN, W. P. *Historical Linguistics: An Introduction.* 2d ed. New York: Holt, Rinehart and Winston, 1973.

MCCRUM, ROBERT, WILLIAM CRAN, and ROBERT MACNEIL. *The Story of English.* London: Faber and Faber, 1986.

MCLAUGHLIN, BARRY. *Theories of Second-Language Learning.* London: Edward Arnold, 1987.

MOLIN, DONALD H. *Actor's Encyclopedia of Dialects.* New York: Sterling Publishing Co., 1984.

MOSS, NORMAN. *British/American Language Dictionary.* Lincolnwood, Ill.: Passport Books, 1984.

PEI, MARIO. *The Story of Language.* Rev. ed. 1965. Reprint. New York: New American Library, 1984.

PEDERSON, LEE. "Language, Culture, and the American Heritage." In *American Heritage Dictionary.* 2d ed. Boston: Houghton Mifflin, 1982.

RHEINGOLD, HOWARD. *They Have a Word for It.* Los Angeles: Jeremy P. Tarcher, 1988.

RIVERS, WILGA M. *Teaching Foreign-Language Skills.* 2d ed. Chicago: Univ. of Chicago Press, 1968, 1981.

ROOM, ADRIAN. *Dictionary of True Etymologies.* London: Routledge and Kegan Paul, 1986.

SAPIR, EDWARD. *Language: An Introduction to the Study of Speech.* 1921. Reprint. Herts, U.K.: Granada Publishing, 1982.

SHIPLEY, JOSEPH T. *Dictionary of Word Origins.* New York: Philosophical Library, 1945.

SHUY, ROGER W. *Discovering American Dialects.* Urbana, Ill.: National Council of Teachers of English, 1967.
STEVICK, EARL W. *Teaching Languages: A Way and Ways.* Rowley, Mass.: Newbury House Publishers, 1980.
TRUDGILL, PETER. *Sociolinguistics: An Introduction.* Middlesex, England: Penguin Books, 1974.
WAKELIN, MARTYN. *The Archaeology of English.* London: B. T. Batsford, 1988.
WALLWORK, J. F. *Language and People.* London: Heinemann Educational Books, 1978.
WARDHAUGH, RONALD. *Introduction to Linguistics.* 2d ed. New York: McGraw-Hill Book Company, 1977.

FOREIGN LANGUAGE DICTIONARIES AND OTHER BOOKS ON INDIVIDUAL COUNTRIES, AREAS, AND FOREIGN LANGUAGES

ANWYL, JOHN BODVAN, ed. *Spurrell's English-Welsh Dictionary.* Carmarthen, Wales: W. Spurrel & Son, 1922.
BAILEY, T. GRAHAME. *Teach Yourself Urdu.* London: St. Paul's House, 1950.
BERGMAN, PETER M., comp. *The Concise Dictionary of 26 Languages.* New York: NAL Penguin, 1968.
BERLITZ GUIDES STAFF. *European Phrase Book.* Switzerland: Berlitz Guides, 1974.
BRAGANTI, NANCY L., and ELIZABETH DEVINE. *The Travelers' Guide to European Customs and Manners.* New York: Meadowbrook, 1984.
BRUCE, GINNY. *Indonesia: A Travel Survival Kit.* Victoria, Australia: Lonely Planet Publications, 1986.
CASTILLO, CARLOS, and OTTO F. BOND. *The University of Chicago Spanish-English, English-Spanish Dictionary.* New York: Washington Square Press, 1961.
CHAMBERS, KEVIN. *The Travelers' Guide to Asian Customs & Manners.* Deephaven, Minn.: Meadowbrook, 1988.
COUSIN, PIERRE-HENRI. *Collins French-English English-French Dictionary.* New York: Berkley Books, 1982.
CROWTHER, GEOFF, and TONY WHEELER. *Malaysia, Singapore, & Brunei: A Travel Survival Kit.* Victoria, Australia: Lonely Planet Publications, 1988.
CROWTHER, GEOFF. *India: A Travel Survival Kit.* Victoria, Australia: Lonely Planet Publications, 1987.
Dictionary English-Cambodian. Lancaster, Penn.: Nha-Sach Xuan-Thu, 1957.
DOKE, C. M., D. MCK. MALCOLM, and J. M. A. SIKAKANA. *English and Zulu Dictionary.* Johannesburg: Witwatersrand University Press, 1977.

DOMHNALLÁIN, T. *Buntús Cainte: A First Step in Spoken Irish.* Baile Àtha Cliath, Ireland: Oifig An tSoláthair, 1967.

English as a Second Language. Vol. 11, *Cambodian Supplement for Beginning English.* Arlington, Va.: Center for Applied Linguistics, 1976.

English-Khmer Phrasebook with Useful Wordlist. Arlington, Va.: Center for Applied Linguistics, 1980.

FISCHER, ARNOLD. *English-Xhosa Dictionary.* Oxford: Oxford University Press, 1985.

FOX, PAUL. *Essentials of Polish.* Poland: Educational Department, Polish National Alliance, 1937.

GREGORY, PAUL, and TATJANA GREGORY. *Contemporary Russian: Grammar and Conversation.* Private printing. Atlanta, Ga.

GRZEBIENIOWSKI, T. *Illustrated English-Polish Polish-English Dictionary.* New York: Hippocrene Books, 1979.

HAMBLIN, CHARLES. *Languages of Asia and the Pacific: A Traveller's Phrasebook.* London: Angus and Robertson, 1984.

HOLMES, R. B., and B. S. SMITH. *Beginning Cherokee.* Norman, Okla.: University of Oklahoma Press, 1976.

HUFFMAN, FRANKLIN E. *Modern Spoken Cambodian.* 1970. Reprint. Ithaca, N.Y.: Cornell University, 1987.

HUFFMAN, F. E., and IM PROUM. *English for Speakers of Khmer.* New Haven and London: Yale University Press, 1983.

KAHANANUI, D., and A. ANTHONY. *Let's Speak Hawaiian.* Honolulu: The University Press of Hawaii, 1970, 1974.

KHEANG, LIM HAK, and DALE PURTLE. *Contemporary Cambodian.* Washington, D.C.: Foreign Service Institute, 1972.

LAMBTON, A. K. S. *Persian Vocabulary.* Cambridge: Cambridge University Press, 1969.

LAY, DR. NANCY DUKE. *Say It in Chinese (Mandarin).* New York: Dover Publications, 1980.

LE BA KONG. *English-Vietnamese Dictionary.* Houston: Zieleks Co., 1978.

LITTERAL, ROBERT. *A Programmed Course in New Guinea Pidgin.* Milton, Australia: The Jacaranda Press, 1969.

MESSINGER, HEINZ. *Langenscheidt's New Concise German Dictionary.* Berlin and Munich: Langenscheidt KG, 1973. (Also published in U.K. by Hodder and Stoughton.)

MIHALIC, F. *The Jacaranda Dictionary and Grammar of Melanesian Pidgin.* Milton, Queensland, Australia: 1971.

MORTON, JACQUELINE. *English Grammar for Students of French.* Ann Arbor, Mich.: The Olivia and Hill Press, 1979.

NEWMARK, L., et al. *Spoken Albanian*. Ithaca, N.Y.: Spoken Language Services, 1980.

NGUYEN-DINH-HOA. *Speak Vietnamese*. Rutland, Vt. and Tokyo: Charles E. Tuttle Co., 1966.

NORTHERN CHEYENNE BILINGUAL EDUCATION PROGRAM. *English-Cheyenne Student Dictionary.* Lame Deer, Mont., 1976.

PETERS, JENS. *Philippines: A Travel Survival Kit*. Victoria, Australia: Lonely Planet Publications, 1987.

REID, DUNCAN. *Elementary Course of Gaelic*. An Comunn Gaidhealach, 1935.

ROSTEN, LEO. *Hooray for Yiddish*. New York: Simon & Schuster, Touchstone Books, 1984.

SALIM, AHMED ALI. *Living Language Conversation Manual: Swahili*. New York: Crown Publishers, 1971.

SANTIAGO, JOSE ROLEO. *Bangladesh: A Travel Survival Kit*. Victoria, Australia: Lonely Planet Publications, 1985.

SCHWARZ, E., and R. EZAWA. *Everyday Japanese*. Lincolnwood, Ill.: Passport Books, 1986.

SHARPE, J., ed. *The Cherokees Past and Present*. Cherokee, N.C.: Cherokee Publications, 1970.

SHIRATO, ICHIRO. *Living Language Conversation Manual: Japanese*. New York: Crown Publishers, 1962.

STEINBERG, SAMUEL. *Living Language Conversation Manual: Hebrew.* New York: Crown Publishers, 1958.

THESIGER, WILFRED. *Arabian Sands*. Middlesex, England: Penguin Books, 1964.

UNDERHILL, RUTH M. *The Navajos*. Norman, Okla.: University of Oklahoma Press, 1956.

VALDMAN, ALBERT. *Haitian Creole-English-French Dictionary.* Bloomington, Ind.: Indiana University, Creole Institute, 1981.

WEINREICH, URIEL. *Say It in Yiddish*. New York: Dover, 1958.

WHEELER, TONY. *Burma: A Travel Survival Kit*. Victoria, Australia: Lonely Planet Publications, 1979, 1988.

———. *Papua New Guinea: A Travel Survival Kit*. Victoria, Australia: Lonely Planet Publications, 1988.

WHITELEY, WILFRED. *Swahili: The Rise of a National Language*. Suffolk, U.K.: Methuen & Co., 1969.

YOUNG, ROBERT W., and WILLIAM MORGAN, SR. *The Navajo Language*. Albuquerque: University of New Mexico Press, 1987.

ZHILONG, FAN. *Essential Chinese for Travelers*. San Francisco: China Books & Periodicals, 1988.

MAGAZINE ARTICLES

CHUA-EOAN, HOWARD G. "A Promised Land?" *Time* (March 5, 1990): 35–41.

"A Crime Even to Speak Turkish." *Time* (June 26, 1989): 11.

CONSTABLE, ANNE. "A Language Under Siege." *Time* (May 29, 1989).

DARNTON, JOHN. "In London, It's 'Estuary English.'" *International Herald Tribune* no. 34,468 (Dec. 23, 1993): 18.

DOWELL, WILLIAM. "A Crag Where Aramaic Lives." *Time* (October 30, 1989): 11.

"English: Out to Conquer the World." U.S. News and World Report (Feb. 18, 1985): 49 ff.

FALLOWS, JAMES. "Esperanto Lives." *The Atlantic Monthly* (Dec. 1986). Reprinted in Social Issues Resources Series, vol. 3, article 51. Boca Raton, Fla.: Social Issues Resources Series, 1990.

GAMKRELIDZE, THOMAS V., and V. V. IVANOV. "The Early History of Indo-European Languages." *Scientific American* 262, no. 3 (March 1990): 110–16.

GETZ, ARLENE. "A Language on the Critical List; Can Afrikaans Survive the Transition?" *Newsweek* (January 10, 1994): 30.

GREENBERG, JOSEPH H., and MERRITT RUHLEN. "Linguistic Origins of Native Americans." *Scientific American* (Nov. 1992): 94–99.

IMBRIE, KATHERINE. "Anatomy of an Accent: Where's the 'R'?" *Providence Journal Bulletin* (March 27, 1988): E1 ff. Reprinted in Social Issues Resources Series, vol. 3, article 69. Boca Raton, Fla.: Social Issues Resources Series, 1990.

In Other Words. Jan–Feb 1989. Huntington Beach, Calif.: Wycliffe Bible Translators.

"Language Differences," *Chronicles* (Oct. 1991): 7.

LESLIE, CONNIE, and DANIEL GLICK. "Classrooms of Babel." *Newsweek* (Feb. 18, 1991): 52–53.

MILLER, RONALD. "'What's Up?' and 'Right On!'" *Faces* 1, no. 10 (Sept. 1985): 34–35.

PEDERSON, DANIEL. "The Cornish Comeback." *Newsweek* (Oct. 29, 1990): 24.

PRATAP, ANITA. "Once Again, Strife Over English." *Time* (Sept.17, 1990): 32.

STUART, DAVID. "Maya Writing and the Calendar." *Faces* 2, no. 2 (Nov. 1985): 20–22.

WRIGHT, ROBERT. "Quest for the Mother Tongue." *The Atlantic* 267, no. 4 (April 1991): 39 ff.

INDEX

Accents, foreign, 71–73, 183
Adjective, 4, 84, 85, 108, 114, 118, 145, 183
AEthelred the Unready (king of England), 9
Affix, 81–84, 86–87, 183, 186, 188, 190. *See also* Prefix; Suffix
Affricate, 65, 183
Afghanistan, 12, 32, 44, 131, 151
Africa: European languages in, 46–47; language families of, 11, 12; proverbs of, 39; regions of: East Africa, 36; North Africa, 12, 35, 36, 45, 46; West Africa, 53, 57, 58. *See also* Algeria; Angola; Ivory Coast; Kenya; Libya; Madagascar; Mali; Morocco; Sierra Leone; South Africa; Tanzania; Tunisia; Zambia; Zimbabwe
African languages, 11, 12, 98, 146, 151; sounds, 66–68, 79; used in Americas, 53, 56–57. Individual languages: Afrikaans, 8, 47; Bilin, 115; Bushman, 66; Ewe, 83; Ge'ez, 34; Hausa, 79; Khoisan languages, 66; Krio, 79; Luganda, 68; Malagasy, 130; Mossi, 39; Ndebele, 46; Senoufo, 109; Shilh, 68; Shilluk, 79; Shona, 46; Tongan, 79; Twi, 56; /Xam, 66; Xhosa, 66; !Xu, 66; Yoruba, 100, 120; Zulu, 66, 79. *See also* Afrikaans; Amharic; Bantu languages; Berber; Coptic; Hottentot; Somali; Swahili
African-Americans, 56–58
Agglutinative languages, 83–84, 87, 100, 115, 183
Ainu, 13

Albanian, 8, 12, 82, 101, 106, 151
Aleut, 12, 51
Algeria, 46, 151
Alphabets, 2, 125–33, 183; borrowing, 125, 128, 132; invention of new, 136–37; Arabic, 33, 36, 99, 127, 129–31, 137, 141; Cherokee, 127, 130–32; Cyrillic, 31, 32, 111, 127, 129–31, 137; Devanagari (Hindi), 34, 99, 127, 131–32, 137; Greek, 127, 131; Hebrew, 37, 38, 127, 129, 131; Khmer, 99, 127, 129, 131; Korean Hangul, 127–29, 131; Phoenician, 127; Roman, 31–32, 125–28; Rotokas, 129; Semitic, 125, 127, 129; Vietnamese, 127, 128
American Indian languages, 28, 49–51, 63, 67, 79, 83, 115–16, 147; families, 11, 12; words, 96, 100, 101; Algonkian, 51; Arawak, 27; Assiniboine, 4; Aymara, 51, 151; Bella Coola, 68; Blackfoot, 4; Carib, 27; Chippewa, 4; Chiquito, 92; Choctaw, 51; Cree, 4, 130; Crow, 4; Dakota, 32; Flathead, 4; Fox, 116; Guaraní, 51, 151; Huron, 40; Iroquois, 40; Karok, 101, 116; Keres, 13; Kutenai, 4, 13; Kwakiutl, 141; Mixtec, 51; Nahuatl, 51, 68, 75; Nootka, 83–84; Olmec, 121, 127; Paiute, 119; Salish, 4; Sioux, 32, 82; Tarasco, 13; Tatuyo, 2–3; Teton-Sioux, 4; Tlingit, 65; Trumai, 13; Yana, 119; Yucatec, 151; Yurok, 68; Zuni, 13. *See also* Cherokee; Cheyenne; Hopi; Maya; Navajo; Quechua; Zapotec

American Indians (Native Americans), 42, 49, 52, 53, 120; Houma Indians, 56. See also Aztecs; Incas; American Indian languages
American Revolution, 40, 49
Amharic, 12, 129, 131, 151
Amish, 61
Anglo-Saxon, 9, 67, 126. See also Old English
Angola, 46, 151
Animals, 101
Appalachian Mountains, 16, 21
Arabian peninsula, 35, 44
Arabic numerals, 99
Arabic, 2, 3, 11, 12, 33, 39, 46, 61, 97, 99, 151, 154; and Islam, 35–37; grammar, 82, 87, 108, 112, 114, 117, 118; levels, 24, 25; sounds, 65, 67, 69; words, 36, 88–90, 96, 102, 104. See also Alphabets, Arabic
Aramaic, 12, 37, 38
Armenian, 8, 12, 44, 61, 129, 151
Articles, 109, 111, 114, 183
Artificial languages, 142–43, 183
Asia, 12, 33, 84, 120
Aspiration, 65, 183–84
Assyrians, 100
Astronomy, 100
Atatürk, Kemal, 136
Australia, 17, 23, 48, 49, 69, 84, 101, 138
Australian aboriginal languages, 11, 12, 17, 35, 49, 67, 68, 98, 101, 115; Mowring, 64; Pintupi, 89; Tiwi, 84; Tyattyalla, 112
Austria, 20, 146
Aztecs, 50, 51, 68, 75, 121

Babel, Tower of, 5
Babies, 64, 141
Babylonians, 100
Bahamas, 53
Bahasa Indonesian, 12, 48, 83, 106, 151. See also Indonesia
Balinese, 117, 151
Baluchi, 8, 12, 44, 151
Bantu languages, 12, 36, 66, 79, 82, 83, 105

Basque, 4, 12, 13, 24, 25, 28, 32, 42, 43, 84, 100, 116, 155
Belgium, 12, 31
Belorussian, 8, 151
Bengali, 3, 8, 12, 32, 70, 95, 129, 151
Berber, 12, 36, 45, 68, 151
Bible, 5, 19, 35, 38, 95; translation, 34–35, 54, 136
Bilingual education, 42, 147
Black English Vernacular (BEV), 57–58
Bolivia, 51, 92, 151
Borrowing of words, 7, 25, 38, 45, 53, 56, 57, 101, 133, 140, 184; from Arabic, 33, 36; from Chinese, 45, 128; from English, 62–63, 74, 101–2; into English, 9–11, 17, 38, 48, 63, 100–101, 109, 134, 141
Bosnia-Herzegovina, 32, 151
Brazil, 50, 52, 151
Breton, 8, 12, 41, 42, 112
British (Empire), 40–41, 45, 48, 52, 53, 140
British Guiana, 52
Buddhism, 34
Bulgarian, 4, 8, 12, 109, 129, 151
Burma. See Myanmar
Burmese, 12, 77, 91, 93, 97, 99, 129, 131, 151
Burushaski, 13

Cabral, Pedro, 50
Cajuns, 40, 42, 56, 63
Calendar, 100
California, 3, 51, 52, 56, 59, 60, 62, 101, 117, 147
Cambodia, 47, 59. See also Khmer
Canada, 18, 40–41, 48, 61, 83, 136, 138
Cantonese, 12, 33, 59, 79, 157
Caribbean Islands, 50–53
Case (of nouns), 86, 110–12, 114, 184
Catalan, 43, 151
Caucasus Mountains, 67, 112
Cave paintings, 120
Celts, 9, 41; Celtic languages, 8, 12, 41, 112

Central America, 49–51, 121
Champollion, Jean François, 124
Charlemagne, Emperor, 30
Chaucer, 71
Cherokee, 12, 79, 127, 130–32
Cheyenne, 12, 26, 75, 156
China, 12, 35, 45, 77, 128, 141, 151
Chinese, 11, 12, 32, 33, 40, 68, 74, 98, 99, 142, 151; in U.S., 3, 56, 59, 61; isolating language, 84, 85, 87, 112, 115; pidgin languages, 52, 53, 56; script, 120–23, 127–28, 131–33, 136; tones, 77–79, 141; words, 6, 91, 96, 103, 157, 158. *See also* Cantonese; Mandarin Chinese
Christianity: Amish, 61; Eastern Orthodox Church, 31–33; Egyptian Coptic Church, 37; Ethiopian Orthodox Church, 34; Mennonite Church, 60, 61; Quakers, 95; Roman Catholic Church, 11, 30–34. *See also* Bible; Missionaries
Clicks, 66
Cockney, 18, 19, 21, 67
Colombia, 3
Colonial languages, 45–52
Columbus, Christopher, 49
Conditional tense, 116
Confucianism, 94
Consonants, 64–69, 72, 74, 75, 125, 126, 129, 130, 132, 133, 184
Cook, Captain James, 101
Coptic, 12, 37, 124
Cornish, 41
Cortes, Hernando, 50
Creole languages, 52–58, 151, 184; French Guianese, 52; Guyanese Creole English, 52; Sranang Tongo (Taki-Taki), 52. *See also* New Guinea Pidgin; Sea Islands Creole English
Crete, 124
Croatians, 31–32
Cuba(ns), 51, 59, 60
Cuneiform, 121, 127, 130, 184
Czech Republic, 31; Czechoslovakia, 31

Czech, 4, 8, 12, 22, 31, 75, 76, 112, 128, 151

Danish, 4, 8, 12, 30, 109, 128, 151
Dari, 8, 12, 32, 151
Darius (king of Persia), 130
Dead languages, 8, 13, 38, 184
Demotic, 123, 124, 127, 184
Denmark, 9, 30
Diacritics, 128, 184
Dialects, 7, 13,14–27, 30–33, 90, 140, 184; feminine and masculine, 26–27; social, 21–26, 189. *See also* England; United States
Diglossia, 24, 185
Dravidian languages, 12, 48, 114
Dutch, 32, 67, 70, 134, 139, 142, 151, 159; in Africa, 47, 66; in Americas, 4, 52, 53, 59, 61; in Indonesia, 47–48; relationship to other languages, 6, 8, 9, 12, 20, 31
Dutch Guiana, 52

Easter Island, 124
Egypt, 12, 35; ancient, 37, 121–23, 125, 127; Egyptian Coptic Church, 37
England, 9, 15–17, 21, 23, 41, 42, 45, 69, 104, 126; dialects, 15, 16–18
English, 2, 3, 6, 48; as a second language, 147; dialects of, 14–21; grammar, 110–11, 114, 115; history of, 8–12, 86–87, 95, 102–3, 105, 126; in Africa, 46–47; in India, 2, 48, 77; sounds, 64, 65, 71, 72; standard, 16, 21–24, 28, 42, 56–58, 107; varieties of: African-American, 57–58; American, 14, 23, 63, 68, 69, 75, 77, 147–48; Australian, 17, 23, 68–69; British, 17–18, 20, 23, 68, 75, 77; Canadian, 18; Irish, 16, 18, 68, 70, 77; New Zealand, 17; Scottish, 16, 18, 23, 67, 68. *See also* Spelling
Erse. *See* Irish Gaelic
Eskimo, 12, 32, 83, 88, 109, 110, 112, 118–20, 141, 151; pidgins, 53. *See also* Aleut

Esperanto, 142–43
Estonian, 12, 151
Ethiopia, 12, 34, 129, 131, 151; Ethiopian Orthodox Church, 34
Etruscan(s), 13, 125, 127
Etymology, 102–3, 185
Euphemisms, 28, 103–4, 185
Europe, 6, 7, 38, 45–48, 59, 84, 99, 120, 137

Family relationships, 6, 39, 90–94; family names, 96–98
Far East, 45, 91, 93, 129
Farsi, 8, 12, 32, 36, 69, 104, 109, 130, 131, 151
Ferdinand and Isabella (king and queen of Spain), 50
Fijian, 12, 151
Finnish, 4, 11, 12, 69, 70, 71, 73, 84, 96, 109, 112, 137, 141, 151
First language, 3, 185; learning of, 64, 181
Flemish, 12, 31
France, 10, 12, 24, 30, 41, 42, 52, 53, 95; Paris, 23
Franco, Francisco, 43
Franklin, Benjamin, 135
French, 3, 80, 102–4, 128, 130, 160; creoles, 53, 56, 61; dialects, 22, 23, 56; gender, 112, 114; in other countries, 4, 40–41, 46, 47, 51, 52, 59, 61; learning, 139, 140, 142, 149, 151; Old French, 102; pronouns, 94–96, 98; relationship to other languages, 6–12, 30, 34, 37, 38, 45; sounds, 68, 70, 73, 75; spelling, 135–36
French and Indian Wars, 40
French Guiana, 52
Fricatives, 65, 185
Frisian, 4, 8, 10, 12
Friulian, 146

Gaelic, 8. *See also* Irish Gaelic; Scots Gaelic
Gender, 96, 112–14, 185
Georgian, 12, 112, 151
German, 3, 28, 32, 80, 94, 101–2, 104, 126, 161; dialects, 20, 22, 24, 25, 60–62, 140; grammar, 86, 87, 108–9, 111–14; in other countries, 4, 31, 52, 60–62, 146; learning, 138, 139, 142, 151; relationship to other languages, 6–9, 12, 38, 47, 53; sounds, 65, 67, 68, 70, 73, 75–77
Germanic languages, 8, 9, 11, 12
Germans, 46, 59
Gettysburg Address, 135
Gilyak, 13
Glottal stops, 67, 185
Gothic, 7
Grammar, 4, 83–87, 107–19, 185; descriptive, 107, 184; prescriptive, 107, 188
Great Britain, 20–21, 49, 52, 138, 140
Greek, 8, 9, 11, 12, 38, 77, 101, 103, 112, 121, 123, 135, 149, 151; accent, 73; alphabet, 2, 125, 127, 131; dialects, 22, 24–26; in U.S., 4, 59–61
Gullah. *See* Sea Islands Creole
Guyana, 52
Gypsies, 12, 43, 44, 151

Haitians, 60; Haitian Creole, 53, 151, 161
Hawaii, 11, 35, 56, 59, 62
Hawaiian, 12, 56, 64, 67, 72–73, 80, 96, 98, 117
Hebrew, 11, 12, 19, 37–38, 61, 87, 90, 114, 127, 129, 131, 151, 162
Hieroglyphics, 121–25, 127, 186
High and low forms of languages, 24–26
Hindi, 3, 8, 12, 20, 33, 34, 61, 75, 99, 151, 163; alphabet, 2, 131–32; as national language, 48, 147; grammar, 95, 109, 112; Hindustani, 33
Hinduism, 33, 34, 121; castes, 95
Hispanic Americans, 59–60, 62–63
Historical linguistics, 6, 186
Hmong, 4, 79, 151
Homophones, 72, 133, 135, 186
Hong Kong, 59
Hopi, 12, 27, 89, 109, 119, 148

Hottentot, 12, 32, 66, 83
Hungarian, 4, 12, 32, 61, 69, 70, 84, 96, 100, 112, 139, 151
Hungary, 11, 59, 73, 139

Iberian, 13
Icelandic, 8, 12, 112, 151
Idioms, 103–5, 186
Immigrants, 38, 58–63, 147, 186
Incas, 49–51, 120
India, 35, 44, 52, 95, 98, 124, 138, 163; alphabets of, 127, 129, 131–32, 136–37, 147; languages of, 2, 6, 8, 12, 20, 48, 66, 67, 146, 151: Gujarati, 12, 151; Kannada, 12, 151; Kota, 68; Marathi, 12, 151. *See also* Dravidian languages; Hindi; Hinduism; Malayalam; Sanskrit; Tamil; Telugu
Indo-European languages, 6–8, 12, 34, 94, 186
Indochina, 47
Indonesia(n), 3, 11, 36, 47–48, 93, 151. *See also* Bahasa Indonesian; Javanese
Indus River Valley, 124
Inflected languages, 86–87, 110, 186–87
Iran, 12, 32, 35, 36, 44, 69, 104, 109, 130–31, 151
Iraq, 5, 12, 35, 44, 130, 151
Ireland, 9, 18, 41, 42, 126; Irish people, 16, 59
Irish Gaelic, 8, 9, 12, 16, 41, 42, 112, 136, 151
Islam, 33, 35–37, 130, 137
Isle of Man, 41
Isolates, 11–13, 187
Isolating languages, 84–87, 187
Israel, 38, 151
Italian, 3, 113–14, 142, 146, 151, 164; in U.S., 4, 59–61; relationship to other languages, 8, 11, 12, 34, 37, 38; sounds, 69, 75, 76; words, 89, 90, 101, 103
Ivory Coast, 109

Jainism, 34
Jamaican Creole, 53, 54
Japanese, 3, 6, 12, 13, 26, 32, 45, 74–76, 80, 99, 102, 151, 165; grammar, 108, 109, 112, 116, 118; in U.S., 4, 56, 59, 61, 101; relationship words, 91–93; sounds, 68–70; writing, 127, 131–33, 136, 142
Jargon, 29, 187
Javanese, 12, 93–94, 129, 151
Jordan, 25
Judaism, Jews, 19, 37, 38, 63; languages of, 37. *See also* Hebrew; Yiddish

Kaddish, 37
Kampuchea. *See* Cambodia
Kazakh, 12, 129, 151
Kenya, 46, 151
Khmer, 12, 32, 61, 151, 166–67; grammar, 82, 83, 108–10, 112, 115, 118; numbers, 98–99; relationship words, 91–93, 96; sounds, 64, 67. *See also* Alphabets, Khmer
King Arthur, 9
King James Bible, 95
Koran, 35
Korean, 12, 13, 32, 39, 104–5, 108–9, 151, 168; in U.S., 3, 4, 59, 61; sounds, 65–66; words, 45, 91, 93, 94, 98, 102; writing, 127–28, 131, 133, 137
Kurds, Kurdish, 8, 12, 44, 130, 151

Language, 1, 2, 4, 30–33, 44, 74, 148; families, 6–9, 11, 12, 187; levels of, 92–94; names, 32; origins of, 4–5; types, 83–87
Language learning, language teaching, 138–51, 181–82
Lao, Laos, 4, 12, 47, 59, 77, 93, 151
Lapland, 12, 89
Latin America(ns), 50–51, 59, 76
Latin, 10, 13, 34, 38, 126, 142, 149; grammar, 86, 107, 112; related languages, 8, 12, 30; words in English, 9, 11, 36, 81, 98, 100, 102, 135
Latvian, 8, 12, 151
Lebanon, 44, 125

Libya, 35
Lingua franca, 36, 46–48, 187
Lithuanian, 7, 8, 12, 151
Logographic scripts, 33, 121–24, 127, 131, 187
London, 18, 19, 21, 23
Lord's Prayer, 9, 55
Louisiana, 40, 51, 56, 62, 63

Macedonian, 8, 12, 151
Madagascar, 12, 130, 151
Malagasy Republic, 130
Malay, 3, 12, 48, 53, 83, 91, 96; Malayo-Polynesian, 11
Malayalam, 12, 98, 131, 147, 151
Mali, 109, 151
Mandarin Chinese, 2, 3, 12, 32, 33, 59, 67, 77–79, 87, 158
Manx, 41
Maori, 12, 17
Martinique, 53
Maya(s), 12, 51, 99, 121, 127, 151
Mayflower, 21
Mexico, Mexicans, 50, 51, 59, 60, 101–2, 151
Middle East, 12, 20, 35, 48, 151
Middle English, 10, 19, 71, 95, 102, 126, 187
Missionaries, 34–35, 126, 128–30, 136
Mon-Khmer, 12, 61
Mongolian, 129, 151
Moors, 36, 99
Morocco, 46, 68, 151
Morphology, 81–87, 187
Müller, Max, 4
Muslims, 32, 33, 35–37, 130, 137
Myanmar, 11, 12, 151. *See also* Burmese

Nahali, 13
Names, 96–98
Napoleon, 123
Native American languages. *See* American Indian languages
Navajo, 12, 50, 61, 67, 70, 75, 79, 119, 169
Nepal(i), 132, 151
Netherlands Antilles, 53, 151

Netherlands. *See* Dutch
New Guinea Pidgin, 53–55, 151, 170
New York, 52, 58, 59, 60, 62, 63
New Zealand, 11, 12, 17, 105, 138
Normans, 10, 45
North America, 49, 59, 101
Norway, 11, 22, 28, 30
Norwegian, 4, 8, 11, 12, 30–32, 109, 128, 136, 151, 171
Nouns, 26, 82, 84–86, 108–14, 141, 143, 187
Number (singular or plural), 54, 82, 85, 94, 95, 111–12, 114, 188, 189
Numbers, 98–100

Old English, 6, 9, 10, 57, 67, 86, 87, 95, 108–10, 112–13, 126, 135, 188
Old Norse, 8, 30, 86, 101, 126
Old Testament, 5, 19, 37, 38
Onomatopoeia, 105

Pacific Islands, 11, 35, 53, 54, 80, 124, 129, 151; Oceanic languages, 12
Pakistan, 12, 33, 36, 44, 48, 67, 124, 131, 151, 163. *See also* Hindi; Sindhi; Urdu
Palestine, 35, 38, 125
Papiamento, 53, 151
Papua New Guinea, 12, 35, 53–55, 84, 148, 151, 170; Kiwai language, 84
Paraguay, 12, 51, 151
Pashto, 8, 12, 151
Pennsylvania Dutch, 60–62
Persia(n), 32, 33, 35, 36, 45, 61, 130, 151; Old Persian, 130. *See also* Farsi
Peru, 51, 120, 151
Philippines, 3, 12, 56, 59, 73, 151. *See also* Tagalog
Phoenicians, 121, 125
Phonology, 64–73, 188; phonemes, 65, 69, 117, 136–37, 188
Pidgin languages, 52–57, 170, 188
Pitch, 76–77, 188
Pizarro, Francisco, 50
Place names, 49, 51–52, 103, 105

Plurals. *See* Number
Poetry, 108
Polish, 4, 8, 12, 22, 39, 59, 61, 68, 73, 75, 76, 112, 116, 128, 151, 171
Politics, 23, 24, 30, 33, 38, 44, 45, 137, 140
Polynesia(n), 11, 12, 53, 101, 151
Portugal, 35–37, 50
Portuguese, 3, 8, 11, 12, 36, 46, 128, 135–36, 151; grammar, 109, 113; in Americas, 49, 50, 52, 61, 147; pidgins, 53, 56; sounds, 70, 73, 75
Prayer, 9, 35, 37, 55, 95
Prefixes, 81, 82, 87, 97, 115, 188
Prepositions, 85, 109–11, 188
Profanity, 28
Pronouns, 86, 94–96, 110–11, 116, 189
Proverbs, 14, 20, 38–40, 120, 138
Puerto Rico, 51, 59, 62–63
Punjabi, 8, 12, 79, 151

Quakers, 95
Quebec, 40–41
Quechua, 12, 49, 51, 151
Quipu, 120
Qur'an, 35

Rates of speaking, 79–80
Religion, 31–38, 60–61, 89–90. *See also* Buddhism; Christianity; Confucianism; Hinduism; Islam; Jainism; Judaism; Prayer; Zoroastrianism
Rhythm, 75–76
Roman Empire, 11, 30, 34
Romance languages, 8, 11, 12, 34, 77, 101, 112, 189
Romany, 8, 12, 43–44, 151
Rosetta Stone, 123–24
Rumanian, 8, 12, 109, 112, 128
Runes, 126
Russian, 3, 6–8, 12, 138, 151, 172; accent, 73; grammar, 86, 109, 111–12, 114, 117, 141; in U.S., 4, 61; proverbs, 39, 40; sounds, 67, 68, 75–77; words, 90, 95, 97, 102–3, 105. *See also* Alphabets, Cyrillic

Saami, 12, 89
Sabir, 56
Saint Augustine of Canterbury, 126
Saint Cyril, 129
Saint Methodius, 129
Saint Patrick, 126
Sanskrit, 7, 8, 12, 34, 44, 127, 132
Sapir, Edward, 141
Saudi Arabia, 35
Scandinavia, 11, 12, 30, 59, 128
Scotland, 9, 21, 66, 67, 97; dialects, 15, 16, 18, 23; Scots-Irish, 59
Scots Gaelic, 8, 9, 12, 41, 42, 69, 136
Sea Islands Creole (English), 56–57
Sejong (king of Korea), 128
Semitic languages, 11, 12, 38, 87, 88. *See also* Amharic; Arabic; Aramaic; Hebrew
Sequoyah, 130, 132
Serbians, 31
Serbo-Croatian, 4, 8, 12, 31, 32, 68, 112, 151
Shakespeare, 16, 28, 57, 71
Shibboleths, 19, 67, 189
Siberia, 27, 151
Sierra Leone, 79, 151
Sign languages, 4
Sindhi, 67, 151
Sinhala, 12, 151
Slang, 19, 27–28, 189
Slaves, 49, 52, 53, 56, 57, 58
Slavic languages, 12, 25, 38, 77, 101, 109
Slovak, 4, 8, 12, 31, 75, 112, 151
Slovenian, 4, 12, 151
Solomon Islands, 129
Somali, 12, 151, 173
Sounds, 1, 2, 4, 7, 15, 19, 23, 27, 33, 53, 64–80, 105, 117; in writing, 121–30, 132–37; learning, 141, 144–45
South Africa, 47, 66, 151
South America, 3, 27, 35, 49–52, 101, 147. *See also* Bolivia; Brazil; Paraguay; Peru; Venezuela
South Korea, 128

Southeast Asia, 12, 47, 48, 59, 77, 79, 83, 97
Spain, 12, 24, 30, 35–37, 42, 43, 50, 51, 53, 151
Spanish, 2, 3, 28, 32, 39, 142, 151, 174; grammar, 4, 82, 86, 108, 112–15, 118, 145; in Americas, 3, 4, 40, 49–53, 59, 61–63, 147; relation to other languages, 7, 8, 11, 12, 30, 34, 36; sounds, 68–70, 72, 73, 75–77; words, 33, 36, 94, 96, 100, 101–4, 149; writing, 128, 137, 141
Spelling, 16, 67, 69, 71, 72, 126, 133–36; American, 136; British, 136; Canadian, 136; French, 136
Sports, 29, 144
Sri Lanka, 12, 151
Standard language, 16, 22–25, 28, 56–59, 63, 90, 140, 147, 189
Stress, 75–76, 190
Subjunctive mood, 115–16
Suffix, 81, 82, 87, 93, 97, 190
Sumerian(s), 13, 100, 121, 127, 130
Suriname, 52
Swahili, 12, 36, 46, 102, 146, 151, 175; grammar, 82–83, 87, 115–16; proverbs, 39, 40; sounds, 68, 75
Swearing, 28, 190
Swedish, 4, 6, 8, 9, 11, 12, 30, 39, 102, 104, 105, 109, 128, 151, 176
Sweyn (king of Denmark), 9
Switzerland, 20; Swiss German, 25, 140
Syllable, 7, 18, 68, 70, 74–76, 79–81, 84, 85, 190; syllabic scripts, 121–25, 127, 130–33, 136, 190
Syria, 12, 35, 37, 44, 125, 130, 151

Taboo, 27, 28, 190
Tagalog, 3, 12, 61, 67, 108, 151, 177
Talmud, 37
Tamil, 12, 24, 91, 100, 105, 108, 129, 151
Tanzania, 46, 146, 151
Telugu, 12, 48, 91, 151
Tense (of verbs), 54, 85, 86, 114–17, 143, 190

Thai, Thailand, 11, 12, 61, 67, 77, 78, 91, 151
Thant, U, 98
Tibet(an), 11, 12, 91, 129, 151
Tok Pisin, 53–55, 151, 170
Tones, 4, 76–79, 122, 128, 137, 141, 190; tonal languages, 77–79, 190
Trade language, 46, 48, 146. *See also* Lingua franca
Transliteration, 2, 25, 68, 111, 117, 153, 190
Tunisia, 46
Turkey, 12, 36, 44, 130, 151
Turkish, 12, 25, 32, 70, 84, 101, 105, 112, 128, 136, 138, 151
Twain, Mark, 113, 149

Uighur, 12, 151
Ukrainian, 8, 129, 151
Umlaut, 70, 126, 191
United States, 28–29, 42, 49, 56, 92, 139, 140, 151; dialects of, 15, 16, 19–21, 57–58, 62; immigrants to, 58–63; languages of, 3, 4, 48, 59–62, 147, 148; place names in, 51–52; cities/states of, 62: Alaska, 51; Boston, 19, 60; Connecticut, 51; Florida, 51, 60; Georgia, 52, 56; Indiana, 61; Kansas, 61; Michigan, 58; Montana, 3–4; New Mexico, 120; Ohio, 61; Oklahoma, 51; Pennsylvania, 16, 60–62; Rhode Island, 16; South Carolina, 56; Texas, 56, 60. *See also* California; Hawaii; Louisiana; New York
Urdu, 8, 12, 33, 34, 45, 61, 131, 151, 163
Uzbek, 12, 151

Venezuela, 13
Verbs, 16, 54, 57, 82–87, 94, 108, 114–18, 143, 191
Vietnam, 45, 47, 128, 151; Vietnam War, 59
Vietnamese, 12, 45, 96–97, 142, 151, 178; alphabet, 127–28; grammar, 84, 85, 109; in U.S., 3, 4, 59–61; sounds, 64, 67, 70, 74, 76–78; words, 90–93, 149

Vikings, 9, 10, 30, 86, 101
Vocabulary, 88, 191. *See also* Words
Vowels, 15, 16, 53, 64, 65, 68–72, 74, 75, 191; Great Vowel Shift, 71, 185; nasalized, 70, 142; written characters for, 79, 125–26, 128–30, 132–33, 147

Wales, 9, 21, 41, 69
Webster, Noah, 135
Welsh, 8, 9, 12, 32, 41, 42, 69, 75, 98, 108, 112
West Indies, 50
William the Conqueror, 10
Word order, 9, 53, 85–87, 108–10, 123, 141

Words, 4–7, 14, 81–106. *See also* Borrowing of words; Logographic scripts
World War II, 67, 70
Writing, 2, 5, 6, 9, 20–25, 31–38, 45, 47, 74, 99, 107, 111, 120–37, 141–43, 147, 191. *See also* Alphabets; Spelling

Yemen, 20, 37
Yiddish, 3, 4, 8, 38, 61, 63, 76, 151, 179
Yugoslavia, 32, 151
Yukaghir, 27

Zambia, 79, 151
Zapotec(s), 12, 51, 121, 127, 151
Zimbabwe, 46, 151
Zoroastrianism, 130